THE GONE ROOM

A Memoir

Eleanor DeVito Owen

For my family.

Non avere paura. Non puoi cambiare il tuo destino. È un regalo.

Do not be afraid; our fate cannot be taken from us; it is a gift.

—DANTE ALIGHIERI, INFERNO

CONTENTS

PROLOGUE

For the world outside our home, the Great Depression started on Wall Street in October 1929. For me, it began in Mama's kitchen a few months earlier when I was almost nine. Papa had come home in the middle of the day in the middle of the week, surprising us, for even on Saturdays, Papa would be out driving one of his big Mack trucks around the boroughs of New York City—breaking up labor union strikes, trucking Prohibition whiskey, hustling customers, bullying Long Island farmers, haggling to buy low and sell high.

I figured something was wrong by the hard kick at the bottom of the door before it swung open and Papa barged into the kitchen, his eyes wild and searching. We seven kids looked up, glances questioning each other, the little ones slurping minestrone. Mama stood at the brand-new gas stove with *Whyte* written in beautiful green cursive letters on the oven door—even though it wasn't white. It was cream-colored with tall, shiny green legs.

Agnes, next youngest to me—Papa's favorite and the only one with curly blonde hair—yelled "Papa, Papa" as if he belonged to her and no one else. But Papa didn't rush to pick her up and twirl her in the air the way he always did. He acted like she wasn't there. Instead, when Mama turned, he caught her eye and tossed his head in sharp, quick jerks toward the archway to the dining room.

Mama stopped ladling soup and followed him, carrying the ladle with her, asking as she went, *"Che cosa?"*

I half expected Papa to start yelling; she had disobeyed his rule forbidding anyone to speak Italian in our home. Everyone —Aunt Mary, Uncle Pete, Giulia Pasquale (Mama's best friend), even Mama's midwife Louisa, and *paisanos* from Italy—knew he didn't want his kids growing up speaking broken English and "going no place."

If we heard it once, we heard it a thousand times: "I don't want my boys digging ditches or my girls sewing in sweat shops. They're going to be Supreme Court judges."

But that day, instead of starting a fight with Mama or talking about Supreme Court judges, he stood still, eyes fixed on the set of new, multicolored, gold-rimmed goblets inside the shiny glass door of Mama's china closet.

He didn't speak right away. Mama studied his face. When he answered her *che cosa* about what had happened, his voice was so low I shushed my younger sisters and older brothers so I could catch every word.

"Today I lost the house on Eighteenth Street."

Lost the house on Eighteenth Street? *Lost a house?* What had happened to Papa? First, he didn't seem to notice when Mama disobeyed his strictest rule, and now he said he'd lost a house. Maybe his Italian nickname—*Pazzo*—was true. Maybe Papa was crazy.

I wanted to shout, "Look out the kitchen window! Look across the roof of your garage. *Look!* The Eighteenth Street house isn't lost. I can see it."

But Mama's face grew long and dark and frightened, scaring me. Her eyes dimmed. They looked like the black woolen buttons on the coat she wore to funerals, reminding me of when five-year-old Petey from down the block caught infantile paralysis and died.

But I didn't say a word. Nor did anyone else.

Albert, one of my two older brothers, and my younger sisters stopped eating, each on edge, waiting for something to happen. Even the air in the room stilled, as though listening. Mama clenched her fingers, making a tight fist, the way she did whenever she wanted to control her quick temper, and she began to gnaw the side of her lower lip, showing her big white teeth. No doubt about it, Mama wasn't just scared, she was *mad*—mostly because she had her heart set on moving a block away, out of the low-ceilinged rooms over Papa's double garage and into that Eighteenth Street brownstone with a big yard and high windows all the way around instead of short ones only in the front and back.

I had overheard her tell Giulia, "Next year, when we move out of here, you can stop complaining about your knees hurting. You won't be climbing three long flights. The Eighteenth Street kitchen is on the first floor, not like here." Mama also hated climbing those steps from the sidewalk, up the steep wooden stoop, and into three long flights of dark stairs; she said it was like living over a horse stall, even though it smelled like hootch, and Papa's garage had no horses.

From where I stood, holding two empty soup bowls—one for me and the other for my oldest brother Francey—I watched Mama's face change. Her mouth clenched shut. Her woolen eyes peeped through tiny slits like the scary cat that slunk in and out of the grapevine fences of Brooklyn's South Park backyards.

Papa looked different too. I had never seen him so still. And I had never, ever seen him look sick. Or scared. His dark olive skin was now a chalky, yellowish green. Even his mustache and thick eyebrows looked different—bigger, blacker. He appeared shorter, almost the same height as Mama. He looked too scared and too sick for me to tell him where he could find the Eighteenth Street house only one block away.

Although Mama and Papa stood side by side facing the shiny china closet holding the new sapphire blue and emerald green goblets, both seemed to have drifted far, far away. Had they gone back to Italy where they were born? Back to their native villages? Papa to the fields of artichokes in Avellino? Mama to her sunny Chieti?

I blinked. No, they weren't gone. Mama stood straight and solid, framed in the archway to the dining room. She lifted her chin, caught my eye, and beckoned with the white enamel ladle.

Handing it to me, she said, "Finish filling the bowls." Then she turned to Papa, her voice low. "You lied to me. You said Eighteenth Street was paid off."

Then, almost snorting, her tone savage, tiny dots of spit flying out of her mouth toward Papa, she flung, "*Bugiardo!*"

Bugiardo was a word I didn't know, but Papa wilted. He looked like he knew. Mama stared at him briefly, her mouth twisting in disgust, and almost grunting, she hurled, "Liar."

She turned her back to him and strode toward their bedroom, her eyes scanning the entire area as though seeking an ally or another foe. The color drained from her face; had Paura, Mama's dreaded apparition of fear, a floating black shroud from Italian folklore, scared her? My chest tightened. I couldn't breathe.

As Mama disappeared into her bedroom, Paura's black shadow darkened the closed door but didn't go inside. Instead, the shadow turned, floated toward the dining room, and hovered over Papa, who sat slumped, his thin body swallowed up by the huge mahogany armchair.

Mama's *bugiardo* accusation echoed from the walls, reminding me of her daily motto: Truth is always in the room. She never goes away.

Unlike other times, that day, I didn't imagine truth flying overhead in a delicate pale blue chiffon gown like the picture on my Holy Communion Prayer Book. That day Mama's words had an ominous reach. I knew Mama had run away from home at age seven because her mother had said she intended to buy embroidery thread for her shop, but she didn't. She met that shoemaker in the park, her hand over his arm, both of them laughing. Now, alone in her bedroom, what was she thinking? Papa had lied to her. Would she run away again? Leave us? Would Papa try to stop her and start a fight and yell, "*La strega. La strega!*" Witch.

Forcing myself to breathe deeply but trying to appear calm so the little ones wouldn't get upset, I tiptoed to the stove and ladled out the warm minestrone into one of the bowls I held. Francey, my oldest brother, almost twelve, stared at me with his long, sad face. I set the bowl at his place, but he didn't sit down or touch his minestrone. Instead, he knelt at the small children's table and helped Evelyn, the baby, balance her spoon without a spill. The rest of us—even fidgety Albert, who always tap-tap-tapped the chair leg while we ate—didn't make a sound.

Caged in silence, we kids watched and waited. Only our eyes moved, roving one to another, sharing and spreading a nameless, contagious dread. Soon, Albert, born after Francey but before me, acted like he had finished his minestrone and dropped his spoon on the table with a clatter.

One by one the younger ones dropped spoons into bowls or set them down on the table. Francey cleared his throat and wiped two-year-old Evelyn's tiny hands on a soft dish towel. Albert gathered up the spoons and tossed them helter-skelter into the sink, pretending not to notice the ruckus. I circled the large oak table, picking up half-full soup bowls and pouring left-overs back into the pot, then nesting them one inside the other, trying not to make a sound—all of us taking quick glances at Papa as his deep, agonized sigh broke the silence.

Papa leaned forward, closed his eyes, and dropped his head into his palms. Looking past him, I stared at Mama's bedroom door, darkened once again by Paura's shadow.

Alone in her bedroom, was Mama gathering the same things she took when she left home as a child? A church dress, her lavender rosary beads, and the hand-embroidered silvery scarf from her mother's embroidery shop? I began to wonder the way Mama wondered, my eyes slid sideways, my lower lip drawn between my teeth. I studied Papa, his eyes covered by the palms of his hands, his body folded. He looked like he had a piercing wound somewhere inside. I wanted to help, but I didn't move. For a moment I felt grown up, as if I had skipped a grade at school, unsure of important lessons I had missed.

If Papa kept acting *Pazzo*, and if Mama left home, would I have to take care of the little ones? Or would Mama take all of us with her? Where would we go?

PART ONE—PROSPERITY

CHAPTER ONE—MAMA'S MEMORIES

1925-1927

Before Papa lost the house on Eighteenth Street, Mama sang all the time. She sang to wake us up, she sang to put us to sleep, she sang to stop the baby from crying, she sang to her homemade gnocchi as they danced in the boiling water. She sang if we laughed, and she sang if we cried.

Her father had been an opera singer in Chieti, a town in the foothills of the Abruzzo region of Italy, where, Mama said, "Everyone who lived there was *cape testardo*—hardheaded, like me." The sun shone year-round, and every morning an old gardener would kneel and arrange the petunias in the entrance to the neighborhood square to display the month and date.

Mama taught us all the Italian operas her father had taught her. If the sun shone, she sang *"O Sole Mio."* If Papa yelled at her and she sassed him, she sang Verdi's *"Sempra Libra"* to his back. In bits and pieces, she interpreted the lyrics, teaching us the only Italian we would ever learn.

Or, for no reason at all, she might stop folding diapers or place a bowl over the mound of ravioli dough she had been kneading and walk across the room. She would crank the Victrola, select a record depending upon her mood, carefully set the needle in a groove and begin to sing along with Enrico Caruso. I loved *"Celeste Aida"* and *Madame Butterfly*, her favorites. When we asked what the Italian words meant, her eyes would grow watery, and her voice turned sad. "Aida is about a brave soldier who dreams of rescuing the woman he loved; Butterfly is about a mother who sacrifices herself for her child." Mama's eyelids would lower, and she remained quiet the whole time she rolled out the ravioli dough.

Giulia, who lived down the block on the second floor of a tenement with dark halls, visited every afternoon. She was much older than Mama. Short, soft, pudgy, and playful. We kids loved her. She smelled of coal dust, like Carlo, her husband, who shoveled coal for a living.

Papa, his voice openly disdainful, said, "Carlo's one of those men going no place. A disgrace to Italian men." His low opinion of Carlo had something to do with Carlo not fathering any children and because both he and Giulia spoke "broken English."

I felt sorry for them, especially Giulia. I thought she came every day because she wished she had a son like Francey. She brought him little treats like jellybeans or Jordan Almonds, which she slipped to him when Mama wasn't looking. If Mama complained, Giulia said it was because Mama favored Albert too much and Francey deserved more attention.

Mama's eyes slid sideways and if she remained quiet, Giulia grew more outspoken. She would carry on about Mama's extravagant spending. She thought Mama was foolish to buy gold lockets which we kids never wore, diamond rings she kept in a tin Hershey's Cocoa box, 14-karat gold-rimmed goblets nobody drank from, and dozens of patent leather high-heeled shoes. Mama also bought yards of silk chiffon and velvet that Miss Budski, the neighborhood Polish dressmaker, cut up and sewed into fancy dresses, not only for Mama, but for Agnes and me.

She bought elegant items for the house, too: a set of blue and white Limoges porcelain dinnerware rimmed with gold, different sets of emerald-green and sapphire-blue gold-plated goblets, and a fancy wooden box full of sterling silver forks, knives, and spoons.

She also bought a dead baby fox with stiff amber fur, yellow glass eyes, and a mouth with sharp, tiny teeth which had been made into a clasp. Mama pinned its mouth to its tail and wore it over the collar of her tan cashmere coat. I could tell she admired it by the way she tucked the fur away from its glassy eyes as she passed the hall mirror before she went shopping. I hated it. Not only did it look fierce, but it also smelled like a closet full of old shoes. And its fur was rough, not like Mama's black sealskin Sunday coat.

· In contrast, according to Mama, Giulia held on to every penny Carlo ever earned. "She walks ten blocks to save two cents on a bunch of soup greens."

After one of Mama's shopping sprees, Giulia would puff, shake her head in disbelief, and bewail Mama's short memory. Had Mama forgotten the years she spent embroidering hundreds of hankies to save the few pennies she had in her pocket when she landed on Ellis Island? And had she forgotten how, after she arrived in America, she saved nickels by walking across the Williamsburg Bridge instead of taking a trolley car? Had she forgotten the long hours she'd worked in Manhattan's lower east side brassiere factory to earn a few dollars a week?

Giulia always finished her chiding with a dire warning: "Eh, *su sposo*, he make-a easy dolla, *fa male*, you trow away money." She mourned a coming day when Mama would wish she had hidden Papa's money under her mattress—as Giulia did—rather than having spent it foolishly.

Often, looking sideways at Mama and sensing she had gone too far, Giulia would sigh loud and long, sometimes hugging one of us on her soft lap. After a brief silence, shaking her head side to side as though reprimanding herself, she would smile and speak to whomever was near or on her lap, acknowledging that Mama was lucky to have relatives like Aunt Angelina and Uncle Tony, with whom she could live after arriving in America. Mama was lucky Uncle Tony had introduced her to Papa. She was lucky Uncle Tony had arranged for Papa and Mama to meet, and that he had been right in predicting Papa would get ahead in this world.

Getting the gist of why Giulia thought Mama was lucky was easy, but I couldn't understand why Giulia said Mama had a short memory. Mama remembered everything. She remembered being a little girl in Chieti and overhearing old men brag about their sons who sent money home from America. Mama remembered them saying the streets of New York City were paved with gold. She remembered how she dreamed of going in and out of fancy shops and walking up and down those golden streets in shiny black patent leather shoes.

Mama also remembered the day she ran away from home. Her mother lied to her about running an errand and instead met a suitor, Pepino. Mama believed this was too soon after her father had died. The nuns taught girls that good widows wore black and never looked at another man for twenty years.

On the day of her mother's wedding to Pepino, Mama said she hung back, packed a church dress and her lavender rosary beads into a silvery scarf, and raced through the cobbled alleys to her grandmother's home, where she lived until her Nonna died when Mama was about fourteen.

Mama remembered how *las maestras*, two elderly sisters who had never married, took her in after her Nonna died. She remembered how they tied three chairs together and made a mattress out of thick woolen blankets. Every night, she lay on those soft blankets and dreamed about the paradise in America.

Las maestras told Mama how everybody who went to America found good jobs with good pay. If only they themselves were younger, they would go too and take Mama with them. According to letters from relatives and neighbors, Italians in America earned more money in a year than peasant farmers in Italy made in a lifetime. They told Mama how, as soon as the men landed, they lived with relatives or in rooming houses, paying twenty cents a night until they saved enough money to open pizzerias, tailor shops, bakeries, shoe shops, or horse stables.

Las maestras said the Italian men who began immigrating to America in the 1870s made America strong. Hundreds of thousands left their villages in Sicily, Calabria, Abruzzi. Those who wrote home boasted about Italian *paisanos* who could plaster walls and shoe horses better than any other immigrants. They got the best jobs and were put on steady work. Especially better than Irish or Polish immigrants who couldn't do anything well except drink away their paychecks every Saturday night. Mama added with a scoff, "Like all Italian men, *braggadoci.* Probably jealous of the tall, good-looking Irish cops."

Often, Mama would pause and repeat why she had disowned her mother. "She lied," she said, then added, "Remember. Truth is always in the room. She never goes away." If Mama thought something was important, she always said it twice.

And I would glimpse Truth as a hazy figure like the one on the cover of my prayer book while Mama continued to reminisce. Mama could not forgive her mother for sneaking out at night, pretending to go to Nonna's or to shop for breakfast biscotti or buy embroidery thread. "I followed her. She lied. She met that shoemaker, Pepino, in the park. She broke her word. I stopped trusting her."

And Mama remembered when she was nine or ten, how her older sister Marietta came to Nonna's house every day carrying fresh cheese or soup and sharing news of their mother and Pepino and the new baby. Marietta also brought thread and taught Mama how to embroider handkerchiefs.

Mama practiced and practiced until she could make even stitches on both sides of the delicate hankies. She said she wanted hers to "be the best." She twisted two or three different threads together, light pink with deep pink, adding a little blue to create beautiful waves of lavender. Her handkerchiefs sold quickly, before Marietta's. She sold each for a few pennies and hid her earnings in a brown jug she kept under her chair-bed.

Mama counted her money over and over until finally, in 1911, when she turned seventeen, she took the jug out from under her bed and counted fifty-two liras—exactly what she needed to set foot on Ellis Island.

CHAPTER TWO—ELLIS ISLAND

1911

One rainy day when we were playing indoors, we asked Mama to tell us the story about her crossing to America during the terrifying storm that almost toppled the ship. In addition to the scary part, we learned if you sailed the Atlantic in the winter of 1911 from the frozen port in Naples, Italy, to Ellis Island in New York City, it cost twenty-two dollars. If you crossed during spring or summer, it cost more—thirty dollars. Mama crossed in December of that year.

Prior to her voyage, Uncle Tony had reserved a middle deck unit on the *Prinzess Irene* for his wife—Aunt Angelina—and their four young children to return to America after their visit with relatives in Chieti. But the children kept getting one cold after another, and before everyone was healthy at the same time, more than a year had gone by. Mama believed the delay was a sign: she was seventeen, and joining Aunt Angelina and her children when they returned to America provided the opportunity to pursue her dream.

She took money from the jug under her chair-bed and purchased a ticket to leave with them.

However, according to Aunt Angelina, a few days before the departure from Chieti to the port in Naples, Mama's mother threatened to go to the Italian authorities to prohibit Mama from leaving, saying her daughter was too young and couldn't support herself. Mama faced her mother for the first time in ten years, picked up a knife and, holding it at her throat, said, "If you try to stop me, I'll kill myself." Her mother relented.

Unfortunately, the delay cost them the reserved cabin. The ship's purser told Aunt Angelina they hadn't arrived in time to claim the deck cabin, and it had been given to another family.

They had two choices: wait for three or four weeks for the next sailing or make the crossing in the hold of the ship. Aunt Angelina wanted to wait.

"Then I'll go alone," Mama said.

Aunt Angelina yielded immediately. Mama said either she wanted to get back to America or she was afraid of what relatives might say if anything happened to her seventeen-year-old virgin niece while traveling alone.

During story time we learned not only about embarking—we learned about landing in America. Before you could step foot on American soil you had to present a healthy body and a sound mind—no signs of any disease, no consumption, no scabs, no coughs, no pinkeye, no limp. In addition to the cost of passage you had to show the Irish American clerks thirty dollars cash in hand—the amount needed in case you were sent back on the next ship because the health exam revealed tuberculosis, syphilis, or another disease.

If Mama said, "It's enough stories for today," a chorus of nos could be heard a block away. We talked over each other, our voices a chorus of reprimands:

"You forgot the best part."

"We didn't have an intermission."

"And you didn't talk about dressmaker, dressmaker."

"And the four brothers?"

Clearly pleased for the encore, she continued to tell us how she spoke with extra care when the Irish clerks asked if she had a needed skill, and the boys wanted to hear the story about the four brothers. Looking pleased, she half-smiled and renewed story time. Mama knew that before the clerks even let the doctors examine passengers, immigrants had to prove they had a "sponsor," an American citizen to live with, as well as a trade America needed. When the clerks asked Mama her trade, she said she cleared her throat and replied, "Dressmaker." She told us, "*Las Maestras* made me practice saying it over and over in English. Dressmaker. Dressmaker. Dressmaker."

Traveling on the ship with Mama were four brothers. Throughout the voyage they helped the sick older men and nauseous children. The brothers held the foreheads of the children while they vomited and lifted the grandfathers in and out of their bunks or steadied them against the side-to-side lashings of the stormy sea as they staggered to and from the foul-smelling latrines, mercifully located at the far end of the hold.

Each of the four brothers had saved enough for his own passage, but between them—in actual cash—they had exactly thirty dollars. Only enough for one return passage. Two of the boys hammered horseshoes and the other two plastered walls.

Mama said, "One looked so sickly, I was sure he couldn't do anything." The older brothers boasted of their strength, flexing muscles, doing pull-ups on overhead rails, but the youngest was frail, seasick the entire trip, throwing up day and night. The whole time his brothers urged him to eat: *"Mange, mange."*

The boys had an uncle who owned a stable of horses in Chicago. They had no idea where he lived, but Chicago was small, they said. Not like New York. They were sure they would find him. Like many early immigrants, their uncle had changed his name from Joseppi Marchiano to Joe March. Mama scoffed at this, saying he lacked Italian pride.

Finally, when the ship arrived at Ellis Island, waiting in line for their health checkup, the four brothers pleaded with nearby women to pray for them. As the oldest moved forward to be examined by the doctors, his brothers made signs of the cross on their chests and gave him light whacks on his back, never taking their eyes off him. When he reappeared, he winked, took the folded wad of thirty dollars from his shirt pocket, and slipped it to the next-oldest brother before he approached the examination alcove. The third did the same.

As the youngest entered the examination area, his brothers stood still as stone statues. A few older women prayed out loud.

Mama said the area sounded like a hushed funeral mass inside a church. The young boy's examination took longer than usual, and the oldest brother lifted his arms and drew his younger brothers close to his thin chest. Nobody moved, all eyes fixed on the door. Mama said the prayers grew softer, and everybody leaned toward the closed door. When the boy emerged smiling, his big black eyes shining and his hand tap-tapping his money pocket, a group of men cheered: *"Bravo! Bravi!"* Women of all ages wept openly.

Starting down the ramp arm in arm, the four brothers broke into song: *"Funiculi, Funicula."*

Some of the passengers yelled *"Arrivederci! Arrivederci!"* Others joined in song, cheering the brothers on as they stepped onto the ferry which would take them to the dock in lower Manhattan.

Mama called out, "Don't change your names. Be proud you're Italian."

CHAPTER THREE—
MAMA'S MARRIAGE

1915

Mama's first years in America were good. She lived with Aunt Angelina and Uncle Tony, who owned a barbershop and made a solid living. Aunt Angelina was a good wife and kept a clean house. And Mama found a job in a garment factory. She was one of the quickest to learn how to stitch double needle. "I knew using a machine with two needles inside the 'foot' couldn't be much different than single needle. You just had to be more careful about turning in the edge. Besides, it paid more than single-needle—two dollars more a week." Then, holding her head high, she said, "I gave the two dollars to Aunt Angelina to help pay for my room and board." Then, to make a point, she added, "Never take anything for nothing in return."

On Friday evenings, as they ate linguini with clams, Uncle Tony talked about a new customer. "Every week, late in the afternoon, a young Italian man comes to the barbershop. He wears a silk shirt and expensive leather shoes." Then, winking in Mama's direction, he added, "He asks about the girl with the beautiful black hair who leaves the house at dawn every morning and comes home after dark."

Mama knew what Uncle Tony was up to. She was almost twenty-one, ready for marriage, and Uncle Tony considered the man a good match.

The stranger kept asking questions, and Uncle Tony explained about his niece from Chieti—how she worked long hours in a garment factory in Manhattan, leaving early in the morning to cross the Williamsburg Bridge on foot to save the five-cent trolley fare for her trousseau.

Mama went to night school with another young garment worker. They both wanted to learn English in preparation for the day they might sign their naturalization papers. Mama said she wanted to become an American citizen on her own, "not because I married an American citizen."

Mama told us the night class had mostly Jewish girls from Poland or Russia with beautiful blue eyes and blonde hair. They studied the hardest and finished their tests first. But the teacher praised Mama for having the best ear. She said Mama spoke English with almost no accent.

The man with expensive shoes started coming to the barbershop more often, sometimes for a shave, sometimes just to get his mustache trimmed. He liked a splash of cologne even though it cost two cents more. Uncle Tony said this customer offered to give Mama a ride to work in his wagon. That way she could sleep a little longer, leave later, and still save the five cents. Uncle Tony said if his intentions were "respectable" this seemed like a fine idea. But knowing Mama's headstrong bent, Uncle Tony told him he would first have to ask her.

"Is he afraid to ask himself?" Mama asked.

Uncle Tony took that as a yes.

The next evening after night school, as Mama approached the brownstone building where Uncle Tony had his shop, a quick-moving man emerged from the doorway. After nodding in Uncle Tony's direction and tipping his hat, he said, *"Buonasera. Permetto permesso?"*

Mama smiled. She liked the feistiness in his voice. *"Si."*

He told Mama he could give her a ride to work. First, he spoke in Italian with a Neapolitan accent, then repeated the words in English. Mama liked his clear English. She thought he might have been born in America; she also thought he was showing off, so she replied "thank you" in her best English, then switched to Italian, telling him she didn't mind walking to work, saying, "I would never ride in a wagon behind a horse. If you had a car, it might be different."

That's how Mama and Papa met.

Over the next few months, Uncle Tony kept dropping Papa's name. Every evening at supper, Uncle Tony would take his place at the head of the table, compliment Aunt Angelina for her tasty minestrone or homemade ravioli, then praise the ripe figs or sweet cherries Papa had dropped off for the family. Or he would mention to Aunt Angelina that Papa had added five steady new customers in Flatbush or Canarsie.

"His business is growing," Uncle Tony would say, without looking at Mama, continuing to address Aunt Angelina.

"The man is ambitious, smart, hard-working. He wears silk shirts, handmade Italian imported ties. Gold cuff links. Good taste. He came from Avalino as an infant, went to American schools. Speaks good."

Uncle Tony's grandparents had immigrated in the mid-1800s, and he had been born and schooled in America. He knew Mama valued good English.

"He owns a strong, healthy horse. Has a well-made wagon, painted with expensive green enamel and decorated with a wide gold stripe. One day some girl is going to live well. She'll have fresh fruit and vegetables every day. Never go hungry."

Uncle Tony let that sink in while he ladled more soup, then continued addressing Aunt Angelina. "He's saved enough money to buy a truck. Hired a helper. He wants to move up in the world. Buys fruit and vegetables cheap from Long Island farmers and sells them high in Wallabout Market. Rents a corner store. Low rent. Hides the profit in a shoe box. Says he's saving money to raise a family. Buys cheap and sells high. The man is going to make it in this world." He nodded to Aunt Angelina and asked for more clams.

Before long, Uncle Tony invited Papa to Sunday dinners. And over time, Papa convinced Mama he was a man who wanted what she wanted—to get ahead in America.

The way Mama explained it, she was twenty-one and didn't want to live with Aunt Angelina and Uncle Tony for the rest of her life. After a year of chaperoned courting, one autumn evening when she and Papa were sitting on the bench outside Uncle Tony's barber shop, he opened a small green velvet box which contained a diamond ring and proposed marriage. Mama was not surprised. She nodded and Papa kissed her on the cheek.

It was 1915.

They married soon after, went to Niagara Falls for a one-week honeymoon, then returned to Brooklyn to live with Papa's parents on Carroll Street. Years later, Papa's older sister—Aunt Mary —said Papa had originally bought the ring for another woman, but when she "gave in to him," he demanded she return the ring; he wanted the mother of his children to be a virgin on their wedding night—a woman who knew how to say no. The way Mama held up her chin when she told us this story, I felt certain she was that kind of woman.

CHAPTER FOUR—LOUISA, THE MIDWIFE

1925

W hen I was almost five, while we kids ate our oatmeal and snow drifted outside our kitchen window, Mama phoned Aunt Tessie and asked her to come over quickly, saying Louisa, the midwife, was on her way. Aunt Tessie had recently married Papa's younger brother, Uncle Pete, after her younger sister (Pete's first wife) died during childbirth. Tessie arrived shortly after Mama hung up the phone. Mama told us kids to obey her and hurried back to bed.

Moments later, Louisa arrived and started bustling about. First, she put clean sheets on Mama's bed. Next, she piled another clean set on the bureau. She scrubbed the big white enamel basin in the kitchen sink and rinsed it with boiling water. Then she poured more boiling water in the basin, stuffed a stack of clean white towels under her arm, told Francey to make sure the rest of us stayed in the kitchen, and headed toward Mama's bedroom. It was December, too cold for us to play outside. Besides, I didn't want to go outside. I wanted to find out why we couldn't go into Mama's bedroom.

Soon Louisa called for Aunt Tessie, who told Francey to keep us out of trouble, then she raced into Mama's bedroom and closed the door.

Every now and then, we could hear Mama. She made sounds like she had a bellyache or had her hand over her mouth to smother a cry. Louisa and Aunt Tessie kept talking over each other: *"Spongere. Spongere!"* "Push. Push hard!"

Shortly, we heard a baby cry. Aunt Tessie, Louisa, and Mama started laughing and talking at the same time, mixing up English and Italian, making it hard for me to understand what they were saying. Francey, Albert, Agnes, Gloria, and I remained huddled in silence exchanging questioning looks.

Within a few minutes, Louisa hurried into the kitchen carrying a baby wrapped in a soft bath towel. We stood on tippy toes to see a tiny baby with a face as red as a ripe raspberry and hair blonde as a canary. Louisa said her name was Genevieve and handed her to me. *"Setta,"* she said, and using her foot, she pulled one of the children's chairs close to the open oven that heated the kitchen. I sat and held the soft bundle. "She pee in you lappa, no jumpa. You jumpa, she scare. She scare, she no talk. Justa hold. Eh *no mova.*" Louisa spun around and bolted back toward Mama's bedroom.

Being selected to safeguard a brand-new baby made me feel important. I smiled as Genevieve's big dark eyes roamed my face. Moments later a hot trickle seeped across my thighs. Pee? I gasped but did not move Genevieve. I was not going to scare this tiny stranger with canary-colored hair, teeny-tiny fingers, and no teeth who had mysteriously emerged from Mama's bedroom. I was not going to be responsible for scaring her into never being able to talk.

Louisa soon returned to the kitchen, picked up Genevieve, and noticed the dark wet spot on my lap. "You mova?" she yelled, her voice half accusatory, half questioning.

"No," I yelled back. "Honest! No." Louisa searched my face. Smiling, she said, "You good mama. Best lilla mama." She stroked the top of my head, spit on one of her thumbs, and smoothed my eyebrow. I felt myself blush with pride. Genevieve had turned me into the best little mother.

In addition to being anointed the best little mother, Louisa often told me I could see what my sisters and brothers couldn't see. She told me every time she visited—and Louisa visited often. After Modestino died, Mama vowed never again to have a baby born in a hospital. Within the next twelve years Louisa delivered all eight of us at home. Throughout those years Louisa came when Mama was carrying a baby, and Louisa came to deliver each new baby. Louisa came if a baby had colic. She came when a new baby was baptized. She came to confirm or dispute Dr. Lupo's advice on any condition Mama might have.

Louisa also came at Easter to pick up one of Mama's homemade ricotta and citron wheat pies. And every Easter, as Mama wrapped the pie in a clean diaper, Louisa would request the recipe because next year, for sure, really for sure, she was going to make one at home for her family.

Mama would look wise, smile, and recite the recipe: "A *frushell*, about three cups. Fresh—really fresh—ricotta. Best from Antonia's. Four fresh eggs, one extra egg yolk. Large. Fresh. A good handful summer wheat you cook the night before with a knucklebone. Some butter. A few tablespoons sugar. Taste. Not too sweet. Cinnamon. Citron and orange rind cut small. You could use juice. Add rum or brandy or vanilla. What you like. Mix with your hands. Taste. Pinch of salt. You could add heavy cream. Rich pie crust. Use lard. Makes flakiest. Put fancy crisscross strips on top. Don't bake too long. Dries out. Before you eat, dust with powdered sugar. It's enough for two pies."

Mama would pause, look at Louisa, smile, and say, "Eh, for sure, really for sure you *won't* make it."

Both would explode with laughter, Mama moving her head side to side, Louisa slapping her thighs and nodding yes, yes, their eyes sparkling with the fun of sharing an annual Eastertime ritual.

At other times, after tending to Mama, Louisa would call to me, "Eleanora."

I stood facing her, while she stroked my hair, wet both her thumbs on her tongue, and smoothed my eyebrows. Moving her head side to side, she would say, "I bringa so many *bambino*—onny you, onny you born with a blue veil. Veil no torna over you heada. No torna veil make-a you see whatta nobody else see."

I understood only that I had been born in a blue sack with its veil covering my head. And according to Louisa—whom Mama insisted knew more than Dr. Lupo—Jesus blessed anyone who entered the world without a torn veil the gift of seeing the unknown.

And I believed it to be true.

CHAPTER FIVE—GOING PLACES

1926

In the months that followed Genevieve's birth, Mama didn't go shopping. She stayed home nursing the baby, scolding Agnes, and spending time with Mrs. Gould, the public health nurse. Mrs. Gould had taken a special interest in Mama, perhaps because Mama loved learning new things, and Mrs. Gould seemed to enjoy observing Mama as she put her new knowledge to work.

Mrs. Gould taught Mama about the importance of giving us cod-liver oil every morning, how to smooth calamine lotion on chicken pox scabs, how to slide Vaseline over the baby's bottom to avoid rashes, and how to rinse the poo-poo diapers in the toilet bowl before putting them in the washing machine.

I was sure Mama already knew how to do this, but Mama respected Mrs. Gould so much, she didn't let on.

Mrs. Gould taught Mama how to check our scalps for head lice, and if one of us had them, we all got treated. We leaned our heads over the sink and Mama doused them with rubbing alcohol, which stung, or a mixture of mouthwash and olive oil that ran down our necks.

Best of all, Mrs. Gould brought small gifts—presents for each on our birthdays: pencils and notebooks with blue lines, round red erasers on tiny wheels with stiff black brushes on the other end, or a dainty hankie with our initials on it. She gave us "toiletries"—a nice, long word that I sounded out under my breath —*toy-let-trees.* And little bars of soap, small hair combs, toothbrushes. She gave Mama a box of awful-tasting baking soda to put on our toothbrushes, which I rinsed off before I started brushing. Mama said Mrs. Gould, who had no children, probably bought these gifts with money out of her own pocket.

While Mama was learning how to raise healthy American children and we kids were enjoying little gifts, Papa seemed to be having a good time, too. He went to meetings, drove upstate on weekends searching for a "gentleman's farm," bought eels and cooked them as if it were New Year's Eve, and kept busy from daybreak until deep into the night. Ever on the move, he delighted in taking me and my older brothers on outings.

"If you're going to be Supreme Court judges you have to learn everything about America." He took Albert, Francey, and me all over the city. On a moment's notice, he would rush up the three long flights of stairs from his garage, crying, "Let's go!" And off we'd go in his big, new Packard.

Although I loved Papa's high moods and spontaneous playfulness, Mama didn't. She complained about how he kept himself in a frenzy, racing around too fast, investing money recklessly, buying expensive machinery on credit without money to back it, hardly ever sleeping. She confided to Giulia, *"Pazzo.* Crazy."

Despite Mama's objections I loved how on Sundays, after Albert, Francey, and I came home from church, Papa would rush everyone through lunch and the whole family would pile into the big eggplant-colored Packard and take off for an adventure.

He took us to the Metropolitan Museum of Art, the Magiani puppet show, and the Bronx Zoo. Once he took us to a late-night feast in Brooklyn's Little Italy where a young boy wearing a girl's dress clung to a rope tied around a telephone pole. The boy was supposed to be an angel talking to the devil. Mostly, he struggled to keep from falling off a tiny platform nailed high up on the telephone pole while half-talking, half-singing to a midget in the bottom of an adjacent building's coal chute that exposed a basement below. Albert tried to shake the telephone pole, and when it didn't move, he kicked it. Then he kicked the door to the coal chute.

At the Barnum and Bailey Circus, we filled the whole front row in a section with fancy padded seats. Three rings were filled with daring animal acts: tigers growled, elephants danced, and lions jumped through hoops. Overhead, skinny girls walked on high wires, one with no net underneath. Outside the rings, walking in front of us were twin sisters stuck together at the hip, and a tall, skinny colored woman from Africa with decorated dessert plates wedged tight inside big holes in her upper and lower lips. The girl on the high wire, the twins, and the woman with dessert plates in her lips made me so queasy I stopped looking.

I didn't like the circus. It smelled of manure and the loud music never stopped.

Another time, Papa took my brothers and me to see Charles Lindbergh when he returned to America from Paris after flying across the Atlantic all by himself in a small plane. We drove to an airfield where hundreds of people waved flags, hooted, and whistled. Papa bought American flags for Albert and Francey and a French one for me.

The crowd was huge. Everyone squeezed together, yelling "Hello, Lindy" and "Welcome home" and "Hurrah for the Lone Eagle," as if they were close relatives. I complained because I couldn't see anything but shoes and belts. Papa lifted me to his shoulders and pushed his way through the crowd, telling the boys to stay close. Lindbergh leaned out of a small plane and waved to me, the only one sitting on her father's shoulders. Papa jostled his way forward and we got so close I could see Lindbergh's eyes.

I yelled to my brothers, "He's got blue eyes! The Lone Eagle's got big blue eyes!"

One sunny spring Sunday we went to the Bronx Zoo. Although I hadn't started school, Francey had taught me how to count. I stopped in awe at the giraffe's area, and when I had counted fifty-seven giraffes, I realized Mama, Papa, and my brothers and sisters had vanished. I called out, but no one answered. I kept shouting, "Mama, Papa, Francey, Albert" over and over again, louder and louder. I didn't know if I should run ahead, go back, or stay put.

A woman approached and tried to comfort me. I could tell she was Jewish because she spoke like the Monday morning peddler who had a pushcart and bought rags from women who lived in tenement houses on our block. She asked, "Are you calling for your mother because you're lost?"

"No, my *mother* is lost," I said. She smiled, then took my hand and said we would find my mother at the police station. I balked and took back my hand. Mama had warned us about never talking to strangers and never, ever letting anyone touch us. Further, I didn't want to go to a police station. But I didn't know where else to go. I recalled Mama's warnings; they always implied never going anywhere with a strange man. Her words rang in my head. I paused.

Mama had never mentioned anything about women strangers. And this woman didn't look strange; she was smiling down at me, and she promised to wait with me at the police station until we found my mother. She also reminded me of Mrs. Gould, the public health nurse. Speaking softly, she said, "I don't need to hold your hand, we can walk side by side. The police station is close. The policemen will find your mother." She took a few steps and waited. I walked to her side.

On the way, she asked my name and where I lived, and she praised me for knowing them. Once inside, she spoke to a police officer who wrote something on a pad. Then he picked me up, swung me around the way Papa swung Agnes and sat me on a huge desk on a raised section above the floor. He told me to wait and smiled at the Jewish lady; he said he'd return soon. When he did, he carried an ice cream cone with two scoops, one strawberry, the other chocolate.

Before I finished the cone, Mama bolted through the door. The moment she saw me she burst into tears. Instantly, the Jewish woman started to cry, then everybody cried except Papa and Albert. The police officer who had given me the ice cream cone laughed out loud and placed me on the floor.

Through her tears, Mama said she was grateful to the Jewish lady, who had stopped crying, and Papa thanked the police officers and told everybody we should be leaving. My middle sister, Gloria, said we would all cease crying if Papa stopped on the way home to buy everyone an ice cream cone. He winked at her, his eyes saying yes. In response, Gloria marched toward the door and started to sing our Car Song.

"They say our Pop has got no pep. But he's got pep in every step." Soon we were all singing. We didn't stop until everyone had an ice cream cone. I still nibbled on mine.

Ever since that day, whenever one of us cried, we all cried. We named it the Police Station Crying Disease.

CHAPTER SIX—PAURA

1927

In 1915, when Papa and Mama married, he had been ped-
dling fruit and vegetables in a horse-drawn wagon. Now, a
little over a decade later, when I was almost six, he owned
two big Mack trucks and employed several hired hands, each at
two dollars a day. He'd bribed several Long Island farmers into
signing papers promising not to sell garlic or broccoli to anyone else. And he began branching out, landing contracts to haul
equipment for government construction projects in Manhattan.

Eager to "connect with big shots," Papa joined the Elks Club,
went to political rallies, and made donations to the Sons of Italy.
At home, he insisted on good manners and good English, which
he said were "absolutely necessary to get ahead in America and
especially to become Supreme Court judges." For good measure
he had nailed a picture of the Supreme Court to the wall of his
garage—nine men wearing what looked like nuns' black bathrobes. I thought it was to show they were all Catholic; I started
to ask but Papa kept talking. He said becoming a Supreme Court
judge was the best job anybody could have in America:

"The job is for life; nobody can fire you. You get a big paycheck
from the government on a steady basis and when you retire you
keep getting your full salary until you die." Although I didn't see
any women in that picture on the wall of his garage, he acted like
he expected me to become one of those judges. I wasn't so sure.

At the same time, in the back room above Papa's double garage, he and Uncle Pete, his younger brother, had a still for mak-

ing whiskey. They sold it to speakeasies in Brooklyn and Long Island.

Although he warned us kids never to say anything to anybody about the still, Papa insisted he wasn't doing anything wrong. "There's nothing in the Constitution about not making whiskey in your own house. And, anyway, the Supreme Court judges are going to fix the biggest mistake they ever made. Prohibition will be kicked out. I'm right. You'll see."

Despite the *Daily News* headlines about police dumping illegal whiskey down manholes, Papa didn't seem the least bit worried. He kept making whiskey in the back room over his garage, and he kept making money on the side. And he and Mama kept spending it. Every other day or two, something new came into the house. A life-size Carrara marble statue of a little girl reprimanding a cat that had killed a baby bird which lay at her feet. A fancy oak icebox with white enamel inside and *two* shelves. A Lionel train set with wide tracks and an engine so big Evelyn could ride on it.

The day Papa drove home with a big, eggplant-colored, brand-new Packard, he boasted to Mama, "Come and look. Pete and I bought ourselves one each. Paid cash." Turning to us kids, he added, "Come next summer, we're all going for a ride along the Hudson River to see a vacation house in the country."

Uncle Pete's plum-colored Packard looked exactly like ours, but his was bulletproof. Albert said it was bulletproof because Uncle Pete was selling hootch in a *Mafioso's* territory. Mama said she didn't want Uncle Pete to park his Packard in Papa's garage. Papa didn't say anything to her. He turned and asked Francey, Albert, and me if we wanted to go for a ride. He was going to an important public meeting in Battery Park in Manhattan.

Before we left the house, Papa got all dressed up in his new Coward shoes, a cream-colored, soft silk shirt with gold cuff links, and his smooth, dark suit with sharp creases in the pants. He put his fancy diamond stickpin on his made-in-Italy pure silk tie and his shiny Elks pin on the jacket lapel. From the bedroom he called out to Mama, "Comb Eleanor's hair." By the rough tugs of the hairbrush, I knew she was upset with Papa's racing around and giving her orders.

Soon we were off, Papa driving the new Packard in a way Mama hated. If she had been with us, she would have lowered her voice and said, "*Aventato.* Reckless. Poor driver." And she would have been right. When he swerved around a corner, an old man yelled, "*Fongool,*" which I knew was a swear word in Italian, but Papa didn't seem to notice or care. He kept talking loud and fast about plans for the new West Side Highway. "It'll be the best thing ever happened to New York City. Exits from midtown all the way down to the Battery Tunnel. Money in my pocket."

I was sure Papa's swerving would end by crashing us into the railing as we crossed the Brooklyn Bridge. We would drown in the water below, and Mama would never know where we were buried, like she had never found out where Modestino was buried after he died. I wished I had stayed home. My chest began to hurt and I was afraid Paura might appear. I closed my eyes and kept them shut until the car finally stopped at Battery Park and I started to breathe.

Papa tried to park near a crowd of people, but a bunch of police officers waved their arms and told him to move on. Papa refused. Instead, he jumped out of the car and started arguing with the police.

"You'll be sorry when you find out who I am."

One of the officers said he didn't care who he was, he couldn't park there. Papa climbed back in the Packard and found another place to park. I thought it was too close to a fire hydrant, but I didn't say a word. He slammed the door so hard, I was afraid to make him more upset.

Papa raced toward a crowd of men gathered in the middle of the street. My brothers and I ran alongside trying to keep up. A small but sturdy-looking makeshift stage had been built several feet off the ground right in the middle of a street at the edge of Battery Park. A row of men sat on the stage behind a long table. The man who sat in the middle, in the biggest chair, held a fancy wooden gavel. The other six or seven men were lined up on either side of him like Supreme Court judges, except they were not wearing black bathrobes. They kept fiddling with their water glasses and none wore a creamy silk shirt as nice as Papa's.

Behind the group stood two big sandy-haired cops. I knew they were Irish because they looked like the tall, husky McNulty brothers, all six of them policemen, who lived on Twentieth Street and ate at Uncle Frank's and Aunt Mary's pizzeria.

The cops on the stage stood stiff and looked uncomfortable. They held tall poles with large American flags. None of the seated men had flags. No one in the crowd waved a white handkerchief or miniature American or French flag the way they had at Lindbergh's celebration.

The crowd was also much smaller. This time, it was easier for Papa to get us up close. And there wasn't as much noise—mostly mumbles and cigarette coughing or men sneezing. Papa held my hand and told the three of us to pay attention, although he seemed to be having a hard time standing still.

After the man with the gavel banged it on the table, the men took turns thanking people for coming. They informed the public about the plans for the West Side Highway. They spoke about how rapidly people would be able to drive uptown to the Bronx, with its expanding population of furniture dealers and hatmakers, and how quickly trucks could cart all the goods that needed to be transported to the boroughs of Brooklyn and Queens. There would be entrances and exits in midtown Manhattan so cars could get on and off. The city would get lots of visitors and everyone would prosper.

Without warning, while the men took turns talking, Papa jumped up on the platform. He spun around and facing the crowd, shouted louder than any of the men on the stage: "And DeVito will do all the trucking! DeVito hauls anything, anywhere."

The men on the stage froze. The street became silent. Nobody in the crowd moved. Nobody coughed. Nobody sneezed. I turned to ice.

The two cops stared at each other, then took a step toward

Papa as if they were about to drop their flags and grab him. I was afraid if they dropped their flags, Papa would be blamed and get in trouble for causing disrespect for the American flag in front of all these people.

The man with the gavel stood up, knocking over the water pitcher, which made a big splash and sent the seated men scrambling away from the spill. The gavel man and Papa spoke to each other, seeming not to notice the water. I couldn't hear anything.

I began to see bright flashing lights and small black holes.

Paura.

She shrouded me like a black cloud and sucked all the air out of my lungs. I tried to breathe, but Paura kept squeezing harder and harder against my chest and swirling her flashing lights.

Gradually, I felt myself begin to disappear and float far away to the outskirts of the silenced crowd, far from the platform, far from where Papa stood talking. But I also stood anchored at the foot of the platform with lights swirling around me.

There were *two* of me. One stood at the edge of the platform barely able to breathe, and one, transparent, stood on the edge of the crowd watching Papa.

From a distance Paura and the twin me watched Papa walk across the platform and shake the gavel man's hand. We watched the two cops step forward and move their lips as if asking the gavel man a question. He ignored them, placed his hand on Papa's shoulder, and pointed to the side of the stage. Paura kept hovering over me as Papa stopped in front of each man seated at the long table. Papa seemed to be talking but he made no sound. He nodded his head up and down and extended his hand for a handshake. The other men looked at each other. The gavel man tried to avoid Papa's outstretched arm. Papa acted like he didn't notice how quiet and still everyone had become. He turned around and clasped the gavel man's hand in both his own, shaking it vigorously. Then he hopped down the steps and came back to where my brothers and I stood.

From the outskirts of the crowd, Paura and the other me watched.

Several people moved aside to let Papa pass, leaving a wide space around us. The men on the stage said something to each other that I couldn't hear. Gradually, as though from a distance, people started mumbling and coughing and sneezing. I felt dizzy and sick to my stomach. To keep from vomiting, I swallowed hard, closed my eyes tight, opened my mouth wide and dragged in a big breath.

She and Paura had vanished.

My brothers and I didn't ask Papa why he had jumped up on the stage, and we didn't discuss it amongst ourselves. Like the men on the stage, we exchanged a series of uneasy, awkward looks. Without uttering a word, we sealed a pact vowing to be quiet all the way back to Brooklyn.

As soon as we returned home and entered the kitchen, Papa told Mama he met in-person a New York commissioner, who approved the contract for Papa's trucks to begin work on construction of one section of the West Side Highway.

Mama asked the three of us why we looked tired.

Francey spoke. "We had to stand in the crowd a long time."

CHAPTER SEVEN—PENN STATION

1927

Shortly after the trip to Battery Park, I lay on the floor underneath the beautiful white wrought-iron cradle, gently rocking it with my foot and counting aloud the loops in the woven design. I heard Papa's quick step up the last flight of stairs and wriggled out from under the crib just as Mama entered her bedroom and checked on Evelyn, the new baby. As he entered the kitchen he called to me and my brothers, "Jump in the Packard. I'm going to buy a new truck."

Mama said the baby had fallen asleep. "Go. Go."

As usual, Papa zoomed through traffic, zigzagging along Fourth Avenue. He stopped the Packard outside a showroom. The building had huge windows, so high and wide you could see a big green Mack truck parked inside. Papa jumped out of the car singing, "Follow me. Come and see. Follow me." He dashed inside and began chatting with two men dressed in church suits and ties. I dawdled, marveling at the size of the showroom window towering above us. Francey circled the big truck while Albert —first checking to see if the men could see him from where they stood—crouched and slid under the bed of the truck. He smirked; I glared and moved close to Francey.

Papa reached into his pocket and took out a bundle of dollar bills almost an inch thick, bound with a fat rubber band. He told the men it held one hundred and fifty dollars and promised the next payment in a month. One of the men counted the money while the other pointed to long yellow papers on the desk. Papa picked them up and studied them like he was about to take a test. Then he reached inside his shirt pocket, took out his bright orange fountain pen with the fancy nib, and signed his name twice. Turning to my brothers, he smiled. "Two new Mack trucks. One for each of you."

"Can I drive mine home?" Albert asked. Francey rolled his eyes, heaved an exasperated sigh, and gave me a look as if to say, "Isn't he impossible?" But Papa and the men laughed and shook hands; they talked about next month and said goodbye.

I didn't mind Papa not buying one for me. Trucks were for boys. I was more interested in the high showroom windows, unlike any I had ever seen, much taller and wider than the windows of Frederick Loeser, the huge department store where Mama sometimes took me when she shopped for fancy shoes and clothes.

As we moved toward the door, ready to leave, I wondered aloud, "How do the windows stay attached to the building? They go up to the roof." I thought they might tip and fall inside or outside and shatter into pieces. No wooden frames, nothing holding them in place.

Papa stared at me for a second. "You think these are high windows? I can show you an entire building made of much, much higher windows. America's Glass Palace."

"America's Glass Palace? Is it far away?

"No."

"Where is it?"

"In Manhattan."

"When can we see it?"

"Now!"

Papa started jumping side to side, imitating Charlie Chaplin from the movies. "Follow me! Come and see. Follow me," he sang, and dashed out the door, the three of us racing after him and piling into his Packard. I slid in front, the boys in back.

As Papa revved the engine and the car headed toward Manhattan, I warned, "Mama said don't be too long. She's cooking gnocchi."

"Seeing Penn Station is more important than gnocchi. Gnocchi can wait 'til we get home." Looking sideways at me, he teased, "You know potato gnocchi take only a minute to dance in the boiling water." After a short pause, he added, addressing the three of us, "If you're going to be Supreme Court judges"—his tone sounded like he was complimenting himself—"you need to see America's Glass Palace. The place is the busiest train station in America. You'll learn how trains come and go from Penn Station to Washington, DC. Even as far as California." Winking and nodding as though confirming our future, he said, "DC is where Supreme Court judges live."

Driving up the incline to the Brooklyn Bridge, he continued talking. "Italian immigrants—bricklayers, masons, ironworkers. They built this bridge. The largest bridge in the world. They built it with their bare hands." He kept nodding, jutting out his chin acting as if he had built it himself. He talked faster and faster about how, without hardworking Italians, America couldn't have won the war with Germany, how more ambitious Italians were coming to America and pretty soon they would be running the country.

While he carried on, he zigzagged recklessly from one side of the road to the other yelling, "Whoo-eee. Whoo-eee. Whoo-eee!" Albert and Francey joined in and pretty soon the car filled with *whoo-eees*. I thought they were acting crazy, and all the swerving in and out was making me sick to my stomach. At one point the car almost scraped the railing. I was sure we would go over the side, drop into the rough waves, and drown.

Why did Papa like to drive like this? Mama was right, he was reckless and his *paisanos* had good reason to call him *Pazzo*. I felt as scared as Mama must have felt on the *Prinzess Irene* when the storm hit the side of the ship, making it rise and fall sideways for three whole days and nights and Paura became captain of the ship.

True to my fear, Paura appeared outside the side window, her shapeless black robe flying alongside the car. I closed my eyes and turned my head, but it didn't help. Paura stole my breath and squeezed my chest till it hurt.

The car screeched to a halt outside Penn Station and Papa pointed toward the tall pink marble columns surrounding the building. "All shipped from Italy," he bragged, as if he had been in charge of construction. "The architects copied the Baths of Cap-acilla in Rome." Tossing his head, he added, "Copycats. They cop-ied the Italians."

Standing on firm ground and viewing the row of solid col-umns helped me breathe again. Papa grabbed my hand and rushed us inside Penn Station. His warm hand calmed me. Paura disappeared.

Inside, everything seemed brighter than outdoors. I looked up. A glass ceiling touched the sky. It was like being in a big church with a view of heaven through brilliant glass arches. Papa was right. Seeing America's Glass Palace was more import-ant than gnocchi.

Albert, on the other hand, seemed more interested in looking down. He moved toward a bank of steps that led to the train tracks on the lower level.

Papa stopped him. "Pay attention. Look at that clock. I want to teach you something." Mounted on one wall was a clock as big as our round kitchen table. Kneeling beside me, Papa grew serious. "See the two hands? What number is the short hand on?"

"Two," I said.

"And the long hand?"

Francey answered "Four—that's the minute hand." Papa sprang up, gave him a quick wink, tapped his index finger to his lips with a little *shush,* and then kneeled again next to me.

"The clock is telling you it's twenty minutes past two."

"Where's the twenty?"

Papa laughed and started to explain sixty minutes in an hour, twelve hours in a day, how the hands had to circle twice to make the twenty-four hours from light to dark and back to light. He kept explaining while I got more and more confused. I wanted him to explain how the windows that reached up to heaven stayed in place.

My brothers looked impatient too. Francey already knew how to tell time, and Albert was more interested in the clanging noise rising from the wide steps that led somewhere underneath us. He kept insisting we had spent enough time looking at the ceiling, it was time to go downstairs, time to watch the trains coming in and going out. Papa gave him warning looks, and I was afraid if Albert kept it up, Papa would unbuckle his belt and give him a whack on his legs right there in America's Glass Palace. But he didn't.

Exhilarated, talking loud and fast, determined to teach me how to tell time, Papa kept explaining how and why the hands moved to let all the travelers know when to board their trains, how they told everyone the earth was twirling around the sun.

Zing! I knew how to tell time. Not only was America's Glass Palace more beautiful than anything I had ever seen, but I had learned how to tell time.

Papa, looking pleased with himself for having taught me something important, finally gave in to Albert.

Facing Francey, I bragged, "I know how to tell time and Albert doesn't." Albert pretended not to hear and leapt ahead as we moved toward the steps down to watch the trains.

Suddenly, Papa stopped and shouted, "Marco! Chenzi!" Three men, facing us from the steps below, froze.

One, leaping up, hailed, "Charley!"

Charley? Only relatives and Mama called Papa "Charley." Who were these strangers acting like family, calling Papa Charley? Everyone else called Papa "Frank." Even the words painted on all his trucks read FRANK DeVITO—We Sell Service.

The skinniest man pumped his fist in the air several times, almost cheering, and shouted Papa's nickname. *"Pazzo!"*

"Chenzi! Marco!" Papa cheered back.

They made so much noise and blocked so much traffic, people glared. When the three of them reached the landing, they began a play fight, hitting each other, not hard, just for fun and to show they could give a good punch and take one, too. Papa nudged Chenzi in his fat belly, and Chenzi rolled his eyes in mock humiliation and laughed. They all spoke at the same time, interrupting each other, some words in Italian, some in English, all so excited that Papa didn't notice they used Italian in front of us kids.

Chenzi poked Papa's bony ribs. "Just like old times. And in the Penn!" Marco doubled over laughing, slapping his thighs over and over. Chenzi and Papa also burst out laughing. I didn't see what was so funny. Another man, who seemed to be with them, stood aside, watching; he didn't laugh.

And for no reason that I could see, Papa shrunk into himself and grew quiet. Was it because he spoke Italian in front of us? He looked at my brothers as if concerned over what they heard or thought. The man who hadn't joined in the laughter continued to be watchful and quiet. Mama would have liked the way this man dressed. He wore a beautiful black fedora tilted sideways over one eye, a snug-fitting navy-blue suit with a matching vest, and a silky-looking pale blue tie. He leaned back, swirling a sweet-smelling cigar at the corner of his shiny lips, taking everything in. Mostly he sized Papa up.

Still laughing and horsing around, Marco said, "*Pazzo, come sta?* Long time no see. Whatcha up to?"

"Doin' good. Keepin' busy, wheeling stuff around Brooklyn. Got a deal with a contractor building the West Side Highway. He keeps my dump truck movin' six days a week. Just bought two new Macks for . . . for hauling."

Then he waved his hand toward me and my brothers. "Four more at home. All girls."

Marco pinched Albert's ear, nodded, and winked at Papa. "*Fa bene.*" Then he pumped his fist in the air five or six times, and the men laughed.

Marco, catching his breath as if he had just remembered something important, turned quickly and nodded his head almost apologetically toward the quiet man who chewed on his cigar, twirling it between his fingers and making the diamond ring on his pinky glitter.

"*Scusa, scusa,*" Marco muttered, then introduced the man to Papa. I missed his name, so I moved closer. "—business partner.

In from Florida. We came to pick him up. Has contacts in Cuba."

Before Marco had a chance to introduce Papa, the man called Business Partner interrupted, his eyes fixed on Papa. "So, you do trucking. Any long-distance hauling?"

Papa nodded, waving both hands in a wide circle, showing off. "Anywhere. Anytime."

"Maybe we can work out a deal." The four exchanged quick looks. I was sure, if Mama were watching, she would say they were planning something they had to hide from the law. I felt the same way and wanted to hear every word.

Turning away from the men, Papa spoke to Francey. "Make your sister practice how to tell time. Albert, listen to your sister and try to learn." Then he and the men stepped away to a quieter spot and stood close together, two facing two, forming a small square. They began talking, mostly in Italian.

Now that I knew how to tell time, I was less interested in the clock and more interested in what the men said with their heads so close together. I hoped to pick up a word or two in Italian, words I might recognize so I could repeat them to Mama.

But their voices fell lower and lower. Soon the men shook hands, slapped each other on the shoulders, and the three strangers started to leave, everyone talking at the same time.

"Arrivederci."

"Addio."

"Good-bye."

"Be in touch."

Papa, Chenzi, and Marco kissed the air on both sides of each other's cheeks, repeating their good-byes and talking too loud. Chenzi and Marco waved to us, and we waved back.

After they left, Albert said, "They seem like old friends. How do you know them?"

"We were—" Papa stopped. His eyes darkened, drifting away from Penn Station to someplace far away, but it wasn't the same as his look when he thought about Avellino. When he spoke, his voice sounded sad. "We were in the same school together." He paused, looked at us almost apologetically, and added, "We were teenagers."

"P.S. 40?" Francey asked.

"No, a school for . . . for boys. Upstate."

Francey started to ask another question and I wanted to know where upstate, but Papa, flaring up, changed the subject. "It's time to head home. Let's go!"

Although Papa drove just as fast going back to Brooklyn, this time he wasn't yelling *whoo-ee* and he didn't swerve back and forth, either. I felt safe.

Once home, he told Mama about meeting some old friends and how he was going to start hauling almonds from a farm on Long Island to customers in New Jersey and Pennsylvania.

"It's a good deal," he said.

Mama snorted. "They can't grow almonds on Long Island. Almond trees need a warmer climate."

Papa turned to the sink and began to wash his hands. "The almonds must come from Cuba." He rattled a few dishes. "Starting next week, I'll be trucking them to a couple places in Jersey."

From then on, Papa's trucks became busier than ever. All day, every day, one truck went in, another truck went out of the garage below our top floor living space.

Mama complained about the noise waking her and the babies during their naps in the middle of the day. In addition to the noise, she fretted about Papa taking on more work than he could handle and putting off fixing the Eighteenth Street house, where, she said, everything would be quiet, and the little ones could nap in peace. I thought she wanted to nap in peace, too.

Some nights, after Papa came home and all the trucks were parked inside, he would ask Francey to go down and double-check the lock on both garage doors. Usually it was when Lonzo, who was Papa's only Italian driver, brought a load of almonds from a warehouse on a farm in Long Island.

Mama, sounding like a teacher, reminded us, "Long Island is too cold to grow almonds. I don't know about Cuba. The almonds must be coming from someplace warm like California or

Florida."

Whether they came from California, Florida, or Cuba, Albert didn't care; he was curious to see if they were Jordan almonds—the sugar-coated pastel ones tinted pale pink, sky blue, or light green that were doled out by relatives at christenings, weddings, birthdays, or holidays. One evening after supper, while Papa read the newspaper in the dining room and Mama put the youngest kids to bed, Albert urged me and Francey to sneak down to the garage with him.

We tiptoed out of the kitchen into the upper stairway, which led past the door to the adjacent building where Papa and Uncle Pete kept their still. The hallway smelled like a mixture of gasoline, engine exhaust, whiskey, and nuts. At the bottom of the long stairway, Francey turned on the lights to the garage, and the three of us headed toward the back where the Mack trucks were parked behind the other trucks. Francey hoisted me onto the lowest side rail, and we climbed up, our bare arms itchy from the rough hemp sacks that poked between the wooden side slats of the truck bed.

On top, huge hemp bags, bigger than pillowcases, were packed tightly together, forming a bumpy carpet. My brothers fished for the openings. Francey, struggling to untie the thick cord of chain stitches, finally got one string unknotted by tugging extra hard. The bag exploded and nuts flew in all directions. Some popped into our laps, and others fell out through the opening Francey had created. Those that dropped below into the truck clunked. They didn't hit more hemp bags—they hit something solid. Metal? Wood?

Without a word, the three of us worked in unison. Carefully, very carefully, like seasoned detectives, we moved the half-empty bag aside, scattering more nuts and making louder clunking sounds. Peering below the bag, we spied brown wooden barrels stacked three deep. Francey and Albert looked at each other as if they had rehearsed it for a play. "Bootleg whiskey!"

The bags of almonds piled along the top, back, sides, and front of the truck hid dozens of barrels of Prohibition whiskey.

Within seconds, we scrambled to scoop up loose almonds. We shoved handfuls back into the bag and tried to flatten it and hide the exposed barrels. For a few minutes, we argued in low tones.

"I am going to tell Mama," I said.

"No, you're not," Albert warned.

Francey agreed with Albert. Then Albert changed his mind. "Yes, Mama needs to know in case the cops come and find the truck."

Then I changed my mind. "It's better if she doesn't know. She'll yell at Papa, and he'll get mad."

In the end we agreed not to say anything for fear Mama and Papa would have a fight. Albert was furious because the nuts were not sugar-coated Jordan almonds. Nonetheless, he stuffed his pockets with the golden shelled nuts, grumbling, "I'll crack them open with a hammer," as if he planned to punish them.

Keeping the truth from Mama made me think more and more about what went on—not only at home, but everywhere. I started wondering what Mama really knew about Papa's business dealings. Her mantra echoed in my head: "Truth is always in the room. She never goes away."

I figured she knew about the barrels of whiskey being trucked around the city; she probably knew that whiskey was being made in Papa's back office. She probably knew things I didn't know. I wanted to know everything Mama knew.

And why did grown-ups pretend nobody knew who had a still and who didn't? On our block, Butch Kowalski's father had a still. My friend Florence La Compte's mother put one in her cellar after her husband ran off with another woman. Papa, Uncle Frank, and Uncle Pete took turns keeping a close eye on the still in the back room over Papa's second garage next door. And everybody knew that everybody knew, but everybody acted like nobody knew, and nobody was supposed to talk about what they knew. Not even Mama.

Now that I was seven and about to start first grade, I wanted to know everything that Mama knew, what everyone knew, and, if truth was in every room, I wanted to know what truth knew about stills and making whiskey.

I decided to go into the room that held Papa's still. Truth would be there and I would know what truth knew. Further, because I believed Louisa when she said I knew things before they happened, I would know if the cops were on their way into Papa's back room and I could warn him ahead of time.

The truck drivers and Papa were out on jobs, and Mama napped. The door between the buildings on the upper landing stood ajar. I tiptoed to the landing, carefully pushed open the door between the two buildings that led to the back room, and peeked in. Uncle Pete looked surprised when he saw me, but he pooched out his lips and put his index finger over his mouth.

I imitated him, adding a soft *"shhh,"* and nodded. I felt like a spy in the know. He smiled, and I smiled back.

Watching Uncle Pete make whiskey proved exciting. Simmering on a large, portable three-burner electric hotplate sat a copper vat with a curved copper pipe in the lid. Steam escaped through a slender glass tube attached to the copper pipe. The whole room smelled like the hard apple cider Papa bought from Mr. Polizzi, the Marlboro farmer. As the steam cooled, beautiful amber droplets drained into a five-gallon jug, sparkling as they splashed.

When I heard Mama moving around, I said goodbye to Uncle Pete. He winked and said, "Don't tell anyone about the still." And I didn't.

When I returned to the hall, before going up the stairs to the kitchen, I sat on the steps and thought. I reprimanded myself for not noticing Truth when I was in the room, but I also wondered why everyone was hiding the truth. Were they afraid? Afraid they would go to jail?

Although some families didn't have a still, almost every block in Brooklyn housed a few, and everybody who had one was mad at the government. There were a few Jewish families who didn't have stills, but they, too, complained about Prohibition, saying it violated the rights of citizens. Mostly, however, it was the Catholics who complained—Italian Catholics, Irish Catholics, Polish Catholics—all with large families, all mad at Woodrow Wilson and Carrie Nation, a dead Protestant lady who looked mean in the *Daily Mirror* newspaper photo.

Even some kids complained. Mostly they were boys about Albert's age, nine or ten, who peddled newspapers on the street corner. They kept shouting about Prohibition riots and policemen dumping barrels of whiskey down city manholes and how Congress wasn't doing its job for the hardworking, law-abiding people.

Both the *Daily News* and the *Jewish Forward*—a newspaper Uncle Pete claimed men who went to the synagogue read backward—had exactly the same picture on their front pages showing a big family of Supreme Court judges wearing matching black bathrobes. The picture looked the same as the one Papa had cut out and nailed to the wall of his trucking garage. The men in front sat on a long bench. Those standing in back had forgotten to button up their bathrobes. Whenever I looked at it, I imagined myself and all my sisters and brothers sitting together on the Supreme Court bench—all of us looking like nuns in black bathrobes, even the boys.

As the first girl born in our family, I was expected to help dress my sisters. I put socks on Genevieve, combed Gloria's hair, and taught Agnes how to tie her shoelaces. I planned ahead. When we got to be Supreme Court judges, I would be sure to check how we looked. I would ask our favorite cousin, Esther, and my friend Florence from across the street to join us. They would be the eighth and ninth Supreme Court judges. And they could help everyone button up their bathrobes before we got our pictures taken.

Papa never stopped bad-mouthing the Supreme Court, the U.S. government, and Protestants. He lectured us during supper on the rights of people who had stills: "Every citizen has a right to hold grudges against the Protestants, the way they force people to sneak around and pretend not to have stills as if they were committing sins." The way Mama nodded her head, I could see she agreed with him.

Papa also had a lot to say about Catholics. He said Irish Catholics became policemen or small-time politicians to influence the Irish politicians who were higher up. He disliked Polish Catholics, primarily because they held secret meetings in basements where they plotted about joining the Communist Party. Papa didn't believe in communism. He said the only people who benefitted were lazy troublemakers. He warned, "If things don't change soon, Al Capone, a big-time Italian Catholic gangster from Chicago, will run for president. He'll show them. Capone will prove to those uppity Protestants that hardworking Italians like me aren't doing anything wrong."

Papa kept predicting that Prohibition wouldn't last. He said hardworking men trying to raise a family had a right to disobey a law that wasn't written in the American Constitution. Besides, only Protestants had voted for it, and now, with more and more Catholics getting their naturalization papers, for sure the law would be changed.

"Italians are harder working than Irish Micks, and the Poles drink on the job. Just wait. Watch. Italian Americans are going to get their way." With extra conviction, he would add, "The smart Jew lawyers are on our side, and they're taking the case to the Supreme Court." He'd catch my eye and remind me, "That's where you're going."

And I would imagine my sisters and brothers and Cousin Esther and Florence all dressed up in our nuns' bathrobes, changing the law so Catholics wouldn't be committing a sin by making whiskey. And I would make sure everyone buttoned their bathrobes.

CHAPTER EIGHT— HOLY COMMUNION

1927

When I was six, Albert and Francey began preparing for their first Holy Communion. They learned new words—words I had never heard before—beautiful, long words. Plus, Mama bought them new suits and new shoes to wear for the ceremony and for the photos that would be taken and put in fancy silver frames.

Cousin Esther, who was Albert's age, visited every afternoon and they practiced reciting the words together. Aunt Mary bought her a fancy white dress with ruffles and a bride's veil with a crown on top. Secretly I envied all of them, so I began to scheme. Even though I hadn't started school, I figured if I learned the words by heart, I too could get a fancy ruffled dress and a veil with a crown. And I could get my picture taken and put in a silver frame on Mama's bedroom bureau next to Tia Marietta, Mama's sister who lived in Italy. Since Mama didn't believe that going to church herself was as important as cooking or sending us to church or being sure we swallowed our cod-liver oil after oatmeal, I felt certain she would give permission.

Mrs. Ryan from across the street—who, according to Mama, had carrot-colored hair that "didn't come from a bottle"—dropped in every day after attending morning mass. She talked about the sermon and who attended mass and thought Mama should at least attend every Sunday. She said Mama "went through the motions but wasn't a real Catholic."

I liked the way Mama sassed Mrs. Ryan right back.

"In my heart I know going to church every day doesn't matter one bit to Jesus. Taking care of my children is more important than," she gave Mrs. Ryan a long look, "showing up at church so neighbors can notice who's got a new hat."

Mrs. Ryan never brought the subject up again.

I waited until Mrs. Ryan left and Genevieve was napping before I begged. "Mama, if I learn the catechism by heart, can I take my first Holy Communion with the boys and Cousin Esther?"

Mama stared down at me. "Well," she mused, "the nuns don't give a writing test . . ." She stepped closer and took my chin in her hand, tilting my face up, fastening her eyes on mine. "If you learn everything, you can take your first Holy Communion with the boys."

Then, as always, she raised the bar. "But only if you learn *all* the words. Every word in its right place."

"Promise?"

"I promise."

Listening to my brothers recite from their prayer books, I figured out what some of the words meant, but when they took me to Mass, I didn't understand what was going on; everybody was bouncing up, sitting back down, then sliding forward and kneeling on the wooden knee benches. I didn't think my brothers knew what was going on either, but squeezed between them on the pew, I didn't ask because I didn't want to break the Never-Talk-in-Church rule. Plus, I was fascinated by the little parade the priest and two altar boys made, walking up one aisle and down the other, swinging a brass bowl full of smoky perfume. It seemed like the parade should have been done outside in a safer place. But I didn't ask about that, either.

I also had a problem with the high holy chanting in Latin. It sounded too much like Italian, and hearing it dredged up how dead set Papa felt about his children learning Italian and speaking broken English and never becoming Supreme Court judges. I stopped hearing the Latin chant by creating movies in my mind. I would make believe I lived in a courthouse in Washington, D.C., with a big kitchen in the back room.

Still, I worked hard, imitating my brothers and Cousin Esther as they practiced. At home, I made sure to practice loud enough for Mama to hear me, and I was careful not to disobey her in anything—I didn't want her to change her mind.

After I learned the Axe of Contrition that began with "Bless me, Father, for I have sinned"—and I knew I had sinned by spitting at Albert when he put a dead mouse down the back of my dress—I started memorizing the ins and outs of the Sins of Disobedience. If you committed any of these sins, you went to Purgatory, which was the scariest place of all, and you stayed there for Eternity—which was all black, like Paura. And you would never again see your mother or sisters. I began to question my wish to take Holy Communion after all, even though Miss Budski had measured me for a white dress with see-through organdy ruffles.

I decided to settle the problem. Although I didn't want to bother Mama while she was putting diapers through the wringer on the washing machine, I had to ask. "If I take my first Holy Communion and disobey you or Papa, will I go to Purgatory and stay forever?"

Mama didn't respond. She kept putting diapers through the wringer. I pressed for an answer.

"If I get hit by lightning and die before I confess and receive abso-lotion, will I go to Purgatory forever?"

"There are no children in Purgatory," said Mama. "All children go straight to Heaven. And you move too fast to get hit by lightning." Then, as she always did when any of us asked too many questions, she gave me something to do. "Go. Learn with the boys."

Relieved, I went back and listened to my brothers. They recited one prayer after another, using words that seemed to be in the wrong place, and they held their arms in strange ways when they practiced. Pressing their palms together, they prayed in phony voices.

"Bless me, Father, for I have sinned. This is my first confession."

Next, they recited the Axe of Contrition, trying to sound holy. I thought they pressed their palms together to look like the head of a hatchet like the one Papa kept near the furnace, and their arms became the axe handle. I imagined that when people entered that dark booth inside the church and confessed their sins, they'd swing their arms up and down so the priest could see them chopping up their sins into tiny pieces like Mama chopped parsley for homemade ravioli.

That part I could figure out.

What kept puzzling me, however, were those special sins—mortal and venial. I had never heard those words from Mama or Papa, or at christenings or weddings, and I wanted to know what they meant, in case the day came when I needed to axe them.

I had some idea of what a mortal sin might be. Last autumn, when the lamb had been slaughtered outside the barn, I heard Uncle Pete say, *"Fa morte."* Although it was forbidden, little by little I had begun to pick up some Italian. I knew *morte* meant "dead." Maybe mortal sin had something to do with a dead lamb, for every now and then the priest or the nuns would talk about Jesus and the little lamb.

But I didn't ask, because I was set on learning every word in its place, whether or not I knew what it meant. Off and on during the week, before we met with the nuns I'd slip in a question or two to Francey, who never lied and always obeyed Mama, but who wasn't quick to catch on to sneaky questions.

Venial was an English word that I was pretty sure Mama wouldn't know, but I decided to ask. "Is venial sin as big as mortal sin?"

"All sins are like sour grapes," she answered. "Some are big, and some are small. None are good." That cleared up a lot of things about sin. I felt ashamed for having doubted Mama's knowledge of English words.

Now I had the full picture. I understood what my brothers meant when they rehearsed their "Hail Marys." I imitated them and memorized the prayer by rote. Now when I recited, "Hail

Mary, full of grapes, the Lord is Withee," I knew what was going on.

I was certain the Virgin Mary came from a rich family. In my prayer book she wore a flimsy blue scarf draped across her belly, which I'd figured out was full of big bunches of grapes. The fabric seemed like the delicate chiffon material in the fancy dress that Miss Budski made for Mama to wear to Cousin Dolly's wedding. And although I wasn't sure if the Virgin Mary was icy cold or even frozen stiff as she hailed down from heaven, I was positive that her father, Lord Withee, held her hand until they landed.

I was equally sure her father aimed straight for a holy wooden stomping vat they used to crush grapes for wine. I imagined all the sour grapes she had under the shawl splattering around in that huge vat. I could see the grapes bursting open, oozing juice the same way they did when my sisters and I stomped them for Papa and my uncles when they made wine after the Fourth of July celebration on the farm. And I was positive the wine sipped by the priests during Mass came from Virgin Mary's grapes.

All this fit right into the big scheme of things. I knew the Virgin Mary must have hurt herself when she landed on the wooden floor of the vat, because in the prayer Albert chanted, I heard him say, "And blessed is the fruit of thy womb." The first-grade teacher had told Mama Albert was having trouble learning to read because he mixed up letters like b and d. I was certain Albert got it wrong when he said "womb." There was no such word. What Albert meant to say was "wound." That made perfect sense.

And I knew all about wounds if you jumped from a high place. We kids jumped from high places all the time: out of trees, over each other, off our horse, from the porch, off beds, down the stairs, and off the back of Papa's trucks. And to avoid the evil eye, we jumped over cracks in the sidewalk. I had learned the rules for a good, holy life.

However, after Francey, Albert, and I celebrated our first Holy Communion Mass, and the nuns had praised me for loving God and memorizing all my prayers so young but saying not a word

about my fancy dress with ruffles or my veil with its crown
of shiny pearls, my brothers and I disobeyed my mother and
jumped out of the hayloft in the barn.

Every fall, hired hands filled the loft with hay to feed Mamie,
the horse, and Bessie, our cow, during the winter. When the
hired hands swung the stiff, dry hay up from the wagon into
the large double door in the loft, stray shafts of hay would drift
to the ground and mound knee deep. After the hired hands left
for the pasture to fill another wagonload, and before the stray
mounds were raked up and hoisted into the loft, my brothers
and I bounded into the barn, climbing the steep wooden stairs
next to the chute and scrambling over heaps of sweet-smelling,
prickly hay to reach the wide opening in the loft.

Francey and Albert stood alongside me, each holding a hand
—just like Lord Withee did when he hailed down with Virgin
Mary—and on the count of three, we all leapt the ten feet or so
into the piles of hay littering the earth below.

I landed in a shallow spot. The fall knocked the wind out of
me, and I could see black and white lights blinking like fireflies.
When I started breathing again, Albert said, "You look like a
ghost." He looked pale himself. And Francey, looking sick to his
stomach, said he thought I had died and wondered if my coming
back to life had been a miracle. Wincing at the pain in my ribs, I
struggled to my feet. Instead of feeling sorry for me, my brothers
made me swear not to tell Mama.

As we walked from the barn to the house, Francey blurted,
"Stop! God punished us for disobeying Mama. Before we get
home, we need to pray for forgiveness and say our Acts of Contrition."

Acts! Say our Acts? Not *axe* them?

Stunned with this new insight and mumbling with the boys,
"Bless me, Father, for I have sinned," I wondered what else I had
learned wrong.

Gradually, whether due to the pain in my rib, Jesus' punishment for my sins, or because I had been humbled by my trans-
gressions, I began to abide by His rules.

That autumn, when school started, we returned to Brooklyn, purged of all sin. I prided myself on being Good. I didn't show off multiplication tables to Albert and didn't call Agnes selfish when she took the marshmallows away from Evelyn. I was quick to obey Mama's every command, doing everything just right according to her standards. I felt—no, I *knew*—I was more "holy" than any of my sisters, brothers, Cousin Esther, aunts . . . holier than everybody.

For some inexplicable reason, going to church during summer vacation had been suspended—like school. And throughout the morning on the first Saturday in the city, I rushed through my chores and couldn't wait to go into the confessional booth at St. Mary's Church. Running fast, I reached the church early enough to stop and pray at each of the fourteen Stations of the Cross mounted along the walls. Studying the colorful plaster renditions, I puzzled over the Agony of Jesus and how difficult it must have been for him to carry that heavy cross. And when he fell three times, I wondered if he scraped his knees.

Choosing a seat as close to the confessional booth as possible, I waited, fidgeting. As soon as an old lady, her head stooped in prayer, parted the heavy green velvet curtain, I dashed inside and knelt in the dark cubicle, pressing my face close to the small confessional door. The moment the door slid aside, I recited, "Bless me, Father, for I have sinned. My last confession was just before we left for the country. I didn't spit at my brother Albert. I didn't put any chewing gum under the minestrone plate, and I folded all the baby diapers without being asked, and I didn't snitch on anybody." Catching my breath, I boasted, "I was perfect."

No response.

Was Father Alonzo there? I peered through the grid. Yes. Although I could barely see him, he was definitely there. Maybe he was hard of hearing. I repeated, louder, "This week I was *perfect.*"

Father Alonzo leaned forward and moved his head closer to

the small metal grid. His sour breath smelled like Uncle Pete's. "You say you have been perfect?" Although he phrased it like a question, he sounded like he didn't want an answer. His voice rose. "No mortal is perfect." He spoke so loud I was sure the old lady in the church had heard him. His voice, harsh and quick and getting louder, threatened, "I know you have had evil thoughts."

Staring down at me, he ordered me to do Seven Hail Marys and seven Our Fathers on the benches without pads.

The door slammed shut.

Stunned, I rose, parted the drapes, and walked toward the tiers of small votive candles flickering at the side altar, palms pressed together, preparing for penance.

Evil thoughts? I didn't know what Father Alonzo meant by evil thoughts. As I walked down the aisle, I choked on the scent of burning candles, waxed pews, and dusty carpet runners. The dim church darkened, then loomed large and unfamiliar, full of black shadows. Paura everywhere. I couldn't breathe, my lungs enclosed in a barbed wire cage. But as I knelt on the hard bench, a peculiar lightness rose in my chest. The flash of fireflies blazed with piercing blue lights. In that instant, I realized I didn't know what Father Alonzo meant by evil thoughts, but I knew *he* knew.

The next day, as my brothers and I sat in Sunday Mass, I studied Father Alonzo. I studied him with a clear, cold gaze. I studied him with Mama's eyes. I judged him with Mama's soul. Leaning forward, I examined him head to foot. A small round reddish-brown spot stained his surplice just below his chin. His black socks didn't match—one was plain woven, the other ribbed. The hem of his white robe fell open in one place, dragging a dirty thread across the floor. His fingernails had dark rims.

When the bell sounded for parishioners to rise and receive the host, Francey nudged me to get up and follow him. I didn't budge. He nudged again. I refused to move. Albert, speaking loud enough for the bratty Ryan boy to hear, said, "I'm going to tell Mama." And he butted against me. I gripped the edge of the pew and refused to rise. Clinging to the edge of the seat, I silently vowed never again to take the host from Father Alonzo.

The moment we dashed through the kitchen door Albert told Mama I must have peed my pants because I wouldn't get up for Holy Communion. Mama looked down at me, her eyes questioning and fearful. "What happened?"

"I don't want to go to church anymore," I mumbled.

"Why?"

"Nothing."

"It's not nothing. Something happened. What?"

I stared at my shoes and didn't answer. She walked toward me and lifted my chin. "Tell me." Her face had grown long and still. She studied me, looking into my bones, not missing the slightest twitch or gulp. "Did anyone *touch* you?"

"No," I answered quickly, unsure why, but certain I needed to avoid alarming her, for as early as I could remember, *touch* was sinful. Getting *touched* was just as bad as *touching yourself*, which made her yell at Francey every time he put his hand in his pocket.

To calm her, I repeated, my voice certain, "No. No one touched me."

"Then what? Why didn't you take communion?"

"Father Alonzo has dirty hands."

Mama looked down at me and searched my face carefully. "I'll tell the boys you're all going to a later mass."

CHAPTER NINE—AMERICAN DREAM

1927

School ended for the boys, and the very next Sunday Papa, Mama, and my younger sisters were waiting in the new Packard outside St. Alphonso's Church for me and my brothers to come out of Mass. We didn't even go home to change our church clothes. Within minutes, we were speeding out of Brooklyn and up along the Hudson River to look at the farm Papa wanted to buy.

Swiveling his head toward the backseat, he said, "For summer vacations. Same as American men with a good business in the city." He sounded proud.

Papa took the Bear Mountain Parkway upstate, with a mountain on one side and a terrifying cliff overlooking the river on the other. I kept searching for bears but didn't see a single one. The whole time Mama kept yelling at Papa to slow down, her voice more and more shrill each time the car swerved around sharp curves.

We kids kept quiet the whole time so we wouldn't make matters worse between them. Finally, the car slowed before a sign that read *Sunny Ridge Fruit Farm*. It was off the 9 W Highway in the township of Middlehope, about a two-hour drive upstate in the Hudson Valley. Papa eased the car into a tree-lined lane with a flowering apple orchard on one side and on the other a waist-high fieldstone wall. The flat fieldstones staggered parallel to a large, leafy, dark-green vineyard, then rose higher and higher 'til the wall ended at a wide circular drive. Papa turned into the drive and stopped behind a small black car parked in front of wide white steps. The steps led up to a spacious porch that wrapped around the front and sides of a big white house that looked like it belonged in a storybook. The front of the house overlooked a huge sloping green lawn that ended where a dense grape vineyard spanned the length of the property along the highway below. Mama appeared impressed, her eyes following a row of pink peonies along a narrow road from the house to a large gray barn.

As soon as Papa stopped the car, we kids jumped out and started yelling to each other:

"Look what I found!"

"Let's play hide-and-seek."

"Is there a horse in the barn?"

Near the back of the house behind a low hedge, a stone path led to an outhouse—a miniature replica of the big storybook house. Francey, looking inside at the long wooden seat with three holes, said, "It's like the three bears doing poo-poo or wee-wee. The largest hole is for Papa, the middle one for Mama, and the small one is for us."

I thought they all looked treacherous. Even the smallest hole gaped open big enough that a kid could fall through it.

And before the summer was out, Agnes did fall into the pit below. Mama pulled her out through the biggest hole, stripped her naked behind the hedge, and sprayed her off with a long hose that Albert threaded through the window from the kitchen sink.

Now, however, with the inspection ended, Agnes and Albert started a fight, both claiming ownership of the outhouse. I didn't care who owned it. It stank, and as I walked away, I secretly feared having to use it.

From inside the big house, a man with a flabby paunch stepped onto the porch; he introduced himself as the owner, Mr. Pavone. He seemed extra friendly, vigorously shaking Papa's hand, nodding and smiling at Mama and the rest of us

I tugged at Mama's elbow and whispered, "Ask him if the house has an inside toilet."

Mr. Pavone laughed. "Yes, and a bathroom with a huge claw-foot tub big enough for three or four of you girls to bathe in at the same time."

Thankful, I turned away, and he started praising everything in sight. Stepping down from the porch he said the grounds had been landscaped by a famous horticulturalist. *Horticulturalist* sounded like part of a song, and I imitated him, mouthing the word horticulturalist over and over under my breath. I also pooched out my stomach behind his back.

Unlike Mama, who believed small words like sin, food, kill, and war carry more weight than long ones, I liked long words. I wasn't sure how much or how little weight horticulturalist carried, or what it meant exactly, but I loved repeating it, quietly raising and lowering my voice. A single word, but long enough to make an aria. I practiced it softly in several different ways, even adding a vowel sound at the end, humming under my breath, *"Hor-ti-cul-turr-raa-li-ist-ah"* to the score of *Aida*.

Mama looked at me and smiled.

Mr. Pavone, now leaning on his car—which Francey immediately baptized Tin Lizzie— the nickname everyone used for Ford's Model T—pointed to the sloping lawn. "Planted with rare trees—no two alike. Those red and green twin maples in the corner just inside the stone wall? And that ginkgo over yonder, near that boulder, size of a wagon? All three imported from Japan."

To investigate his remarks, we kids, dashing around like detectives, started comparing the delicate fan-shaped, pale-green leaves of the ginkgo with the seven-fingered pizza-sized leaves of the horse chestnut tree. Best of all, we discovered an "upside-down" mulberry tree. My sisters and I hid inside, standing upright under its huge drooping branches. We marveled at the unripe little green berries that decorated what I thought would be a perfect stage setting for make-believe.

When Mama said the mulberry tree reminded her of sunny Chieti, Mr. Pavone perked up. Pointing his hand upward, he said she could get a better view from the main bedroom window upstairs. He encouraged her to go check it out. She smiled and disappeared inside, carrying Evelyn. Mr. Pavone turned his attention to Papa.

"Down below, two full acres of concord grapes. Best grapes for Chianti," he said, pausing to let that sink in, as if he knew Chianti was Italians' favorite wine. "You can't see it from here, but there's a brook in the middle of that lower vineyard. Runs the length of the property in line with the 9W. Potential for commercial . . . good stretch right on the highway."

Albert and Francey took off to find it. Gloria, who was always the first to notice a poo-poo diaper or sour milk or a moldy orange, asked about a strange scent.

"It depends," Mr. Pavone said. "Which one? That far-off odor is skunk spray. The French put tiny amounts in expensive perfume. The musty smell? That's fresh cow manure. She's for sale, too." He gave Papa a long look. Papa studied the barn, scrunched up his chin, and nodded tentatively. Mr. Pavone scribbled something in a little notebook, and said, "Fine Guernsey. Richest milk. Docile."

Then, testing us as if he were an uncle, he said, "Close your eyes. Breathe in hard. Can you smell where that fresh-cut grass is coming from?"

We pointed toward the area we would later learn to call the Westlakes – our neighbor to the north with the flowering apple tree we noticed during our drive up the lane. "Now guess which way the peach orchard stands?"

Gloria guessed the quickest, and, as always, she was right both times.

A week or two later, Papa signed the papers that included the Guernsey cow and Mamie the draft horse, and we spent our first night in that big storybook house. Albert refused to go to bed. He raced around outside in the dark capturing fireflies and imprisoning them in a glass canning jar he found in the cellar, magically turning it into a flashing lantern. Mama was furious and demanded he let the fireflies go free.

Disgruntled and pretending to obey, he released his bounty. As they escaped, he crushed and smeared them on his bare arms. Racing around the gazebo on the side lawn, waving his arms wildly, he yelled, "I'm king of the lightning bugs. I'm king of the lightning bugs." Then, ignoring Mama, he immediately began recapturing fireflies and filling up the jar again.

One of the first things Papa did at the farm was install a flag-pole on the front lawn. The pole seemed as tall as the telephone poles in the city. He bought it at the Brooklyn Navy Yard, where they sold leftovers from the First World War. Papa wanted it in place for the Fourth of July, which was a week away.

He hired a few day workers who dug a hole as big around as a bushel and as deep as a barrel, added a bag of gravel, and tamped it down hard. Next, they fumbled around, trying to hoist the tall pole. The men staggered and struggled to maneuver it, the whole time Papa demanding they hold it upright.

At one point, he lost his temper. "You're lazy niggers, not men," he shouted. The men said nothing but exchanged quick, knowing glances from their language of looks.

I could tell they didn't like what he said. Uncle Frank, who had been mixing concrete, shot Papa a reprimanding glance and filled the hole with the mushy mixture. Papa dismissed Uncle Frank's warning look and took a level to the pole, yelling "this way" and "that way." Finally, his voice louder, he demanded, "Hold. Hold. It's level." He and Uncle Frank helped the hired men to hold it upright.

We kids watched in silence while Papa periodically checked the concrete until it solidified, and he told the men to stand back. The pole stood tall and straight. Papa looked proud. I thought Papa was the smartest man in the world, but I wished he under-stood colored people like Mama did and hadn't hurt the feelings of the three hired hands. As the somber-faced men walked away from all of us and opened packets of Lucky Strikes, I wished I could have heard what they mumbled to each other through cig-arette smoke.

But the best was yet to come. On the morning of the Fourth of

July, Uncle Pete, Papa, and Mr. Ike built a sturdy wooden scaffold on the flat, open lawn near the flagpole. The scaffold was longer than the new Packard and taller than Uncle Pete, who was taller than Papa. The scaffold was even taller than Uncle Frank, the tallest of all our relatives.

When they finished putting it together, they emptied boxes of firework wheels and nailed them to the frame. They also built a makeshift table to hold a pile of small fireworks. Albert wanted to help, but Uncle Frank said it was too dangerous and insisted he and the rest of us stay back. Then, to appease Albert, Uncle Pete promised to give us sparklers in both hands when night came.

Throughout the assembly process, Papa kept busy supervising or jumping in and doing things himself, bad-mouthing one person, praising another. One of the black men tossed a bent nail aside. Papa picked it up and examined it. He grunted in the direction of the man and said, "You should know better than to throw a nail on the grass where a kid could step on it." Then, with exquisite delicacy, Papa began to tap the curved nail. He rolled it around and around on a small flat rock with one hand while gently hammering it with his other until it was absolutely straight. Holding it up and eyeing it, he put it in his pocket and used it later.

More proof that Papa *was* the smartest man in the world.

The entire time the men set up the fireworks, Josephine, a friend of Aunt Mary's, kept hanging around, bumming cigarettes, and asking Papa if he was thirsty, then bringing him a glass of Chianti. She did the same thing in Brooklyn. If Josephine came upstairs after joking around with the men in Papa's garage, she never offered to help in the kitchen like Giulia, and she never talked to any of us girls the way Mrs. Gould did. Instead, after lighting a cigarette, she would walk over to the sideboard and pour herself a glass of red wine or cut herself a piece of cheese. After she left, Mama said she had no manners. "She's common. Only uneducated *cafones* would do that without being asked. And she fills the kitchen with smoke." I could tell Mama didn't like her. Neither did I.

Josephine had dark, densely curled black hair, a raspy voice which Mama said came from smoking too much, a faint dark fuzz on her upper lip, and a single, inch-long hair growing out of a small mole under her chin.

But now Josephine was standing near the fireworks scaffold talking to Papa. I couldn't hear what she said before she turned toward the driveway. Papa, talking extra loud, said the concrete base had cured, as if it had a disease. Then he asked Francey to get the package containing the American flag out of the Packard and to notify everyone to come and watch the flag raising. The house was full of relatives who had come up from Brooklyn and Long Island: aunts, uncles, cousins, and some *paisanos* I had never seen. Uncle Frank and Aunt Mary had closed their pizzeria for the day and come up on the Hudson River steamer with all seven of their children, even Ralph, their only son, whom we kids seldom saw because he spent most of his time in his bedroom studying to become a doctor.

There wasn't a quiet moment. Dogs barked and romped. Grownups laughed and teased, half in English, half in Italian— which Papa didn't seem to mind. Aunts reprimanded any kid for grabbing a cannoli from another kid, and older cousins scowled at the boys for cupping hands under their armpits and making fart sounds. The day was like one long school recess without monitors.

Mama finished making gnocchi, then took off her apron and put a Caruso record on the Victrola. She opened the parlor window so everyone could hear the music outdoors.

Uncle Pete opened a bottle of Chianti and filled glasses for all the grown-ups. Papa turned toward Francey, who cradled the flag, warning him, "Don't let it touch the ground. Show it respect. Let me have it."

Then he and Uncle Pete unfolded the flag and anchored it to loops on the long line which hung from the top of the pole. Together, they tugged on the rope, hand over hand as if they were sailors who had done it a thousand times. They hoisted it way,

way up to the top, where it waved in the wind. We kids clapped and shouted the same way we applauded the Brooklyn lamplighter when he lit the gas wick and flooded Seventeenth Street with light. The grown-ups clinked glasses, and Mama, looking up at the flag, almost singing, called, *"Brava, brava."* I liked learning the American flag was female.

During all the hubbub, I noticed Josephine heading down the driveway and asked her where she was going.

"Back to the Palatine Motel where it's quiet. I have a headache." I told her the Palatine Motel was a mile away. Would she be back in time to see the fireworks after dark? She shrugged her shoulders and kept walking. Shortly afterward, as Papa headed for his Packard, I asked where he was going. He said, "To buy more fireworks before dark." As he jumped into the Packard and drove off, Mama's face grew solemn, and she began to chew the side of her lower lip. Like Mama, I began to chew my lip but didn't know why.

Later that night, as Papa lit the fireworks, cars stopped on the 9W below. First one, then two or three, then a long line of cars and pickups stretched along the highway the length of our property below the deep slope of the lawn and beyond the grape vineyard. At intervals, the firework wheels anchored to the scaffold twirled and glowed with different hues of blue and green and red. Rockets flew high above the lawn, streaming bright colors that lit up the sky with streaks of dazzling brilliance. Before the last grand display—when Uncle Frank was needed to help set off the wheels and rockets at the same time—Papa yelled for us kids to form a circle and twirl our sparklers. Everybody celebrated America's Fourth of July. Everyone but Josephine, who didn't come back to see the fireworks. When I asked Aunt Mary why she brought Josephine if she didn't want to see the fireworks, she said, "Go look for any empty glasses and put them in the sink."

As the last streak of colorful light dimmed and disappeared from the sky, darkness returned. Down on the road, horns blared and headlights flashed; a few guys whistled as the cars drifted away, and nothing was left but silence.

CHAPTER TEN—MIRIAM

1927

That fall, back in Brooklyn, chaos reigned. Mama and Papa squabbled constantly, and we kids did, too. I thought it arose partly from the confined space of the apartment and partly from Josephine's hanging out in Papa's garage, but it was also due to Papa's daily frantic presence and constant complaints. He liked a neat and clean house. He loved to show off and wanted everything to reflect how successful he had become as an "American businessman."

He didn't mind Mama spending money—he liked fancy things even more than she did—but he hated disorder as much as Mama hated housework. They fought about it day and night.

One winter evening, he came home and found the kitchen a bigger mess than usual. The day had been rainy, and instead of the diapers drying outside on the clothesline strung over the garage roof, dozens were slung over chair backs, on cabinet doorknobs, over a corner of the icebox, and covering the beautifully written *Whyte* under the horizontal handle of the oven door. Papa glared and grunted at the mess.

His black eyes roved over the small table where the three littlest ones ate, the surface still smudged with dried oatmeal from breakfast, gooey blotches smearing the white enamel top, hiding its pictures of rabbits and turtles. He smirked at the sink full of soiled dishes stacked helter-skelter. The room smelled of a poopy diaper.

Papa continued to look around, his neck veins bulging. He

shouted at Mama, *"Sporca. Sporca."* Dirty. Dirty.

Within moments, the kitchen became as noisy as the Barnum and Bailey Circus. Papa turned his back on Mama, stomped to the sink, rattled pots, and splashed water over the soiled dishes.

Mama, her eyes flashing and her face getting redder and redder, picked up a metal pot lid and hurled it across the room. It landed close to Papa's feet. First, she mimicked him, her voice low and harsh, *"Sporca. Sporca."* Then she shrieked, "If you want everything clean, you better get used to cleaning the house yourself. I'm busy taking care of seven children. Cooking. Washing diapers. Cleaning floors."

When she stepped toward Papa, Francey jumped up and held her arm. Ignoring him, she muttered, as if we weren't supposed to hear, "If you slept on the floor instead of my bed, I'd get more sleep. I'd have more time to empty the sink and put away pots and pans."

Papa pretended she hadn't said a word. He turned on the faucet full-force and scrubbed and splashed until no soiled dishes or even a spoon remained in the sink.

Later, as we ate our minestrone, we kids took extra care to avoid making slurping noises, our eyes warning each other. Mama and Papa were also quiet, paying far too much attention to their plates. Mama didn't really eat or even sit down for more than a moment or two. Mostly she acted as if the Public Health Nurse were coming and she needed to straighten up the kitchen, putting cups away and nesting clean oatmeal bowls in the dish cabinet. We kids had seen this before; we knew she didn't want to sit at the table facing Papa.

The very next afternoon, Papa came home with Miriam.

The moment Papa entered the kitchen with her, he tossed his head toward Mama. Facing Miriam and swinging his arm to take in the entire room, he said, "The wife can make a feast out of a handful of flour, one egg, a few tablespoons of olive oil, and a little milk, but she's a lousy housekeeper."

I could tell by the way Mama and Miriam shot looks at each other that Papa's put-down didn't sit well with either of them.

Mama gave Papa an angry look and snorted. I knew she resented being referred to as "the wife." Like Mama, I wished Papa would stop saying it.

Miriam scanned the six of us finishing lentil soup, then looked steadily at Papa. "By my way of thinkin', seem she mighty busy birthin' babies left and right. Nursin' babies tires a woman." I loved the way Miriam strung out *t-i-r-e-s*, her voice rising and falling like a song I wondered if all black women sang when they spoke.

Mama shifted slightly on her feet but her scowl disappeared. Clearly, Mama also enjoyed hearing how Miriam sang and dragged out *t-i-r-e-s*. Or maybe she liked seeing Papa put in his place. Mama's face brightened. She looked extra proud and grew a little taller. Papa studied both women, no doubt noting how their eyes talked to each other. He said he had to get back to work and left without slamming the door.

Mama and Miriam became friends from that moment on. I marveled at how Miriam picked up the little ones and cuddled them on her plump hip with her left hand as she dusted the dining room with the other. She had a wide space between her two front teeth, moved at a slow, steady pace, and smelled of Fels-Naptha laundry soap. She lived in Harlem and rode the subway to and from our house every day. In the months that followed, she introduced Mama to corn: corn pone, corn soup, corn grits—the same as polenta, Mama said—corn muffins, corn on the cob, corn *off* the cob, corn fritters, corn pudding, corn crackles, corn dodgers. Even corn husks filled with corn kernels, bacon, and chopped red peppers.

Miriam taught us kids about corn too. On rainy days, she kept me and my sisters busy kneading and flattening rounds of corn dough into thin wheels for the crackles and dodgers she fried into crisps. She said we were old enough to learn the recipe:

"Two cups corn meal. Two tablespoons lard. Pinch salt. 'Nough hot water to make a stiff dough. Mix all together. Knead dough on a floured board. Cut into circles. Let dry for about an hour. Let me or Mama fry. Best in bacon fat."

She kept an eye on our dough making while wiping walls, washing windows, helping with the babies—keeping the house clean the way Papa liked it.

Sometimes in the late afternoon, after Mama had her nap and when Giulia wasn't visiting, Mama and Miriam sat together like old friends at the kitchen table, both folding diapers, matching socks, or sewing a missing button or two on a knee-high winter legging. They told each other stories about where they came from and what their childhoods were like. Miriam said her mother and her grandparents had been slaves in Mississippi.

Miriam was twelve when her grandmother passed, and her mother put her on a Greyhound bus headed north to go live with her Aunt Gardenia. Miriam would grow quiet, study her hand, and rub her thumb along her fingertips. Mama wouldn't say anything. She waited until Miriam spoke. Later, we learned Miriam's mother died shortly after Miriam took the Greyhound to New York City.

When she spoke again, her voice was low but clear. "The law say slavery weren't no more, but nothin' change in Mississippi. Colored man couldn't hardly find a day's work. Hardly ever." She paused and they both sighed. "Started house-work when I turned thirteen."

Looking at Miriam, I couldn't tell if she was old or young. Just strong. Once, when I asked if she had children, she said, "No more young'uns. All growed."

Mama loved stories and would ask question after question to prompt Miriam. She learned that Miriam had survived two husbands. Of the first, Miriam said, "Jason be a good man. Died of consumption. Second man didn't take to my children. Ran him off."

Mostly Mama listened, but one afternoon, she shared how she, too, had earned a few pennies—to help her Nonna pay the nuns for her schooling in Italy. Twice a week, she carried milk from an old peasant who had a cow in her shed on the edge of town to another old woman who lived in Chieti and made cheese on her porch.

She confessed to Miriam that before delivering the milk, she would hide behind a huge tree trunk and tuck her hair behind her ears so no strands would fall into the pail. "I drank and drank until my belly was so full, it bulged. My Nonna seldom bought milk."

They both smiled, nodding their heads as though they shared a secret.

"I thank them for my good teeth." Mama and Miriam laughed. Mama said she learned how to milk a cow and make cheese from those old ladies. "The one who owned the cow lived to be one hundred and four."

One day we were all listening to "Ave Maria" on the Victrola. Mama folded clothes, Miriam jiggled Genevieve on her lap as she folded towels, and I polished the "E" on my new gold bracelet. Mama got up to flip the Caruso record. As she walked toward the Victrola, Miriam asked Mama if she had any records with gospel singers.

"I never heard of gospel singers," Mama said.

Miriam smiled and slowly rocked Evelyn back and forth. Rhythmically moving her head side to side, she carried on about a colored man from Texas named Blind Lemon. He was a famous gospel singer who played the guitar and made records for Paramount Pictures.

"On Sundays, the whole Baptist congregation be singin'. We be singin' back and forth, singin' back and forth with the whole choir."

Mama looked surprised and asked her to sing one of those songs.

Miriam beamed. She cleared her throat, rearranged Genevieve on her lap, and began to sing a sad song about four motherless children living in a railroad boxcar. Her voice was low-pitched and heavy, not high and light like Mama's. More like a cello than a violin. From then on, every day, rain or shine, Mama and Miriam took turns singing as they did chores. Although all the songs Miriam sang were sad, she and Mama seemed happy working and singing together. I thought they were playing house.

However, it was because of Miriam that Mama ended up hitting Albert.

Albert was Mama's favorite. She never, ever swatted him like she did the rest of us. I believed it was because he was brave and fearless. He shot at pigeons with his homemade bow and arrow. He started fights with bigger kids. He walked along the edge of the garage roof, which was three stories above the street, pretending not to hear Mama's screams of "Get down! Now! Obey me!" He knew that when he jumped to safety or brought home a dead pigeon for her to cook or scared her with a rat he had trapped, she would never punish him.

Instead, her eyes always lit up with pride.

None of the rest of us matched him in daring, especially not Francey, even though he was a year and a half older.

But one day, Albert did something that Mama would not tolerate. It was Easter vacation, and the neighborhood kids gathered around our stoop. Teenage boys played kick-the-can in the middle of Seventeenth Street, Gloria skipped rope, Agnes played hopscotch, Francey stretched rubber bands and added them to his fist-size bouncy ball. I babysat three-year-old Genevieve on one of the stoop steps, and baby Evelyn was in her crib upstairs with Miriam.

Albert and one of the Kowalski boys played keepsies with marbles. They had scratched a circle in the patch of earth in our small front yard next to the stoop. Albert was in a mean mood. He had lost one of his favorite marbles—a clear emerald-green aggie with a yellow tiger eye—to Butch Kowalski, who gloated.

And Albert was a poor loser.

He was a sharpshooter and had insisted they play for keeps. Now Butch wouldn't swap two marbles for the return of the tiger eye aggie, and Albert fumed.

He bad-mouthed Poles in general, mocking their round heads and sneering at their drunken parties on Saturday nights. He said they never saved enough money to buy a house or start a business like the Italians, and he tossed in a put-down about how Butch smelled like dried pee. Albert was talking so fast that spit flew with every word. He got more and more revved up. I was sure he would punch Butch and was relieved to see Mama coming home from a shopping spree.

As she neared our stoop, she heard Albert bullying Butch.

"And you don't have a nigger maid like us."

Quick as lightning, Mama slapped Albert on the back of his shoulder. Hard—so hard he almost lost his footing. Harder than she had ever smacked me. And in front of Butch!

Albert's mouth opened and his eyes, showing lots of white, flickered. He stared at Mama in disbelief. But Mama didn't soften one bit. She stared back, her face hard, mad, and mean.

"Don't you use that name with Miriam. Miriam deserves *respect*. She's helping your mother day in and day out. Miriam's an honest, hard-working *colored* woman. And *colored* people are very *sensitive*."

The way Mama emphasized *respect* and *colored* and pronounced *s-e-n-s-i-t-i-v-e*, everyone stopped talking, as if all the neighborhood kids needed to learn the lesson Mama intended for Albert. For a moment I thought Mama, with only an eighth-grade education, could be the principal of Public School 40.

Still fretting and glaring at Albert, Mama began to climb the stoop. Deliberately ignoring him, she called out, "Girls, come inside, I bought a record with gospel songs. Miriam can teach us to sing back and forth. Like they do in her Baptist Church on Sundays."

CHAPTER ELEVEN—THE WORLD OUTSIDE THE KITCHEN

1928

Although Miriam kept the apartment clean and orderly, everything else felt lopsided. Papa and Uncle Pete came and went all hours of the day and night, almost never stopping to pat me on the head or give a playful reprimand. And Mama came and went, too. Once or twice a week, she left us with Miriam and shopped at Frederick Loeser department store on Fulton Street. She came home with boxes of fancy clothes, elegant goblets, Victrola records, suede or patent leather high-heeled shoes, embroidered silk pillow slips, and a pair of elbow-length soft leather gloves that matched her camel hair coat.

Sometimes when Mama went shopping, she took one or two of us with her. Once inside the elegant store, I couldn't wait to board the elevator and watch the man in a green uniform close and open the expandable metal gate on the second floor where there were yards and yards of fabric. While Mama shopped, I wandered around, fingering bolts of cloth or asking clerks or strangers what the fabrics were called and where they came from. I loved the feel of the various materials—flimsy chiffon, smooth silk, shiny satin, soft flannel, stiff muslin, wispy veiling, and best of all, see-through organdy. *Or-gan-dee-e*—its name sounded like a song.

At home, merchants came and went. One delivered a gleaming oak ice chest with two white enamel sections inside and bright brass handles on the outside; another delivered the gas stove with *Whyte* written on the cream-colored oven door. I loved the way the cursive green letters matched the long, shiny green enamel legs of the stove. I traced and retraced them with my finger. Once a week, Mama gave money to a salesman for furniture on layaway for the following year, when she planned on moving us into the Eighteenth Street brownstone.

Mama dismissed Giulia's objections and misgivings when three delivery men, their shirts wet under their armpits, maneuvered a dark brown upright piano up three flights of stairs, through the kitchen, and into a corner of the dining room.

"It's for the children. It's for the children," she said, sounding like a schoolteacher, reprimanding Giulia. "They need music lessons while they're young."

Along with the piano came two violins and auburn-haired Madame Hambrouges, who, according to Mrs. Ryan from across the street, had been a former stage performer. Madame Hambrouges' appearance fascinated me. Although she was very, very old and had dry, paper-thin, wrinkled skin over high cheek bones, she rouged them in flame circles to match the fake reddish color of her hair. She spoke with a throaty, heavy French accent, and her stiff, short hair smelled of cigarettes. Once, she leaned across me as we sat side by side on the piano bench, and her entire head of hair slid sideways.

Madame Hambrouges came twice a week to teach me piano and the boys violin. Francey seemed to enjoy taking lessons, and he liked Mrs. Hambrouges, who praised him for always finishing assignments. Albert hated both the lessons and the teacher.

In the evening during practice time, Papa, reading the *Daily News*, lamented, "Between them, they can't come up with one musical note." He shook his head, turned a page, and looked at Mama. "It's a good thing I have a real business for the boys to take over. They'd never make a living as musicians!"

Mama pretended not to hear his comment. "Knowledge of great music is the sign of an educated man." Her voice made the words sound like a putdown. I wondered if Supreme Court judges played musical instruments or listened to Caruso singing great operas on the Victrola in the evening.

All the squeaky music didn't stop Papa from paying for the music lessons or shopping for equipment to expand his thriving trucking business. Every few weeks he bought something new: a steam shovel, a dump truck, heavy lifts. He hired more men and put money down on an empty lot to house all his new machinery.

Despite all the buying and selling and hiring and firing men, he often got into ugly arguments. He had a mean temper with his employees. I couldn't figure out why, if he didn't like colored men, he kept hiring them, but I never asked him. However, I did ask Mama. "They work for less money." I thought maybe shouting orders and watching them obey made Papa feel superior, like a successful American businessman.

However, despite his frantic rushing about, Papa found time to walk me to school on the first day I started at Public School 40. The entire three blocks he held my hand and said I was on my way to becoming a lawyer, reminding me that speaking good English and getting a good education were the first steps in getting appointed as a Supreme Court judge.

When we got to Fifteenth Street, he knew exactly where to go.

The school building was huge, and dozens of noisy kids shoved and yelled and butted into each other. Before mounting the first step, I balked. Peering inside the dark gray concrete building, I spied an even darker entryway. It led to a shadowy hall that looked like an endless walled cave. Wild, unfamiliar kids disappeared into open doorways along the endless hall. The thought of being left in this strange place terrified me. The hallway blackened. Paura? No. Papa's warm hand held mine. He didn't seem disturbed. I moved closer to him as we walked down the hall.

Shortly, Papa stepped into a doorway that opened into a huge room with rows of bright orange wooden desks and half-drawn, dark-green window shades. A tall, thin woman with large blue eyes behind thick eyeglasses greeted Papa.

"Miss O'Reilly," he said, "here's my third."

She smiled down at me and pointed to the first row on the window side, nearest her desk. She said I could sit in the front seat because I was small.

Papa said, "She's small, but she's quicker than the two boys."

I liked hearing Papa praise me to a teacher. It felt like getting a head start. For a moment I felt maybe he liked me as much as he liked Agnes even though I didn't have blonde curly hair.

I slid into a wooden seat anchored on one side to its desk, both framed by wrought iron sides that resembled those of Mama's treadle sewing machine. Papa leaned over and told me I was in good hands in the best place in the world and to do what the teacher said. He smiled at Miss O'Reilly, then left.

Soon, strange kids, everyone bigger than me, began scrambling for seats, boys scuffling and pushing girls out of seats, girls whining. Miss O'Reilly didn't seem to notice. She turned from me and went to her desk. I wanted to leave and catch up with Papa before he got too far down the hall, but I knew I had to obey and stayed seated. Speaking above the din, Miss O'Reilly said that when the bell rang, we should all be quiet.

A thunderous bell echoed throughout the building. Three times.

Like magic, the room became silent. It seemed quieter than home had ever been, quieter than church. No noise inside the classroom, no noise outside in the playground, no noise in the hall. The soft hum in the air that followed the bell created a song. A school song. I loved school.

Miss O'Reilly's calm voice floated above our heads. "Good morning, class."

"Good morning, Miss O'Reilly," I whispered, showing good manners as Mama had instructed before I left home that morning. No one else responded except a boy in the back, who snickered. Miss O'Reilly's big blue eyes stared at him; she smiled at me and whispered, "Thank you, Eleanor."

My love of school increased. I loved it more than church or going to Aunt Mary's for cream soda. Even more than going to our vacation farm.

From all my First Holy Communion practicing, I was good at memorizing the alphabet and careful at copying each letter Miss O'Reilly wrote on the blackboard. I imitated how she started and stopped writing numbers or the alphabet. I loved writing the different letters, first with a pencil and then with a pen. I focused on tracing them over and over, first lowercase, then capitals. I liked the fancier capital letters best and concentrated on drawing each new line exactly over the previous mark, so the letter kept looking the same, only darker and darker.

At home, after I had put all the supper dishes in the sink, emptied the tray of water under the ice box, and rocked Evelyn in the cradle until she fell asleep, I practiced making letters with the pencil and notebook Mrs. Gould gave me when she learned I had started school.

Later in the school year, to prepare for cursive writing—a word that sounded like swearing, which didn't seem proper—Miss O'Reilly demonstrated how to make a series of circles. She held her pen in a raised hand but kept her lower arm on her desktop and rotated her arm without stopping, making small circles from the left side of the paper to the right, keeping tiny spaces in between. If you did it right, it looked like a round black tunnel.

Once most of the class had made rows and rows of circular tunnels, we practiced writing the alphabet in fancy cursive where each letter was attached to another, like sleeping three to a bed. Finally, we learned to write our names in cursive. As a reward, Miss O'Reilly said we were each going to get a book. She placed a stack of readers on the front desks of each row and asked us to take one book and pass the rest to the student behind. The readers had a soft olive-green cloth cover Mama identified as Irish linen. It was beautiful and it smelled like the fabric department in Frederick Loeser's. And it was mine.

"Today we are going to learn to read," Miss O'Reilly said. "Open to the first page and sign your name in the top space of the sheet that's glued to the back of the cover. It's your reader."

I signed my name exactly in between the top two lines and secretly praised myself for doing it right, certain I had done it better than any of the boys in the class.

Having my very own book was glorious. Although Papa read Elks Club brochures and leaflets about his equipment, and Mama read the *Daily News*, the only books we had at home were prayer books. My reader was the best present I had ever been given. Better than the pencil and notebook or the toothbrush Mrs. Gould had given me, better than my First Holy Communion dress— even better than getting my picture taken.

Miss O'Reilly stood in the center of the room and held the book open in front of her flat chest so we kids could see where she pointed. She asked us to tap the pictures of the cat, the dog, the cow. Then she pointed to the three different words: Cat. Dog. Cow. She said she was going to read a story about the cow, and we should point to each word as she read. She had gone through a few pages when *zing!* I could read! The printed letters had turned into words, and the words turned into a story. Oh, if only Mama could have been here. I almost shouted. Instead, I went on to the next sentence and finished reading the whole story along with Miss O'Reilly.

When the bell rang and school was over, I dashed out of the room and ran all the way home without waiting for Francey to fetch me. As I ran up the three flights, I screamed, "Mama, Mama, I can read! I can read!" Mama's face lit up. She took the book out of my hand, put it on the kitchen table, opened it to the first page and placed her hand over mine.

"Point," she said, sounding like Miss O'Reilly. "Say the words exactly like the teacher."

"Dickie Dare went to school. On the way he met a cow. Moo said the cow."

As I recited, Mama read along with me, our hands sliding along the page. Gradually, we were reading together like twins in a chorus. I was teaching Mama how to read in English!

Later, proud of my accomplishment, I told Gloria and Genevieve, "I taught Mama how to read." That evening, I bragged to

Albert about my reader and how I taught Mama to read in English. He burst out laughing.

Furious, I sneered, "We pointed to the words together and she said the words same as me."

"You think you're so smart? You're one hundred percent stupid. Mama was testing you to see if you really knew how to *read*. Not just *memorize* like you did Hail Mary and Our Father."

If Mama hadn't been nearby, I would have spit at him. Albert was right. His smug look jolted my memory. Mama told us she had gone to eighth grade in Italy and to night school almost as soon as she landed in America so she could get her naturalization papers. But I was so mad I convinced myself he was being spiteful and kept believing I taught Mama how to read in English. I don't remember ever changing my story to Gloria or Genevieve.

On the last day of school before the bell rang at the end of the day, Miss O'Reilly asked the class to clean out desks and drop trash in the wastepaper basket. Everyone bustled about, running back and forth from desk to wastebasket. Her voice rose above the shuffles. "Class, when your desks are empty, I want each row to pass your readers from the back to the front desk. I need to collect them for next year's first grade students."

I couldn't believe her words. She wanted *my* reader!

Seven readers landed on my desk. In a ritual of dazed obedience, I added mine to the stack and watched in horror as she placed stack after stack in the wall closet. Smiling, Miss O'Reilly walked to my desk and took my reader along with the pile beneath it. She moved across the room, set the stack on a shelf next to the others inside the closet, and locked the door. My stomach churned as I stared at the large metal lock.

As soon as the three o'clock bell rang and Miss O'Reilly wished us a happy summer vacation, I fled home, rushed into the kitchen, and burst into tears.

Mama shrieked, "What happened? Did anyone hurt you? Tell

me!"

I shook my head side to side, snot sliding out of my nose, and sobbed uncontrollably.

"Did anyone *touch* you?" Mama's eyes blazed.

"Miss O'Reilly took away my reader. She took my reader," I blubbered.

"What reader?"

"*My* reader. My book with the green linen cover. Remember? Dickie Dare went to school.'"

Mama stood very still, her eyes gripping mine. Her voice softened. "The reader wasn't yours. It belongs to the school."

"Miss O'Reilly told me to write my name in it. It's *mine.*"

Mama's chest heaved a big sigh. She swept my hair away from where it was stuck on my face. "I'll buy you another book."

"It won't be the same!" I turned and stomped into the girls' bedroom. As I changed out of my school clothes and tugged on a play dress, I kept thinking about how I should have stolen my reader. I could have hidden it inside my sweater. I also decided I didn't want to become a Supreme Court judge. Instead, I would become a teacher and keep as many readers as I wanted.

That night, unable to sleep, I imagined a Gone Room where I could keep my reader and anything that was lost or taken from me. Like the French flag Papa gave me at Lindberg's celebration. I couldn't find it after Florence La Comte from across the street and I played grown-ups and I never saw it again. And maybe I could put Albert's lost tigers eye marble in the Gone Room, too.

The next day Mama returned from Frederick Loeser's and handed me a small package covered with shiny green paper. Inside, I found a book about a little orphan girl who lived in a boxcar with her sister and two brothers. I liked the story, but the cover was cardboard, not soft olive-green Irish linen.

CHAPTER TWELVE—ERRANDS

1928

N ow that I was seven and allowed to walk to and from school by myself, Mama sent me on errands. "You're quicker than the boys," she said, handing me a nickel to buy soup greens from the corner vegetable store on Eighteenth Street. I loved this chore.

As I waited for Mrs. Fotina to finish with a customer, I stared at her daughter, Violetta, who sat with her head bent, sewing at a huge factory sewing machine in a section of the store which led into their living quarters. The huge machine had the same kind of wrought iron sides as my school desk and Mama's treadle sewing machine.

Violetta looked to be about sixteen or seventeen. I marveled at how she never looked up, not when a customer entered or left her mother's store, not even when I stood next to her. Fascinated, I watched as she grabbed a shiny oval cloth about the size of a dinner plate from a pile on one knee, placed it under the needle, and stitched several tucks into the edge.

Without stopping, she would grab a different oval of dark navy blue wool from another pile on the side of her machine, make several similar tucks in it, then sew both together. Finally, she grabbed a circular strip of matching blue leather from her other knee and carefully sewed on a rolled edge. She snipped off a few loose threads and placed the hat on top of a pile that looked like dark blue woolen pancakes. In the five minutes or so that I stood waiting and watching, Violetta had made a hat.

Mama said she did piecework. "She makes tam-o'-shanter hats. Maybe earns a nickel a hat. She might make more than your father's truck drivers."

Mrs. Fotina always knew what I came for. Without asking, she grabbed a sheet of yesterday's *Daily News*, tossed in a big bunch of Italian parsley, a few stalks of celery, two carrots, and a small onion. I passed her the nickel.

I thought Violetta's hats were a better buy. I wanted to learn how to make one for myself.

When I returned home, I begged Mama to show me how to sew. She smiled, picked up a clean diaper, sat in front of her treadle machine, and said, "Watch. Keep your fingers away from the needle. Look at my foot. Go slow. Look at my hands. Go straight. Slide. Slide. Keep your fingers away from the needle." And ever so gently she rolled the raw edge, tucked it under the fold, held it taut, slid the folded flannel cloth under the wiggly pressure foot, and hemmed a straight edge down one side of the diaper.

Finished, she stood up and said, "Try." I sat, managed to reach the treadle with the tip of my toe, and imitated Mama. Soon, every diaper in the house had hems. I felt a little like Violetta, but mostly like Mama.

Besides sending me out to shop, Mama would also send me to Giulia's. If Giulia didn't show up at her usual visit time, I would go down the street to the tenement apartment where she and Carlo lived, to check and see if she was okay. Giulia didn't have a phone. She said she didn't need one. The only person she knew in America was Mama, and we lived within walking distance. A phone cost too much.

Giulia was soft and round and playful. She loved to tease me by unexpectedly shoving her false teeth in and out, knowing it made me retch and turn away. Unlike Mama or Papa, she had infinite patience. She never raised her voice, never scowled. If I scooted from her lap, she would beg me to come back and tempt me with, "We make-a suga titties." It always worked.

She and I would sit close and make sugar-titties for the younger children. I felt grown-up, like her girlfriend. Giulia would start by pulling the dark crust from chunks of Italian bread, tearing the white part into small bits, and tossing them into a bowl with dots of butter and a pinch of sugar. Then she would sprinkle it with milk, mix, and squeeze the moist bread into little balls the size of Albert's glass marbles.

After putting the dark crusts into a jar where scraps were turned into breadcrumbs, she would pick up a clean hankie or a torn square from a soft, worn diaper and drop the little round clump into its center and ask me to hold onto it while she snugged a rubber band around the bottom of the ball, forming a tight little knob. Next, we would trade jobs; I would make the sugar-titty, and she would hold the blob for me to secure with a rubber band.

Inside your mouth, the sugar-titty became a sweet, watery pacifier. I never sucked on one. I didn't like the way you looked, walking around half the afternoon with a rag hanging out the side of your mouth.

When Mama wasn't present, Giulia snuck one to Francey, who really was too old for a sugar-titty. If Mama caught sight of Francey with one in his mouth, she yanked it out and then yelled at Giulia—not like she yelled at Papa, more like a schoolteacher reprimanding a naughty student.

"He's the oldest and you treat him like a baby. He'll never grow up."

Giulia would laugh at Mama but never talk back. Instead, she would look sideways and reassure Francey with love in her eyes. I felt she wished she had a son like him. And despite Mama's objections, on many of her her daily visits, Giulia would sit at the table, settle into her soft, squat body, make sugar-titties, and continue to sneak them to Francey.

I loved Giulia not only for teaching me how to make sugar-titties, but because she loved holding us on her lap—one or two at a time—just for fun. She smelled of lavender soap with a hint of coal soot in her hair because of Carlo's job shoveling coal.

If we were running around playing tag and one of us got near her, she would reach out and grab us. She'd gently squeeze us onto her lap and close her soft, warm arms around our bodies and rock us like babies.

Mama only held us if we fell and had a bruise, or if we had a fever or a cough that wouldn't go away. And even then, it was never for long.

Once, while Giulia and I worked in the kitchen, the phone rang. It was Mrs. Ryan, who lived across the street and had thick, bushy hair as orange as a carrot. Mama put the phone down and called to me. "Mrs. Ryan needs a little help. She had a hard time delivering the baby. She's not supposed to get out of bed for at least another week."

"Why can't her bratty son help? He's nine. He's two years older than me."

"Bryan is staying with his uncle. Anyhow, he's a boy. Just go. Mrs. Ryan left the door open." As I headed toward the stairway, she said, "Wait."

She ladled warm chicken soup from a pot simmering on the stove into a Kerr canning jar and wrapped it in a dish towel. "Be careful. Don't drop it," she warned, handing it to me. "Be quiet so you don't wake the baby. Look both ways before you cross the street. Look twice. Bring back the towel."

Mama always gave two or three orders in a row.

I climbed the stone stoop at Mrs. Ryan's, imagining what I'd say to her son about how boys can't even help their own mothers.

When I peered into a strange dark hallway, I balked. Why wasn't her son doing this chore? Pressing the soup to my chest, I tiptoed down the narrow hall, pushed open the door at the end, and entered Mrs. Ryan's kitchen. A big clawfoot bathtub next to the sink was covered with a wide wooden board piled high with newspapers, cereal boxes, a half-full jar of ketchup, and a stack of dishes, some clean, others soiled. The room smelled old. It was messier than Mama's kitchen had ever been. Papa would have thrown everything into the trash bin.

If the Ryans ever took a bath, it would take them all morning to move the pile of stuff off the board. As I shoved some cups aside to clear a place for the chicken soup, I started plotting. The next time Bryan acted like a know-it-all, I'd say he smelled like he never took a bath.

Mrs. Ryan's loud whisper, "I'm here in the front bedroom," interrupted my imaginings. Following her voice, I tiptoed through several dark rooms to where she lay. Close by, in a small wooden crib—not nearly as ornate as our cream-colored, wrought-iron cradle that swung back and forth—a baby lay sound asleep, orange hair peeping out of a lacy white cap.

When I approached the crib, which stood near the window, Mrs. Ryan pressed her finger to her mouth and whispered, *"Shussh."* She beckoned me toward her side of the bed and tossed back her bedding. I had never seen a naked adult. Lying before me, flat on her back, was a fat woman with a huge orange bush growing between her thighs.

"Here, take this Kotex," she said, reaching between her legs. "Wrap it in some newspaper you can find on the bathtub and put it in the garbage pail under the sink." Blinded by the flaming bush, I stood frozen until Mrs. Ryan spoke again. "First bring me a fresh one from the box on the bureau."

Dutifully, like a sleepwalker, I picked up a blue Kotex box on the bureau, and as I set it on her bed, Mrs. Ryan reached down, pulled what looked like a thick bloody sock from under the bush, and holding it by one tip, handed it to me. The bloody clump weighed a ton and its stench made me queasy. Holding my breath, arm stretched ahead of me, I carried what she called a Kotex through the dark rooms toward the kitchen.

Without warning, the area darkened and tiny lights flashed on and off like fireflies. Preceding me, another *me* continued into the kitchen. The other me dropped the Kotex on the stack of newspapers covering the bathtub. She pinched the edges of several layers of newspapers and folded them around the warm, bloody Kotex. She dropped the clump into the garbage pail. When it thumped, she disappeared.

Unable to breathe, my stomach convulsing, I headed out the kitchen door and raced down the narrow passageway. Outside, I vomited on the stoop.

When I entered the kitchen at home, Mama, dusting her macaroni board with flour, looked up and asked, "What happened? You came up the steps slow." She studied me. "You're pale. What's wrong?"

Unable to find words to match my feelings, I concentrated on my shoes. I finally said, "I forgot to bring the towel back."

"That's all?"

I continued to avoid Mama's penetrating eyes and moved toward the sink to wash my hands. "Crossing the street, I didn't look twice."

Mama said nothing, but she never sent me to Mrs. Ryan's again.

CHAPTER THIRTEEN—THE ATTIC

1928

Every year after school let out, we moved to the country farm for the summer, but Papa stayed in Brooklyn to run his trucking business. He came on weekends, and knowing how he felt, we kids took extra care doing our chores. If everything was clean and neat the way he liked, he wouldn't get mad at Mama and yell, "Sporka. Sporka," and she wouldn't get mad at him and throw a pot—or whatever she had in her hand —across the room. And we kids wouldn't have to be go-betweens when they had something to say to each other.

One Friday, it was my turn to sweep the large upstairs hallway, including all the steps and both landings that zigzagged inside the big three-story Victorian house. As I slid my broom under the small night table on the upper landing, taking care not to tip the votive candle in its stubby red glass or disturb the picture of the Virgin Mary, I heard a faint rhythmic sound coming from the attic. A mouse? I tiptoed closer. The sound continued. Slowly and quietly, I started up the steep, rough wooden stairway into the dark attic where Nick, a guest, slept.

Nick had come home with Papa a few weekends earlier. He seemed too young to work in Papa's garage or drive one of the Mack trucks. Besides, instead of gasoline, he smelled of pomade and he combed his oily hair flat. As soon as he and Papa came through the back door into the kitchen, Papa started to speak to Mama in Italian, disobeying his own rule prohibiting anyone from speaking Italian in front of his children.

From the little Italian I had picked up listening to relatives, and from Papa's lowered voice, when he said *polizia,* my interest picked up. A *compagno*—one of the brothers from Brooklyn's Little Italy—had asked Papa for a *favore.* Could his *figlio,* Nick, stay at the farm *"uno o duo mesi?"*

Recalling Papa's hushed tone when he arrived with Nick, and intrigued by the faint rhythmic sound, I continued up the attic stairs. Less than halfway up, my head level with the thick wooden floor at the top of the open stairway, I saw my younger sister Agnes sitting on Nick's lap. She was facing him, her legs straddling his knees, rhythmically sliding the sole of her sandal back and forth along the side rung of the heavy oak chair.

Nick's back was toward the only small window on that side of the attic; I couldn't see his face clearly, but his eyes seemed closed. His knees, held firmly together, extended beyond the folds of my apple-green school dress that Agnes, looking smaller and frailer than usual, hadn't quite grown into. The front of the dress was pulled up near her belly button, laying bare her knee and small thigh, both caught in the light from the window. She was looking up into his face, wearing a strange expression I had never seen before, her mouth partially open, her cheek pulled a little high, as though smiling, but not in a way familiar to me. Her head was titled slightly toward Nick's hand, which wasn't quite touching her small frame. His dark forefinger twirled inside one of her shoulder-length, soft blonde curls. I couldn't see his other hand.

Why didn't they notice me? They could easily have done so, but both seemed far away in another place, visible only to them. Enclosed. Although Agnes' foot was still gliding along the rung of the chair and Nick's finger was still slowly twirling around her curl, I had the distinct sensation that both were still, not breathing.

I stared in wonder. Some part of me, as yet neither nourished nor awakened, sensed something new.

Paura struck a sharp painful jab in my chest. *I* had stopped breathing.

Confused and ashamed of my spying, I backed down the
stairs, leaning on the stiff broom bristles to lighten my footsteps,
not making a sound. At the landing, I hurried past the red votive
candle, jumped the few steps down into the upper hall, turned
again and raced down the long flight of stairs until I reached the
landing above the three steps that led into the kitchen.

Mama, humming and rhythmically kneading and rolling
gnocchi dough into long, round logs, glanced at the broom and
sprinkled flour over the dough. "Done?"

Catching my breath, I hesitated. "Agnes is sitting on Nick's lap
in the attic."

Mama turned to face me, her eyes penetrating mine. "Call her
down. Quick." But before I could obey, she yelled up into the
hallway, her voice high, almost shrieking, "Agnes. Agnes! *Venga.*
Come!"

We both waited. Within seconds, we heard Agnes' light step
—skipping, almost dancing—as she descended the attic stairs
onto the small upper landing, down three steps into the upper
hallway, then down the stairs leading to the kitchen. When she
stopped on the lower landing, I didn't move aside; I wanted to
get as close as possible. I wanted to get a better read of the expression I had seen on her face. It was gone. Now her expression
was completely familiar—primed and ready to make a demand,
the same as always.

Cheated, and feeling a mixture of betrayal and envy, I stared
at her sandals.

Agnes stood on the landing looking down at Mama, who
stared back, her eyes like dark wool, and for a moment I felt both
had disappeared from the kitchen and rendezvoused some place
unknown to me, leaving me on my own, invisible, excluded. Motionless, they stared at each other. Mama was first to drop her
gaze.

"I don't want any of you girls going into the attic," Mama
hurled. Turning away from Agnes, Mama clutched a clump of
gnocchi dough, slapped it hard against the dark walnut macaroni board, and began to roughly knead and reshape the dough.

As she did so, her eyelids lowered. She bit into the side of her lower lip, sucking in her cheeks, making her whole face shrink. Then she turned to me and signaled with a sharp toss of her head. "Go tell the small ones." As I headed out the kitchen door, she added, "Tell the boys, too."

Uneasy, my thoughts dwelled on how Mama and Agnes had stared at each other. I didn't like the way it reminded me of the game the neighborhood boys played: Flinch First, You Lose. Why did Mama flinch? I went outside to find my younger sisters, mulling over what I had been unable to resolve.

The next morning, we learned that Papa had left for Brooklyn instead of spending the weekend. He had taken Nick with him. We never saw Nick again.

CHAPTER FOURTEEN—THE DAY I SHOT AGNES

1928

That autumn, back in Brooklyn, returning from school, Mama waited at the bottom of the stoop. She wanted to take me and my younger sisters with her to pick up mozzarella cheese at Aunt Mary's. My first-grade classmate Florence, who lived across the street in the only wood frame house on the block (where she may have hidden my French flag from Lindy's celebration) told Mama we had planned to play Grown-Up with Mama's high heeled shoes and veiled hats. "Besides, my mother won't allow me to go off Seventeenth Street. Can Eleanor stay home?"

"Stay, stay," Mama said. "Don't get into trouble. Eat a tangerine. Change into play clothes."

Mama left, carrying Evelyn; Gloria and Genevieve tagged alongside. Agnes stayed behind. She said she wanted to play Grown-Up, too, and the three of us went upstairs. We ate tangerines and arranged the pits on Mama's macaroni board to make funny faces. Agnes told me to change out of my school dress, and I tried on Florence's green coat with a new kind of fake leather and imitation lamb's wool collar. Florence said she wanted to wear Mama's black suede high-heeled shoes, and could she wear the dead fox with the tiger eyes?

Agnes turned to Florence and said, "You're picking out the best. Shush. I hear someone in the hall downstairs."

I peeked out the door from the top of the stairs and saw no

one. But it stirred a long-held curiosity. I could get the gun Papa hid in the closet in the boys' room. Papa had shown it to the boys, saying it had a pearl grip and wasn't for girls. But I wanted to see it up close, too. And we could get a good look at it before Mama came back and my brothers were playing kick-the-can in the street below.

We kids had been forbidden to touch the gun, but we were alone. No one would know. It would be a quick peek. I moved toward the boys' bedroom, and the girls followed. The three of us tiptoed into the dim room, lit by a high window that spanned the length of the room. Light came through from the adjacent girls' bedroom with its large windows on the street side. Mama hated this room, said the wall with the window had been put up to make two rooms out of one. I dragged a large chair from the dining room and asked Florence to get one of the small kiddie chairs from the kitchen. "So I can reach."

"You're not supposed to do that," Agnes warned. "I'm going to tell Papa." Ignoring her, I stacked the small chair on the seat of the big chair and boosted myself up. Standing on tiptoe, I reached into the back of the closet's highest shelf and slid my hand between the linens from one end of the wall to the next.

I touched a cool object and grabbed the small pearl-handled pistol hidden under the pile of pillowcases and slipped it out. Success!

Looking up, Florence said, "Let me see it." The room was too dark to really examine it. I jumped down and we trooped into the kitchen. The three of us stood around admiring the beautiful pearl swirls on the gun's grip. Florence said it looked like the inside of a shell. As I turned it over to see the other side, a loud bang shattered the silence. The gun spun out of my hand from the force of the shot, thudded on the table, shivered, and lay still. Agnes screamed and raised her left arm. Blood oozed out of her elbow and circled into a dark red puddle near the gun. Florence grabbed her coat and headed for the door.

"Don't leave," I pleaded. But Florence, her face an unfamiliar mask, disappeared; her footsteps sounded like pellets dropping on the steps.

The puddle lengthened. Blood dripped off the table and splattered on the floor. I turned to Agnes and said, "I'll take you into the bathroom and wash away the blood."

Within seconds, the kitchen filled, crammed with people. Papa and Uncle Pete came racing up the stairs from the garage. Mama arrived home moments later. Gloria and Genevieve began wailing at the sight of Agnes' bloody arm. The phone rang. Nobody answered it. Everyone fired questions at me. I couldn't hear what they were saying. Paura squeezed my chest and stole my breath—the kitchen darkened, then flashed with blue lights and black holes.

Through the swirling blue lights and suffocating dark air, the *girl* wearing a blue and white after-school dress like the one I had changed into appeared across the room. She stood in Mama's kitchen, but also didn't; she appeared like a see-through image. She looked straight at Papa.

He kept asking her where she stood when the gun went off. He kept insisting, "Where, where? I'm trying to find the bullet." He kept asking her to show him exactly, exactly, exactly where it had landed.

She didn't answer.

She couldn't.

She didn't know.

Papa got more frantic, running his hands along the walls and the door frames, his gaze darting back and forth. Uncle Pete peered under the table, both arms outstretched, moving like a swimmer as he searched along the floor. He asked for newspapers or a rag to wipe up the blood.

"Where? Where?" Papa kept asking, his voice louder and louder. "Where were you holding the gun? Where were you? How did you find it?"

Each time he asked, the girl moved farther away. I remained trapped inside Paura's cocoon of whirling lights. Finally, she spoke. "I stood on the chairs in the boys' room . . . we heard a burglar. We were looking at the handle. It was on the table.

When I turned it over . . ."

"Where were you standing?"

"On the chairs."

"No. Not the bedroom. The kitchen. Standing on what side of the table. Where?"

Papa continued to run his grease-stained hand over the walls and doors, studying the ceiling and the window frames. The girl began to move about the room, sometimes leading, sometimes following.

"Was anyone else here?"

"Florence."

"Did she see what happened?

"Yes."

Papa looked at Mama, who held Agnes in her arms. Both were pale and frightened. Paura's black shadow hovered between them.

Uncle Pete swore in Italian. "Her goddamn mother screws every Irish dick in the borough. If she calls the police, we're done for. They'll find the still. They'll search the garage. I'm moving my truck out." Stomping toward the door, he spoke to Papa, in a mean, bossy voice. "If the cops come, keep your mouth shut. Callucio will be after us if you say a word about the runs from Cuba to Long Island."

But before he reached the door Mama screamed, her eyes fierce: *"Femari.* Stop! One of you get Dr. Lupo. Now. Go. Now. *Now."*

Papa and Uncle Pete froze. They stared at each other like gangsters in a newspaper photo. Uncle Pete mumbled something to Papa in Italian; then, their heads hanging, both fled out the door.

Agnes screamed for Papa to come back. Mama looked inside the towel she held against Agnes' arm, dropped it in the sink, and picked up a bunch of clean diapers from the shelf near the bathroom. She pressed them lightly against Agnes' arm, and Agnes wailed. Mama did not look at the girl or me. She kept her face turned away the whole time we waited for Dr. Lupo. Paura kept squeezing my chest so hard I couldn't breathe. The see-through girl waited in the archway to the dining room. Agnes screamed in pain. I thought I would vomit.

Soon, the downstairs door banged open, and footsteps sounded on the stairway. Mama opened the kitchen door. Papa barged in first, followed by Dr. Lupo, and then Uncle Pete and Chenzi—Papa's driver for the almond truck. Dr. Lupo glanced at Mama, greeted her in Italian, and put his black leather satchel on a kitchen chair. He asked Mama to place Agnes on the kitchen table. Agnes wailed louder.

Dr. Lupo removed the bloody diaper from Agnes' arm and peered at her elbow. The rest of us peered at him, our eyes following his eyes. The room became silent; no one moved until Dr. Lupo spoke. "Lie still. Stop screaming. Don't move."

He sounded angry. Agnes must have thought so too; her screams rose higher. He said something in Italian to Mama, who put a pile of clean diapers on the table and tried to prop Agnes' forearm on top. Dr. Lupo struggled to hold her arm still. Mama helped. Agnes wailed. The men looked like scared boys. Everyone watched in silence. My stomach turned.

Dr. Lupo felt around the bloody area. He turned to Mama, and speaking half in Italian and half in English, said a sharp object had pierced her flesh and might still be in her arm. He said she was lucky. Very lucky. He shook his head and muttered something in Italian that made Papa stare at the floor.

Leaning back, he said, "We have to get her to a hospital. It's got to be removed. I'll call ahead for the surgeon."

Papa, Uncle Pete, and Chenzi exchanged frightened looks. Papa's face turned a pale yellow-green and Mama's turned even paler, almost white. Gloria and Genevieve started to wail, causing Papa to explode with anger.

"Go into your bedroom," he yelled. "Tell nobody. Nobody knows she got shot. Nobody." My sisters didn't move, but from across the room the girl stirred, peered at Papa, and mouthed, "But everybody knows."

She knew, and across the street, Florence knew. I wanted to

run down the steps, go to Florence's house, and beg her not to tell her mother, or her mother's boyfriends, but Paura's shadow kept squeezing my chest and wouldn't let me breathe or move.

Mama seemed unable to calm Agnes, and turning to Papa, she said, "You try." Papa, tenderly holding the bloody diapers under Agnes' arm, cradled her to his chest and carried her into Mama's bedroom. While settling her on the bed, he turned to Chenzi and whispered, "Move my truck."

Dr. Lupo followed Chenzi out the door. "I'll be back with a surgeon," he said. "Make space in the bedroom for the X-ray machine. We have to see where the bullet is lodged." Then, sounding like a police officer, he said, "Hold her still to stop more damage. Don't let her move her arm."

At this, Agnes began to kick and squirm and scream louder. Dr. Lupo ordered them to tie her free arm and legs to the bedposts if she didn't stop. Papa and Uncle Pete tried to soothe her, but Agnes kept struggling and screaming. A sharp peach pit poked into the lining of my stomach. Although I was standing at the foot of the bed, unable to move, the other me, the girl, stood in a haze at the far corner of the room, darkening the space around her.

Within an hour, Dr. Lupo came back with a big machine and a young doctor with shiny blond hair and a fancy wristwatch. Speaking softly, the young man asked everyone to stand back while he placed a big box on the bed next to Agnes' arm and asked Mama to hold Agnes motionless while he took the X-ray. Dr. Lupo stared into the machine and seemed to be studying what he saw. Everyone else stared at him as if they might glean some knowledge from his expression. Both doctors pointed to the image. They mumbled to each other. The young doctor opened his black leather satchel and asked Mama to place a clean towel on the bed. He took out a bunch of shiny tools and placed them on the towel. Dr. Lupo removed the box and placed it on the floor.

The young doctor put on a pair of long, stretchy gloves and asked Papa and Uncle Pete to hold Agnes as still as possible. "It won't take long, but it's going to hurt."

Agnes screeched, and Mama put a moist face cloth on her forehead.

The men looked like giants holding a screaming doll. Uncle Pete, his face shiny with sweat, pressed her thin little body firmly against the mattress. Papa, looking sick, held her arm against the towel. Mama's face turned gray. The peach pit in my stomach twisted.

Agnes screamed and screamed while the young doctor probed and probed and probed with his shiny tools. First, he used a small probe with loops on one end and clamps on the other, then a larger one that looked like pliers. Finally, his expression changed, and he clamped onto something solid. With a sure, quick stroke, he twisted his hand upward and pulled out a bloody clump which he set on the towel.

"Please keep holding her still. I need to put in a few stitches." He tossed his head sideways to swing a lock of his blond hair away from his eyes, leaned close to Agnes' elbow, looked up at her, and in a soft voice said, "I'm sorry." He began stitching the wound.

Agnes wailed like a kitten whose paw had been caught in a trap. The sharp peach pit pierced the walls of my stomach. Soon the young doctor sat back, his job done. He reached for the bloody clump, examined it, wiped it with the edge of the towel, then dropped it into Papa's palm. Everyone moved closer and gaped at the tiny metal bullet the size of a cockroach lying in Papa's grease-stained hand.

The young doctor went into the kitchen, washed his gloves, shook them until most of the water was gone, and put them in his back pocket. Then he washed his hands, dried them on a clean diaper, went back to the bedroom, picked up the X-ray machine and his black leather satchel, nodded to all the grown-ups, said something about emergency rooms, and left.

Agnes, her face wet with sweat, kept screaming. Papa stroked and smoothed her hair, and Mama tried to wipe her forehead with the moist towel, but Agnes kept tossing wildly, kicking her legs.

The taste of vomit rose in my throat, but trapped inside a cocoon, I couldn't move. The peach pit kept stabbing my belly, and I couldn't tell anyone how much it ached because what happened to Agnes was my fault. And I couldn't change anything.

Perhaps the girl disappeared along with Paura when I vomited in the kitchen sink, or maybe later that night, after I hid my face in the pillow and cried myself to sleep without letting anyone hear. I dreamed of seeing the cockroach bullet on Papa's greasy palm in the Gone Room.

A few days later, Dr. Lupo came back, changed the bandages on Agnes' elbow, and put her arm in a black sling. Standing tall, he spoke to Papa. Clearing his throat and sounding like Father Alonzo, he lectured: First, Papa should never have a gun where kids could get it, and second, if he kept the gun, he should know better than to leave it full of bullets. "Next time, you won't be so lucky."

I couldn't figure out why Dr. Lupo said Papa was lucky and that Agnes was also lucky. Papa was nodding as though he agreed. I was sure Agnes wouldn't agree. Looking at the two men —my father, the smartest man in the world, and Dr. Lupo, a doctor—I decided both were wrong.

CHAPTER FIFTEEN—AGNES' CURLS

1928

The whole time Agnes' arm healed, Mama hardly spoke. She didn't look anyone in the eye. She never sang any arias. She didn't even swat or pinch any of us. She kept checking the bandage and made Agnes special eggnogs and beef tea with baby *pastina* to help her arm heal and grow stronger. She never looked at me or asked me to help set the table or rock the baby or fold diapers. I couldn't tell if she was mad at me, mad at Papa, or mad at herself.

Like Mama, I became quiet—except in school, where I began to get into trouble. I wouldn't let the boy monitors on the playground boss me around, and if one of them tried to shove me because I refused to get in line when he asked, I'd spit at him. In class, I lied and said somebody else must have stuck the chewing gum under my classmate's desk. I stole and ate several Jujubes candies from my closest classmate's desk. When she accused me, I said she was lying—she ate them, not me.

Meanwhile at home, I tried hard to be good. Extra hard. Without being asked, I set the table for soup, rocked Evelyn to sleep, and turned the black rubber nipples inside out, washing them with sudsy water, then rinsing them with cool, clean water. I scrubbed the glass baby bottles until they gleamed. I washed oatmeal bowls every morning. I constantly went out of my way to please Mama. I wanted to hear her sing.

I wanted her to notice me.

I feared Agnes would never be able to move her arm again.

Sometimes I woke at night from a dream where Agnes' arm was paralyzed. In the morning, before we left our bed, I would fix my eyes on her arm and pray for it to move.

Gradually, her arm healed, and she could use it the same as before. Still, Papa kept giving her extra attention. Sometimes Agnes pretended her arm hurt even when she had been playing jacks with no trouble at all or had just poked Albert with it. If she began to whine and make Mama mad, I would—quick as I could —do something extra, extra good, like fold all the baby diapers into neat triangles and stack them one on top of the other, ready to use.

After a while—I don't remember when it started—Mama began to notice me. To praise me again. A lot. Often. And it made me feel important again because Mama always told the truth. She never said anything she didn't mean. She never pretended.

She appeared to forget about the gun, and much to my delight, she often grew angry with Agnes, who kept reminding everyone that I shot her and that the doctors didn't use any pain medicine to remove the bullet, and how awful it hurt when they held her still, and that she would never get over hating the cruel surgeon who could bring a big X-ray machine but no pain medication. I would have agreed with her if she hadn't said it so often and to everybody on the block.

Further, Agnes repeatedly reminded Papa and Aunt Mary that Mama should never have left us alone. She found fault with Mama over the least little thing, like the *pastina* not being thoroughly cooked or overcooked, or Mama not coming quick enough when she said her arm hurt, or Mama not giving her as much cocoa as she gave Albert. And when Albert told her to shut up, the moment Papa came through the door she whined and said everyone was picking on her. Papa would smile, pick her up in his arms, and twirl her in the air.

The more Agnes whined to Papa, the more Mama praised me —for putting the spoons away and rinsing the dishes, for finding matching napkins when our aunts came to visit, for rocking Evelyn in her cradle, for folding diapers. She praised me when we were alone, and she praised me when my aunts came to visit. She praised me to Mrs. Gould, to Mrs. Ryan, to Giulia, to the ice man. To everybody.

"I don't know what I would do without her," she said. "She's the best help. She is the most responsible. She always does the best."

Inside, I beamed.

As Agnes' arm healed, Papa continued to pay her extra-special attention. He brushed her curly blonde hair and twisted it tenderly around his finger to form long, shoulder-length curls. During breakfast, he buttered thin strips of toast and dipped them into her soft-boiled egg, coaxing her to eat. He never noticed she pretended to be full. Teasing, he urged, "Just one more bite. One little bite. Papa wants his little Minky to take one more bite."

Finally, after endless coaxing and feeding her, one little bite at a time, Papa left for work. At the door, he turned and winked. "Goodbye, Minky." Agnes smiled. She was the only one Papa had given a nickname.

The moment the door closed behind him, she shook her head sideways, making her curls soar. "I'm the only one with blonde, curly hair. That's why Papa makes my curls," she bragged. She spoke the truth, but it infuriated me to hear her say so.

Earlier that morning, before breakfast, Mama had been cutting diapers from a new bolt of white flannel, and now she was in the bathroom washing out the stiff sizing. She had left the scissors on the table. Agnes kept twirling her head, swirling those beautiful blonde curls.

The scissors beckoned. As if moved by a puppeteer, my hand reached out, picked them up, turned toward Agnes, and cut off a dangling curl.

Horrified, both of us watched it drift to the floor. I waited for Agnes to hit me or scream for Mama. Instead, we froze, our eyes fixed on the yellow curl, which lay like a dead canary at our feet.

Growing nauseous, I slunk toward the bathroom and stood

in the doorway, mute, ready for punishment. Mama stopped swishing diapers in the washing machine. "You're pale. What happened?"

"I cut Agnes' hair."

Mama looked puzzled.

"I cut off a front curl."

Mama turned off the washing machine, lifted her apron, dried her hands, and approached me. I waited for the usual hard yank on my hair, which happened whenever she felt I needed to be taught a lesson. Nearing me, she raised both hands, moistened her thumbs across her tongue, leaned forward, and smoothed my eyebrows. Gently. Very gently. Twice.

"You told me the truth without being asked. That's the best truth. The curl will grow back." Taking the scissors from my hand, she added, Agnes has the curliest hair. But yours is the shiniest."

I had the best mother in the whole world.

CHAPTER SIXTEEN—THE BAGS

Mama was unpredictable. If we disobeyed or lied, Mama would do one of two things: if you happened to be near her, she would grab your hair and pull you across the room, slap her free hand on the wall, and bounce your head against her hand. One or two light bounces meant easily forgiven; three or four bounces meant never do this again.

But she was also approachable.

Once, I asked her why she placed her hand against the wall. "I want to know how hard I'm hitting. Teach you a lesson. I don't want to damage your smart brains."

Mama had another standby method to instill or reinforce obedience to rules. It consisted of Bags. These invisible Bags were constantly being filled and emptied—their contents sometimes known, sometimes not. If you happened to be out of reach when you committed a transgression, she would warn, "I'm putting it in the Bag," implying you deserved a slap right then and there, but she was too busy at the moment, or you were out of reach.

Mama kept a tally for each Bag, stuffing it with every minor or major wrongdoing: if you didn't come when called, if you peeled a chicken-pox scab, if you hit a younger sibling, if you lied— everything went into the Bag. Then, out of the blue, if you happened to leave the water running or left the door of the chicken coop unlatched, or, more predictably, if Mama had on the reddish-brown dress she wore for almost a week every month, any one of us could get a quick swat for no apparent reason at all. The first one who noticed the dress whispered to the others, "Mama's wearing *the dress*."

Often, while wearing what we nicknamed her '
Mama would lose her temper over nothing. If you ...
enough, you'd get an extra-hard pinch wherever she could grab,
or two or three rough tugs on your hair. Puffing, she would end
the ordeal by sliding and slapping her palms together as though
wiping sins off her hands, warning, "Now the Bag is empty. Keep
it that way."

If you looked quickly before turning away, her face might
register a message: satisfaction if you had learned a lesson, or
a tinge of remorse—a lingering plea—checking to see if she had
yanked or pinched too hard.

Agnes thought the Bag was a discarded chicken feed sack decorated with the picture of a rooster, like the pillowcases we made
from feed bags. She was certain all our sins went into the same
bag, yet she puzzled over Mama's ability to keep track of who did
what. She wondered how Mama sorted out individual wrong-
doings and reprieves in that sack full of sins.

Unlike Agnes or Gloria—who thought the Bag had lots of
pockets, one for each of us—I imagined my Bag as a crumpled
brown paper sack; I was convinced that Mama's mysterious skills
enabled her to keep accurate scores for each of us. Besides, I had
such a strong vision of my own crumpled brown paper Bag being
constantly filled and squashed flat, I was sure Mama had a different Bag for each of us. Except Albert and Francey—her favorites
—who didn't have Bags.

With all of Mama's demands for obedience, with all her boss-
ing us around day and night, with all that swatting and pinch-
ing, you might think she had a whole bunch of rules for us to follow. Not so. She had three, each cast in stone:

Never steal. Not a penny, not a diamond ring. Nothing. Never.
Always tell the truth. All the truth. Everything. Always.
Stay a virgin until you marry.

Every day as we lined up for school, mouths open like fledgling birds, we received the same lecture. Looking into our eyes,
Mama poured a teaspoon of slimy cod-liver oil down our throats,
followed by a sliver of tangerine. "Swallow! Chew."

One at a time, she lectured us with variations of her three rules. "Obey the teacher. Do nothing to make your mother ashamed. "

"Hold your head high." Mama reinforced these rules by greeting us after school with "What happened at school? Tell me." If we paused, she would add, "The truth."

I had firsthand experience with the first two rules but wanted her to explain the third. She dismissed me with, "You'll learn about that when you grow up."

I put number three aside for later, but not before I figured out that staying a virgin until I married had something to do with the virgin olive oil Mama put on salads; I was certain it was what the Virgin Mary used.

I planned to check this out on a day Mama wasn't wearing her once-a-month dress.

CHAPTER SEVENTEEN— STEALING LIPSTICK

1929

It was an early Saturday afternoon in Brooklyn when the phone rang. Mama stopped mincing parsley and garlic and I had just finished washing the oatmeal bowls. Cousin Jenny was turning twelve, and Mama said I could go to her birthday party, even though I was only eight—a prize for being her "best helper" since Miriam seldom came on Saturdays. Cousin Esther, Jenny's younger sister, had called to plead with Mama. Since Mama had made the cake for the party—everybody said her beautiful lemon custard sponge cake was the best—she should be there to sing "Happy Birthday" when Jenny blew out the candles.

Giulia, sitting near the kitchen table, rocking Genevieve, urged Mama, "Go. Go. Me watcha da baby."

Mama could never say no to Esther. Nobody in our family could, especially Francey, who Albert said had a crush on her. We all loved Esther, and Esther loved Mama. I thought she loved Mama more than she loved Aunt Mary, her own mother. Once, when we were playing Make-Believe, Esther said she wished her mother didn't speak broken English and wished she could sing Italian arias like Mama. And she wished her mother wasn't so old-fashioned and would learn to drive a car like Mama and pile us into Papa's Packard and take us to Coney Island. And I wished Esther were my older sister.

Mama's face would light up whenever Esther asked her to

sing, and sometimes they sang together. Cousin Esther would tease Mama and make her promise to teach her how to drive the way she taught her to sing. Mama once told Aunt Mary that Esther had an "ear for opera and should study music," which made me study Esther's ears and wish mine were a little bit bigger. Then maybe I could carry a tune as well as Esther.

But Aunt Mary had scoffed and said, *"Perché? Why? Sheeza* girl. She gonna helpa da pizzeria, an' getta marry."

Mama's face grew serious. "That might be all right for some Italians, but our girls should do better. They need to make something of themselves. Have a career of their own. Same as men. Hold their heads high."

Aunt Mary laughed and said something in Italian I didn't understand; whatever it was, the conversation ended, and Aunt Mary never gave Cousin Esther music lessons.

As we headed for the party, we walked more slowly than usual. I thought it was because Mama's belly was getting fat and she was "carrying." When we were about to cross Fourth Avenue, a wide, busy street, my sisters and I braced ourselves, dreading the "Crossing a Busy Street Ritual." Mama would stretch out both her arms, grab each of our index fingers one by one in one of her fingers, and, with a vise-like grip, pull all four of us across the street, two on each side, all struggling to stay upright as she dragged. Safely across, she would release her hold and beam. "Good. No complaints."

As we approached Aunt Mary and Uncle Frank's pizzeria, Mama reminded us not to argue, talk loud, or ask for anything —especially the cream soda stacked in brown bottles in a big wooden, walk-in refrigerator. "Wait until Aunt Mary offers *three* times. Three times before you say yes. Remember to say thank you." To the little ones she said, "And don't drink and walk. You might fall and spill."

Esther, the first to greet us, led the way through the restaurant into a big backyard with a bocce ball alley and a long table inside a gazebo shaded with green grapevines. Aunt Mary had set the table with more than a dozen matching dishes, each framing a pink or green curled, crinkly paper toy that sprang out as long as your arm and tooted when you blew it. Beside each plate sat a little white organdy gift bag filled with fancy blue, pink, and green Jordan almonds and tied with a gold ribbon.

Aunt Mary decorated the table like Italian families always did when they celebrated a daughter's engagement or a son's graduation from high school: a spotless white tablecloth, white linen napkins, fancy glasses, shiny silverware. Sunlight flickered through the grapevines overhead. Mama selected a Caruso record and wound the handle of the Victrola that sat near an open window inside the doorway, and everybody danced on the grass or sang Italian street songs.

Mama had secretly told me it was the backyard parties—especially now, during Prohibition—that "made the dollar" for Uncle Frank and Aunt Mary, not the pizzas they sold for twenty-five cents.

Only girls and women came to this party, small girls like my younger sisters and my cousins Tina, Rosie, and Esther, but also grown-ups: Cousin Jenny's older sisters Violet, Dolly, and Frances, Aunt Tessie, Aunt Esther, my godmother Aunt Frances, and wavy-haired Aunt Lou who as a child had returned to America on the *Prinzess Irene*, the same ship Mama sailed on when she left Chieti and landed on Ellis Island.

We squeezed together at the table, and if anyone left her chair momentarily, one of the younger girls would slide into it to sit closer to one of the aunts. Sitting next to aunts or older cousins meant breathing the sweet scent of lilac or rose perfume. Even the pale pink rouge on their cheeks smelled fancy, mixed in with the scents coming from the kitchen. I couldn't wait to smell like lilacs and wear pink rouge from a shiny compact with a mirror.

Boys were not allowed. Not my two brothers, nor Tina's brother Cousin Sol. Not even Cousin Ralph, Jenny's big brother, who was upstairs in his room over the pizzeria, studying to become a doctor. Mama disapproved when he changed his name from Sorrentino to Sorley after he graduated from Columbia University and started his training at Bellevue Hospital.

"To get American patients, you don't need to change your name—you need to be the best doctor in Brooklyn. That's how a doctor gets new patients. Word of mouth." She had said this only at home and to Giulia, not to Aunt Mary. Not even in front of Cousin Esther.

When we finished eating ravioli with *braggioli* and eggplant *parmigiana,* all the kids had cream soda and all the grown-ups had red wine. Esther whispered to Jenny, the birthday girl, to ask Mama to cut the big round sponge cake topped with peaches and whipped cream. I had helped whip the eggs for the cake, the whole time thinking, *When I grow up I'm going to make the best sponge cake, just like Mama.*

While everyone ate the cake, Jenny opened her presents: an orange fountain pen, a card full of barrettes, and a box of colored chalk. Later, we kids took the chalk upstairs and drew pictures on a big bedroom wall Aunt Mary let us use like the blackboards at school. Aunt Tessie, who never had any children, gave Jenny a delicate silver necklace with a dangling heart and a dime to go to Woolworth's and buy herself a matching shiny bracelet.

I was curious why a wool store would sell metal bracelets, so when everybody started to head home and Jenny said she was going to Woolworth's, I begged, "Mama, I've never been to Woolworth's. Can I go? Jenny can walk me home." I knew she was in a good mood from hearing everyone praise her sponge cake.

"Go. Go. Be good. Look twice before you cross the street."

Woolworth's was on Fifth Avenue, about five long blocks away. With each step, I felt more and more grown-up, eight years old and out shopping with my twelve-year-old cousin.

When we entered the store, I couldn't believe all the gadgets that surrounded me. At eye level were small teddy bears, toothbrushes, crayons, packages of safety pins, can openers, sparklers, towels, comic books. Each demanded my attention. On the walls hung fancy curtains, yellow brooms, and framed pictures of cats and dogs. Above them, a sign decorated with bright red letters read *Fifty Cents* in beautiful cursive writing better than mine and bigger than the wording on the gas stove's oven door.

Inside the front door next to a cash register sat a fat lady with thick glasses that made her eyes bulge like a frog's. When somebody paid for an item, she put the money and a slip of paper inside a small metal cylinder the size of an empty tomato-paste can and slid it into a see-through slotted metal pipe. Like a bullet, the can shot up the wall and across the ceiling, disappearing inside a room behind a big glass window, where a man methodically opened the can and took out the money. He looked at the slip of paper, stamped it, and sent it flying back across the ceiling and down the pipe to the fat lady. She opened a sliding door on the can and took out the change. Everything happened so fast it felt magical.

Jenny told me I was going to get a stiff neck if I didn't stop staring at the ceiling and tugged at me to follow her. Heading down the aisle, I couldn't resist imitating the lady with the eyeglasses. I bulged out my eyes and jumped like a frog. Jenny shushed me and tried to stop laughing, shoving me along toward the back of the store. Rows of tabletop flat bins with green felt bottoms held all sorts of amazing items. We stopped at a bin containing small red square compartments filled with trinkets and bracelets. While Jenny examined the bracelets, trying on one after another, I gazed in fascination at the shiny tubes of lipstick that lay in green squares alongside the red squares. Lipsticks like my grown-up cousins kept hidden in their pocketbooks.

"Jenny, you're twelve. Why don't you get a lipstick?" I dared. She turned and started to examine the shiny lipsticks. She fondled black ones with little gold wedding bands around the middle, plain red ones, and one shiny gold tube smaller than the rest.

"You're almost grown up. You can start practicing now," I urged. "Buy the gold one."

"I like the black one." She picked it up and headed toward the front of the store while I kept staring at the little gold one. It was so pretty. I didn't want to leave the only gold one there by itself. I could take it, and nobody would know. An invisible puppeteer reached out and curled my fingers around the shiny gold treasure. Instantly, my heart lurched. What *joy!* My body felt hot all over. I almost sang out like I did when Papa said we were all going to the Barnum and Baily Circus. I had a grown-up lipstick all my own. I felt like I had won a prize for an act more daring than any of the high-wire acts in a circus. More daring than Albert.

"Come on," Jenny snapped from halfway up the aisle. "Do I have to take your hand?" Clutching my golden treasure, I ran to catch up. As Jenny put her dime on the counter to pay the fat lady, out of nowhere an extra-large peach pit pierced the insides of my belly. I looked away from the fat lady and stared at the sticky wooden floor, my fist shut tight.

As soon as we stepped outside, Jenny stopped and removed the cap from her lipstick. She looked at her reflection in the glass window and carefully drew a bright red mouth on her face.

"Doesn't that look pretty?"

I peeked, glancing up from the sidewalk. Was she talking to me or to herself? I didn't answer, unsure if she looked pretty or like the clowns in the circus, comical. Mostly my stomach ached.

After we crossed the street, the peach pit stopped piercing my stomach. Jenny licked her lips and said it tasted like sugary olive oil and raspberry soda. I didn't pay any attention. Instead, I imagined myself painting my lips in our bathroom with nobody watching.

At home, I put the lipstick on—not so bright anyone would notice—and went outside.

I had misjudged Papa.

He was working on the big engine under the hood of his Mack truck parked in the driveway. As I passed, he turned, stared straight at me, and wiped his hands on a greasy rag lying on the green fender. A long, fat, bluish vein popped up on his neck. "What's that lipstick on your mouth?" he barked. I wanted to bolt, but my feet stuck to the ground. "Where did you get it?"

I gulped. "At Woolworth's." Flailing for an excuse, I added, "With Jenny."

"Did she buy it for you?" His dark eyes flashed and his face grew red. I thought he would start yelling at me the way he yelled at Cousin Dolly when she came to visit with her lips painted red. Papa had glared at her and told her to either go home and never come back or go into the bathroom and wash that filthy grease off her mouth.

In a fury he had turned toward Aunt Mary, who had brought Dolly. "She's seventeen and you let her wear lipstick? Next, she smokes cigarettes, becomes a *puttana,* catches syphilis, and dies with so many scabs, you can't even have an open casket."

Now those words clanged in my head and the lipstick in my hand weighed a ton. My tongue stuck. I couldn't speak.

"Answer me! I'm your father. How did you get it?" Although he whacked my brothers on their shoulders or knuckled their heads and sometimes took his belt to their legs, he had never hit me or my sisters. Glancing up, I thought he looked like he was about to.

"I . . . I took it."

"Did you pay for it?"

"Yes," I lied.

"Who gave you the money?"

Trapped, I couldn't utter a sound. The peach pit in my belly began to move around. It hurt so much I began to cry, making sucking noises.

"You disobeyed your father and mother. You lied. You stole." He grabbed my shoulders and shook me hard. His face was almost purple. He shouted, "If you ever *need* something and you can't pay for it, tell me. I'm your father. If you *need* it, I'll buy it. And if I don't have the money, *I'll* steal it for you." Instantly, he hit his head with his palm and groaned, *"Marone."* I didn't know what *Marone* meant, only that I had made him mad at himself.

"We're going to Woolworth's right now," he grunted, "and you're giving it back. Tell them you stole it." He wiped his hands fast and rough, then threw the rag down so hard it thumped on the fender. He ordered me to get the lipstick. I raised my hand and uncovered my palm, revealing the lipstick. Turning, he grabbed my other hand and squeezed my fingers together so tight none of them could move.

We didn't even stop to tell Mama where we were going.

Now the shiny gold tube began to hurt my hand like the peach pit hurt my gut. I wanted to toss it away, but I knew that would enrage Papa even more. He would stop and force me to pick it up from the street no matter how far away it rolled. I wished the peach pit would come up or go down. But all the hurt places stayed stuck inside me, and slimy, salty snot began to slide out of my nose into my mouth.

We rushed across the street, Papa walking faster and faster, holding my hand so tight I had to run to keep from tripping. The whole way I never looked up. I saw only the front of Papa's black shoes and the dirt between the granite slabs of the sidewalk. Half-pulling, half-lifting me off the ground, he roared, "Why did you steal it? Lipstick is only for whores." He didn't seem to care if anybody heard him.

I focused on the cracks, trying to avoid them because stepping on cracks brought bad luck, but the way Papa dragged me along made it impossible. Snot kept dripping from my face, wetting my dress, and I couldn't avoid stepping on the cracks in the sidewalk.

"Answer me. Answer me. Why did you steal it?"

I blurted the truth. "I just *wanted* it."

Papa was silent for almost half a block.

When he finally spoke, his voice was calm as if he were thinking out loud, trying to understand himself. "People always *want* something. It's human nature. Sooner or later, everybody lies and whether people admit it or not, everybody steals." He repeated, "It's human nature. But that doesn't make it right. It's always wrong to steal or lie just because you *want* something." Every time he said *want,* his voice grew extra loud. After a long silence, he said, "Do what I say, not what I do."

His gait slowed and when he started talking again, his voice almost a whisper, he began to tell me about his life as a kid growing up in Brooklyn. His words sounded so soft and sad that I began to cry again, but without the snot. I knew I was supposed to listen and learn.

He hated school because American boys called him "wop," ginny, "garlic breath," and "dago." Big kids taunted him on the way to school, during recess, after school. They shouted, "Go back to where you came from and take your mother and father with you—and all your sisters and brothers and cousins too. You wops are like rabbits—the only thing you're good for is making babies."

If he passed a gang on the street corner, they yelled, "Go back to Italy. You don't belong in our neighborhood."

But he didn't take it lying down. He punched and kicked and called them stupid Irish micks—even though some weren't Irish. He told them their fathers were drunkards and too lazy to put in a day's work for a day's pay, and without the Italian bricklayers, the Brooklyn Bridge would never have been built. And Columbus discovered America, so an Italian came here before they did.

Papa's grip on my hand relaxed. He started talking about his best worker, Vincent. Not many Americans were like him, and anyway, Vincent was mostly German. The Germans were the best tool makers in the world. Papa said too many Americans watched the clock and were afraid to get their hands dirty.

"I never flinched," he said. "I told those kids to shut up. If they didn't run away, I'd punch one of them as hard as I could. His buddies would gang up on me. When one finished, another began. They said we were all in the Mafia and that's how we got ahead, and we all belonged in prison."

"Is that when you went to the boys' school with Chenzi and Marco? Remember? Penn Station?"

Papa didn't answer. He said, "I made myself a promise. When I grew up, I'd do whatever I had to do—anything—to give my children an education so they could become Supreme Court judges, make a good salary for life, be proud, show what Italians are made of."

My head dropped lower, and I started crying louder. I knew I wasn't supposed to say anything because Papa seemed sad, an' he wanted me to see how brave he was. And I did. But it made me feel worse. And I didn't know how to tell him he was brave.

By the time we got to Woolworth's and stepped inside, the peach pit dug into my gut. Only now it hurt even more, and I was afraid I might puke it up and make a horrible mess all over the Woolworth's floor. I lifted my free arm and wiped at the snot leaking out of my nose into my mouth, tasting saltier and saltier.

Papa spoke to the lady at the cash register, "My daughter has something to tell you."

I didn't look up, but I could see she was the same lady with the thick glasses. Through my sobs, I managed to blurt, "I . . . stole this."

My fingers uncurled, and I dropped the golden tube on the green linoleum counter. The lipstick started to roll, but the eyeglass lady picked it up. Nobody spoke. I stared at the green countertop. Papa stirred and put his closed fist in front of my chest, waited a second or two, then uncurled his fingers. A shiny dime with the beautiful face of Lady Liberty rested on the dark cracks that lined his open hand. Was this a test?

Looking at it made my chest hurt and my breath go in and out faster and faster. Papa didn't say anything. The eyeglass lady set the lipstick upright on the counter. She didn't say anything, either. Papa didn't move his hand. They just waited.

I looked at the golden tube and shook my head sideways, back and forth, sobbing, "I don't want the lipstick. I don't need it."

Papa put the dime in his pocket and took my hand. We left the store and headed home. After a long silence, Papa said I could stop crying. "You've learned your lesson."

But now I was crying because I dreaded what Mama would do.

Unlike Papa, who didn't whack the girls, Mama did. Worse, she could shun. And I knew what she would do. The head bouncing against the wall never hurt as much as her silence or dark
sappointment. They were the worst punishments of
as sure when she heard what I had done, that's what I

would get. Even if Papa didn't tell her, Mama would *know.*

The minute I walked into the room, Mama could look at me and she would know if I had done something good or if I had committed a sin. She even knew if it was a big sin or a small sin. She always knew. Sometimes her face would grow long and dark. She would turn to Giulia or my sisters, but really, she was talking to the me—the sinner. "Whenever you lie, you are stealing. Stealing from truth. Two sins." Then she would add, "Truth is always in the room. She never leaves. Never."

Mama believed in repetition.

Stealing the lipstick was one sin, lying about it another. Two big sins. When she saw me, she would *know.*

And that's exactly what happened.

Papa mumbled a few words to Mama, half in Italian and half in English, then left the kitchen and went back to work. Mama gave me one long, dark look, and without saying a word, turned her back to me. She remained silent. I felt like I was in a separate room, alone with truth.

Mama didn't talk to me the whole time she prepared dinner. She either turned her back toward me or acted like I wasn't there. Then she called to Agnes and, speaking in a soft tone, asked her to set the table.

My job!

She always praised me for doing it "the best," getting the plates evenly spaced around the table, putting the spoons on the right and the forks on the left. I stepped forward. Mama ignored me and continued speaking to Agnes, reminding her where to place the spoons and forks.

Her face grew darker and darker with disappointment. After a while, she caught my eye and held it. She took in a quick breath, turned away, and started to sob, causing me to cry, too.

She didn't talk to me during minestrone, and not even when I went to bed and hid my face in the pillow so no one could hear me cry. She didn't even say she was putting it in the Bag.

Just before I woke up, I saw the lipstick next to my reader in the Gone Room.

Perhaps Mama had a Gone Room, too, for she often remin-
isced about her childhood in Chieti. Her father, a local opera
singer, had died when Mama was five, two years before she ran
away from home. Mama missed her father teaching her Italian
operas. She missed his humming in the morning and how, on
her birthday, he hid Jordan almonds under her pillow or inside
her folded napkin or behind the curtain on the windowsill. And
when she found them, her father would twirl her in the air and
break out in song.

"I still miss him," Mama said, her eyes moist. "One Sunday
after Mass, Marietta, my older sister, and I were finishing minestrone. My mother was unusually quiet and had barely touched
her soup. Then, without looking at us, her eyes on her lap, she
announced, 'Pepino asked me to marry him.'"

Mama had slapped her spoon down on the wooden table and
warned, "If you put that man in my father's bed, I will never step
foot in this house again."

On the day of the wedding, Mama hid in the shadows of the
doorway to her mother's embroidery shop. When the small wedding party disappeared around the curve at the bottom of the
cobblestone alley, she hurried back up the stairs to the tiny bedroom she and Marietta shared. She grabbed her things, bundled
them in a scarf, and rushed out of the house, taking the shortcut
through the back alleys to her grandmother's house.

"I waited on my Nonna's stone step and never stepped foot in
my mother's house again."

My sisters and I gasped.

Mama seemed surprised at our reaction and said her mother
had been "too loose." She disobeyed the nuns' teachings about
good widows: they wore black for twenty years after their husbands died. And a truly good widow never again looked at another man. Ever.

Mama's face would grow pensive. "My mother must not have
loved my father. Not as much as I did." She paused. "It was too

soon after my father died, too soon to find another man."

Mama had seen her mother with Pepino in the village square, sitting in the shadows under the big fig tree. She knew her mother had lied.

Mama's eyes sought ours. "Remember. Truth is always in the room. She never goes away. Never."

CHAPTER EIGHTEEN—
THE SPEAKEASY

1929

In the autumn, after we had returned to the city and shortly before Papa said he lost the house on Eighteenth Street, upstate New York had a sudden deep cold spell. Papa was looking for warm gloves. "I need to go to the farm and check on the pipes to keep them from freezing. I'll be back tomorrow night."

Agnes pulled Papa's sleeve and pleaded, "I want to go too." He nodded yes. Mama said okay but thought she was too young to go alone, and I should go with them.

Agnes and I scurried around helping Mama find warm clothes. I rummaged through the closet for woolens and leggings. Mama found mittens and pulled warm hats over our ears. We promised to keep our coats buttoned up. She gave Papa a big blanket to put over us for the two-hour drive and handed him a floppy orange bag. "Fill it with hot water and warm their bed. Make them hot cocoa before they go to sleep."

We left at dusk. The car was cold, and Agnes pulled most of the blanket around herself to avoid the cold leather seat. She snuggled against the soft leather and fell asleep before we crossed into Manhattan.

When we got to Newburgh, Papa stopped at the Elks Club to get milk. I said, "I have to go pee-pee." We left Agnes sleeping in the car and went up the steps to the front door. From outside, I could hear music and lots of people talking. It sounded like a party.

Papa knocked with two short raps followed by a light slap with the palm of his hand. A man with a mustache just like Papa's peeked out the door before unchaining it from inside and opening it all the way to let us in. The hallway looked foggy and smelled like cigarettes. Papa pointed to the ladies' room at the end of the hall.

"Wait here when you're done," he said. "I'll be right back."

When I came out of the smoky bathroom and he wasn't there, I walked down the hall toward the music and looked around the corner. Dimly lit chandeliers hung over a huge room with a raised stage at one end. The song coming from the Victrola wasn't an Italian aria, and it wasn't Miriam's gospel music—it was jazz. The same as I heard on the radio. Everyone in the noisy, crowded room was drinking. Some people stumbled like Uncle Pete, whom Mama wouldn't invite for dinner—even after his first wife died and he married Aunt Tessie. "He drinks too much. A bad influence. Bad influence." Repeating something meant Mama considered it important and you better learn that lesson.

Papa stood across the room close to a skinny lady with a flat belly, not like Mama's stomach, which was getting bigger and bigger every week. He was drinking from a milk bottle. The skinny lady wore long beads over a short, silky dress. When she talked, her bobbed hair, wavy from a curling iron like Florence's mother's and longer on one side, swung around her cheek. I liked the way she had tucked her black hair over one ear with a shiny blue barrette. She held a cigarette in a long silver holder in one hand. Giulia would have called her a *puttana,* but I was fascinated with the way she twisted her body back a little and reached out to push Papa's shoulder, not hard, just enough to make him laugh. He lifted his arm and tugged her ear like they were playing. She laughed with a musical lilt.

Tipping her head back a tiny bit, she did a little dance step to the music. Papa poked fun at her by imitating the way she danced. They both laughed and she shoved his shoulder again. This time he almost lost his balance. He put his hand over the top of the milk bottle to keep it from spilling, laughing the whole time.

While regaining his balance, Papa turned his head and noticed me watching. He came over to me right away and we
headed toward the exit door. As we left, he glanced back, and the
skinny lady waved and smiled, her bright red lipstick framing
pretty white teeth. She mouthed, "See you."

Walking to the car, I didn't say anything to Papa about
the barrette lady being a cigarette-smoking *puttana* who would
catch syphilis and die with so many scabs her mother couldn't
have an open casket. And I didn't say anything to him the whole
time he drove too fast the last few miles to the farm. I poked
Agnes awake when we were almost there.

Once inside the house, Papa started doing everything in a
hurry. He turned on the lights and told Agnes and me to shut all
the furnace dampers in every room but our bedroom. Then he
got an armful of newspapers and logs from the hall and started a
fire in the furnace. Next, he heated a pot of water on the electric
stove and filled the water bag with hot water. Handing it to me,
he said, "Rub it between the sheets, move it around top to bottom to warm up the bed. I'm making cocoa."

He did everything in a rush, and the cocoa didn't taste as
delicious as Mama's. She always stood by the stove and kept an
eye on the milk until it was "just right." Then she would take it
off the burner, add the cocoa with a little sugar, and whip it with
the eggbeater until it was thick and frothy so we kids could make
cocoa mustaches with the heavy white foam. Papa didn't add a
pinch of sugar or whip up a froth, and the milk tasted too luke-
warm. I wanted to remind him but feared he might get angry
and yell at me the way he yelled at Mama.

"It's late, your bedroom should be warm. Time for you to go
upstairs to bed. I'm going to bank the fire with coal and check
on the pipes in the kitchen and bathroom." He added, "Keep your
socks on if your feet feel cold." When we got in bed, Agnes grumbled and told me to stay on my side, so I didn't tell her about the
skinny lady with the shiny blue barrette. But I couldn't sleep. I
kept wondering why Papa didn't get mad at the skinny lady for

wearing lipstick like he did with cousin Dolly.

I also thought about how much fun Papa and the skinny lady had playing and teasing each other. Maybe if Mama learned to dance, she and Papa might play that way, too. My wondering stopped when I heard the crunch of gravel as the Packard rolled slowly down the driveway. I slid out of bed and looked through the window. Halfway down the lane, the Packard's headlights flashed on, and a few moments before it reached the highway, the engine started. The Packard turned left toward town.

The next morning, Papa's whistling in the kitchen woke me. He had our oatmeal ready and said if the weather stayed cold, we might have to come back next weekend. I stirred my under-cooked oatmeal and asked about the skinny lady.

"She's a dancer at the club," he said.

Later that week, after Agnes and I came home from dancing lessons, I asked Mama if she would like to take lessons. She laughed and said, "Dancing is for children."

"I think Papa likes to dance."

"What makes you think so?"

"He danced a little at the Elks Club when he got us milk for cocoa."

Mama looked at me, her breath coming fast but her head very still, her eyes darkening.

In a different voice—quicker, higher—she said, "He took you inside?

"I was afraid I'd wet my bloomers."

"Who did he dance with?"

"I don't know her name."

"What did she look like?'

"She was skinny, with a sparkly blue barrette in her hair." I didn't say anything about the cigarette or the lipstick.

"Did she talk to you?"

"No, but she talked to Papa."

"What did she say?"

"When we left, she waved and said, 'See you.'"

Mama's eyes turned woolen, and she withdrew deep inside herself. When she bit her lip and showed her teeth, I knew she was upset, so I asked her to sing *"Celeste Aida."*

"Not now."

That evening, as soon as Papa came through the door, Mama, sounding hoarse, spat, "So you have to go to Newburgh this weekend." Her tone caused us kids to pay close attention.

Papa didn't answer. I was certain he had heard. He walked to the sink and began washing his hands. The air grew thick with silence. Francey and I stopped setting the table and Agnes ceased reading the nursery rhymes inscribed into the children's enamel tabletop. The younger girls near Agnes didn't move.

Papa cleared his throat. "Yes, if it's still cold." He kept washing his hands. His voice was barely audible over the splashes.

"And is it *hot* in the Elks Club?" Mama's voice was sarcastic and shrill.

"What are you talking about?" He kept washing his hands, his back to Mama.

"Answer me," Mama demanded, her face tight, her back straight and still. When he didn't, she taunted, "So, you forgot how to lie?"

Papa turned and shouted to us kids, "Go to the other room." But before we could move, Mama pressed on. "Are you afraid for them to hear the truth? You're screwing around with other women and making a fool out of their mother and—"

Quick as lightning Papa lunged toward Mama and struck her in the face. Twice. Hard. First with an open palm on one cheek and then with the back of his hand on the other. We kids turned to stone.

Mama grabbed a knife from above the stove, raised it above her head and beat the air. She started to call him names—some in Italian and others in English.

"Whoremaster. *Cafone.* Bastard."

Paura's shadow darkened the room and filled it with flashing blue lights. A sharp barbed wire net squeezed my chest. I couldn't breathe.

Mama's face changed to a fiery red. "I curse you," she said, her voice a slow, low growl. "You raised your hand to me. One day a man will raise his hand to you . . ." Her tone terrified me. "You'll die from some man's hand! Die alone in the dirt for worms to feast. That's my curse."

Papa's face lost color. *"La Strega. Strega!"* he yelled.

Mama waved the knife toward him. "Get out! Get out before I take this knife to you."

Papa rushed to the door and slammed it behind him. Paura followed. Mama tossed the knife back toward the stove top, but it ricocheted onto the floor. Instantly, Francey stopped it with his foot. The room turned so cold; his face had turned white as snow.

Mama sank into a kitchen chair, and as one, we kids moved to her. A trickle of blood oozed out of a corner of her mouth.

When we tried to comfort her, she covered her mouth with both hands in a futile attempt to stifle her sobs. Instantly, we older girls began to cry. Three-year-old Evelyn, her eyes blank, stared at me and Francey, searching our faces. One side of Mama's face had begun to swell, and blood from the other side of her mouth slid from her chin, making a dark blotch on the collar of her dress.

On and off, all through the night, she wept. Unable to sleep, I wondered: Would Papa ever come back? Would Mama not have thrown a curse at Papa if I had said nothing about the skinny lady who danced in the Elks Club?

Would Mama's curse come true?

The next afternoon, Giulia dropped by with soup greens. She seemed to know without asking why Mama's face was swollen and turning purple on one side. They talked in Italian for a short while and then Mama began to sob. She told the boys to go outside and asked me to take the younger ones to play in the girls' bedroom and close the door. I left it open a crack.

"Here I am, five months pregnant. I don't know what to do. I wish I could die." She kept weeping and catching her breath. Giulia said nothing, her expression attentive. In small bursts, Mama continued. "First, it's Josephine, now another one. I want to die, but I can't leave my children. They need me. They are the only joy in my life. They need me." I was glad to hear we brought her joy, and I was glad to learn why her stomach was growing fat, but I started to cry. And I couldn't figure out why she mentioned Aunt Mary's friend Josephine.

A few afternoons later, Aunt Mary and Aunt Esther dropped in. Aunt Mary carried fancy Italian pastries in a pink box tied with red and white barber pole string. Aunt Esther, who was younger than Aunt Mary, sat at the edge of the chair nearest the door. She smelled like lavender soap, and her blouse had crisp creases. Mama said Aunt Esther kept her house scrubbed so clean you could eat off the floor. Now she kept looking around like she wanted to tidy up the kitchen, but once she sat, she didn't stir.

During the entire visit, she didn't say a word; she kept looking at the pile of dishes in the sink and the diapers piled helter-skelter on the small children's table. Mostly she seemed like she was getting ready to leave.

Mama stood close to the table during the whole visit, her right thumb squeezed tight inside her fingers, looking down at Aunt Mary, who kept pointing toward the box of pastries, urging Mama to open it while Aunt Esther looked more and more like she wished she had stayed home.

"*Setta. Setta.*" Aunt Mary urged Mama to sit in the empty chair. Then, sounding as preachy as Father Alonzo, she told Mama that she was too quick with her temper, and it was dangerous for Papa to break the law and sleep in the cold Eighteenth Street building he no longer owned. She said Mama should try to understand men better because they all had other women from time to time, particularly when their wives were pregnant. Especially if the man was real macho. That's how Italian men were.

Mama snapped, "You think I'm a *cafone* like your family?"

Instantly, her expression apologetic, Mama turned to Aunt Esther. She shook her head as if to imply she hadn't intended the Italian slur—ignorant, lowlife—for Aunt Esther. Aunt Mary's lips became a thin, tight line and she cleared her throat. She removed her hands from the table where the pastry box lay and stared at the tablecloth.

"If that's how all Italian men in America act," Mama said, "I'll never let any of my daughters marry an Italian man." Her voice rose. She stared hard at Aunt Mary. "You have no pride. You can stoop low and come begging me to take back your brother, a coward, a rotten bastard who hides behind my innocent girls to go screw whores and catch syphilis. I'll never sleep with him again." She snorted like an angry horse. Towering above them, she slapped her hand on the table and gave Aunt Mary a long, hard look. "Watch your own chicken coop. Keep an eye on your own rooster. He could be screwing around and catching syphilis. Then I want to see how much understanding you have. Until that day, don't tell me what I should do!"

As I peered through the crack, it was clear to me that none of them understood each other. Mama was furious. Aunt Esther wished she had never come. Aunt Mary looked worn out. And I wished my aunts would leave so Mama could calm down and I could open the box of pastries.

Mama never explained why, after a week or two, Papa came home for dinner and slept in Mama's bedroom again. None of us caught syphilis, so I guessed Papa didn't either.

CHAPTER NINETEEN—CONTAGION

1930

Mama hardly left the Brooklyn house at all. She never went shopping, not to Fredrick Loeser's, the fancy store in Flatbush, not to the neighborhood vegetable stand for five cents worth of soup greens, not to the corner drug store to buy talcum powder for the baby's bottom. And she didn't send Francey or me on errands either. "Too dangerous," she would say.

And each day when my brothers and I left for school, after Mama gave us the teaspoon of cod-liver oil followed by a sliver of tangerine, I found it hard to tell if she was mostly fearful, mostly angry, or mostly sad. Was it because she had to tell the furniture salesman she would be cancelling the order for twin beds for my brothers? Or maybe it was because Mama's best girlfriend Giulia had told her about thirteen-year-old Tricia O'Meagen from down the street. Like her two older sisters, Tricia had died of TB and was lying in a coffin in their parlor wearing a bride's gown with a veil covering her face. Or maybe it was because Papa had stopped taking us on weekend outings in his Packard. Or was it because Papa said he lost the house on Eighteenth Street—and we could see it same as always?

Whatever the cause, Mama had become strangely silent. Silent when we woke up, silent when we ate, silent when we went to bed. But in between those silences she had unpredictable outbursts. She screamed if Agnes forgot to turn off the light after leaving a room. She grunted if I accidentally spilled a few drops of milk when filling Evelyn or Genevieve's baby bottles. She screamed, "Careless. Careless," if Francey left the downstairs door open and caused a slight draft into her kitchen.

She never turned on the Victrola, and if we asked her to sing, she acted like she hadn't heard. Worse, she seldom looked us in the eye; instead, she stared at the floor as though seeking answers from the green-flecked linoleum.

Before the day Papa said he lost the house on Eighteenth Street, frightened or not, Mama stood tall, her head held high, her thick black hair braided into a fat bun on the top of her head, her big dark eyes bright. Bright with pride as she set a platter of homemade gnocchi on the table, or bright with anger after Papa had yelled, "*Strega. Strega.* Witch," and she sassed him back quick and mean.

And even when she was frightened, like the time Petey from down the block died of infantile paralysis, she responded by calling us indoors and bringing us close. She would sit, straighten her dress across her lap, turn her eyes inward and, after a deep sigh, tell us a story.

Some stories were from her childhood, from operas, or from more recent times, like the day she told us about Modestino, her firstborn who had died of infantile paralysis a few days after he was born, and how he was quarantined and buried in a group grave along with two thousand other children during New York City's infantile paralysis epidemic of 1916.

In between words she would sob, and Agnes and I would sob with her, especially when she said she never knew where Modestino was buried. "I'll never forgive myself for allowing the nurse to take him from me," she sobbed, vowing never to have another child in a hospital. And she would look at me, her mouth trembling, her cheeks moist with tears, and say, "Maybe when you grow up you could find his grave and say a goodbye prayer to him for me."

I had no idea where to look, but managed to say, "I'll do my best."

We kids also dreaded the deadly disease. Every November 18,

Mama would sit at the kitchen table, light a red votive candle, make a small sign of the cross over her lips, and vow never to forget Modestino. Weeping, she would look at Francey and say, "Your father jumped on me too soon. The whole time I carried you, I drank nothing but tears."

She sobbed and whispered as if she were alone, "The next year you were born on the same day Modestino died. When Louisa put you in my arms, I wanted Modestino." Her chest heaved, and in between sobs she uttered, "It was worse the following year when I lit the candle. Outside in the street everyone was cheering, celebrating. Celebrating the whole week for the end of the World War." Sobbing, she would cover her eyes with her apron. "Everyone celebrating and I never said goodbye to my firstborn."

Francey stood very still and never said a word. On one of those November eighteenths, he leaned under the table and untied his shoelaces, slowly retied them, and quietly left the kitchen. I watched him leave and wondered if Mama had noticed. I began to cry again but didn't know if I cried for Mama or Modestino or Francey.

Perhaps the slight sound of the door closing behind Francey caused Mama to press the apron to her eyes, dry her cheeks, and drop it into her lap. Looking skyward, she pleaded with Jesus, "Keep my children safe from the disease."

Although most people were frightened of TB and Infantile Paralysis, I thought Mama was more terrified than any of my aunts or neighbors. Terrified that we would catch TB and die like the O'Meagan girls, or be paralyzed for life like the rag peddler who dragged one leg as he pushed his wooden cart up the street every Monday morning and chanted, "Rags for sale? Rags for sale?"

During this time and before we moved to the farm, Mama had flung open the door to my second-grade classroom, startling Mrs. Klein, the teacher, who gasped.

"Quick! Come." Mama yelled.

I jumped up and ran to her. Mama grabbed my arm, and lifting and pulling me through the doorway, we headed down the hall.

She stopped at Albert's third-grade class, put her head in the door, beckoned and yelled again, "Quick! Come." Off we bolted to Francey's fourth-grade class, where she did the same thing. On the way out of the building, as we passed my classroom, I hoped Mrs. Klein hadn't noticed my mother's smudged housedress. I had no idea where we were going or why.

Outside the school, Vincent, Papa's best mechanic, waited behind the steering wheel of our eggplant-colored 1928 Packard with leather seats that smelled like a horse saddle. My four younger sisters, looking relieved at the sight of us, sat crowded together on the backseat.

"Boys. Quick, get in front," Mama yelled as she and I squeezed into the back next to Agnes. Mama puffed a loud sigh and reached over to pick up Evelyn—fretful and fidgeting on our middle sister Gloria's lap—and we settled in for the two-hour drive to our summer home in the farm country of upstate New York's Hudson Valley.

But before we were out of the city, she called out to Vincent. He nodded and tilted his ear toward her. Sounding brave, she said, "You have to teach me how to drive. I want to take my children out of danger myself." None of my aunts, and not even my most grown-up cousin Frances, drove a car. Would Papa allow Mama to drive his brand-new Packard? I was sure this would start a fight and Papa would yell, *"La Strega! La Strega!"*

And I wouldn't know if he meant Mama was a witch, or that he didn't want her to learn how to drive. Especially his Packard.

PART TWO—THE GREAT DEPRESSION

CHAPTER TWENTY—
THE AFTERMATH

1930

After the day Papa barged into the kitchen and said he had lost the house on Eighteenth Street, everything got worse. Worse in the world outside our home and worse inside our home. Outside, men jumped out of Wall Street buildings, banks closed, storefronts were boarded up with scrawled messages that read CLOSED or MOVED. The Daily News carried pictures of long lines of hungry men standing for hours, ankle deep in snow, for a bowl of soup.

At home Papa flailed about, trying to regain his financial footing. He left the house before we kids woke up and didn't come home until our bedtime. And when he spent time at home, he didn't answer our questions or talk to Mama. Everywhere you looked people seemed scared. And without understanding why, exactly, we kids and Mama moved back to the farm after summer vacation.

Mama brooded openly. She hated the isolation and loss of largesse. She missed Giulia, her best friend. She missed Mrs. Gould, the public health nurse. She may even have missed Mrs. Ryan's gossip.

But early one autumn morning while we kids ate oatmeal, our neighbor Mrs. Westlake phoned. A slim, carefully combed busybody with grown-up children, Mrs. Westlake had too much time on her hands, according to Mama. She smiled pleasantly. Nonstop. Mama called her *Americana*, meaning she was too guarded, too formal, too polite, not worthy of a confidence. If Mama felt that way about her, I did, too.

Mrs. Westlake called to tell Mama that school started that day, and if we were going to spend the winter on the farm, all school-age children in the township were required to be at Middlehope School by 8:30.

Mama panicked. "Albert, Francey, Eleanor. Get dressed. Quick. You have to go to school. Right now. Quick. *Quick*."

Within minutes, we three were on our way. As we dashed out the door, Mama, her voice shrill, reminded us, "Obey the teacher. Do nothing to make your mother ashamed." She didn't even bother about the cod-liver oil. At the last minute she shouted, "Be safe. Run facing traffic. Watch the cars."

And so, we did. The three of us, breathless from having sprinted nonstop along the 9W Highway for more than half a mile, arrived in the schoolyard where clusters of kids milled around.

"Who's the principal?" Francey asked a group of kids. A boy pointed to a short woman with gray hair, one of two adults chatting near the entrance.

Walking up to her, Francey said we were new. I was in second grade, Albert in third, and he was in fourth. The principal called one of the taller girls in the schoolyard and asked her to show Francey to one room and Albert and me to another. Before dismissing us, she said to give the teachers our names and address. Then she complimented Francey for taking on the responsibility of registering us "just like a parent." He looked proud, but because she went on and on asking if we had a father and was Mama at home, I felt the praise was meant to criticize Mama and Papa for failing to register us themselves.

I didn't know our address. Francey said, "Sunny Ridge Fruit Farm. On the 9W." Albert bent down, picked up a pebble, and tossed it against the fence.

Unlike P.S. 40—a huge concrete building with separate rooms for each grade—this school looked more like somebody's house. It had faded, yellow wooden siding on the outside and only three classrooms inside. Each room held three grades.

Mrs. Fowler, the teacher of first, second, and third grades, assigned me to the last seat in one of the two second-grade rows. I had never sat in the last seat, behind taller kids. Never. I felt the teacher had dismissed me. She didn't notice I was small for my age.

When the lunch bell rang, she announced, making a point of looking at Albert, who had been involved in a small punching match during morning recess, "Nobody leaves the school grounds during lunchtime."

Outside on the playground, Francey, Albert, and I spent a few frantic minutes trying to locate each other. Shortly, feeling like outcasts, we conferred. Unlike Brooklyn, where we went home for lunch every day, at Middlehope School children brought sack lunches.

"I'm going home," Albert announced.

Francey and I tried to convince him otherwise.

"We can't disobey Mama." Francey feigned authority.

"Or the teacher," I chimed in.

Albert scoffed. Jerking his chin derisively at the building, he said he knew more than the buck-toothed teacher, and he began bad-mouthing the know-it-all brat who sat in front of him. I suspected the know-it-all brat had been the other kid in the brawl. Determined to go home for lunch, Albert gave a final grunt of revulsion, turned, and headed out of the schoolyard toward home.

Before he was completely out of earshot, the know-it-all boy who sat in front of him in the third-grade row shouted, "Good riddance. Not only do wops send their kids to school without lunch, your mother doesn't even know how to iron your shirt."

My face flamed. It was true. Albert had grabbed a shirt from the pile of clean clothes heaped on the dining room table, and Mama hadn't noticed the wrinkled shirt. Neither had I.

Albert glared at the boy and spit on the ground but kept walking toward the 9W Highway. I half-wished he had hit the bratty kid.

When Francey and I arrived home at the end of the school

day, Mama had hot chicken soup with *pastina* waiting for us. Neither Francey nor I mentioned Albert's wrinkled shirt. As soon as I finished my soup, I ran upstairs, changed my school dress, then hurried back down. I was on a mission. Our ironing board was in Brooklyn, and I searched the dining room closet for a loose table leaf to begin construction of what would become a permanent fixture in the dining room.

I dragged the big armchair close to the electric wall outlet, padded the wooden table leaf with several bath towels, wound them around the board, and pinned the edges together underneath to eliminate wrinkles, the whole time plotting how Albert and I could gang up on the bratty kid. After balancing the leaf on the chair arms, I plugged in the iron and selected two shirts from the pile of clean clothes still heaped on the dining room table.

Mama, standing in the dining room doorway, looked puzzled and asked what I was doing.

"I'm playing Make-Believe. I'm Miriam." I truly missed Miriam and wondered where she was working and if she were teaching some other school-age girl how to flatten dough for corn dodgers. I didn't know her address, either, so as I ironed in silence, I sat her in the Gone Room in her favorite kitchen chair.

Before bedtime, I ironed every item in the pile that had been sitting on the table for weeks.

The very next day, just before lunchtime, Mrs. Westlake appeared in the classroom doorway carrying a large basket. It held a soup pot wrapped in a plush floral dish towel, three matching white bowls, three matching shiny spoons, and three matching white paper napkins. She said something to the teacher, who asked me and Albert to remain in the classroom while the other children ate at their seats or took their sack lunches outside.

Mrs. Westlake set a bowl in front of me. "I've brought you some warm soup." It looked like the tomato gravy Mama cooked on Thursdays to go over gnocchi.

Without looking up, I said, "I only eat tomato gravy over spaghetti and—"

"Oh, this is Campbell's tomato soup. You'll like it." She spoke in a strange voice, as if she were talking to a toddler.

"I have my lunch," I mumbled, avoiding her eyes while unwrapping my sandwich from my carefully ironed linen napkin. Immediately, the air had a noticeable scent of eggplant, olive oil, and garlic.

Did Mrs. Westlake move back slightly?

I kept my eyes on my sandwich, nibbling at a corner of the crusty Italian bread.

Mrs. Westlake stepped closer. She leaned on my desk and her starched dress made a crunchy sound. It smelled of clean, fresh air and starch. Speaking to me—again, as if I were a three-year-old—she urged, "You'll enjoy the soup. It's good for you. It's delicious and very nutritious."

My face warmed, partly because I felt defiant, but mostly I resented her for smelling so pleasant and for using such nice rhyming words like *dee-lish-ee-us* and *new-trish-ee-us*. She made me feel mixed up, standing above me, too tall and too close. I began to tuck the napkin around my sandwich.

"I don't need any soup. My mother's sandwich will fill me up." I managed to speak while sliding sideways across my seat, away from her. I stood up and took my sandwich outside.

I felt her eyes follow me out the door but didn't turn my head. I regretted not saying thank you. After school, when I went home, I didn't tell Mama.

I hated Middlehope School, yet a few weeks later when we packed up and unexpectedly moved back to Brooklyn, I wished we had stayed in the country. The autumn of 1930—maybe it was due to the Wall Street Crash or maybe it wasn't—started a series of confusing moves, back and forth between country and city, from one school to the other.

After having had the run of a huge house with big rooms and large windows, riding horseback, climbing trees, playing Romeo and Juliet in the gazebo mounted on long stilts tucked in the forested area near the barn, taking quick dips in the nearby Hudson River, and falling asleep with the faint, exotic scent of far-off skunk spray, we were now confined to the small living area over the garage.

Compared to our country home, the low ceilings and dark bedrooms seemed airless, tight, and cramped. Kitchen windows fogged over from simmering soup and the bathroom smelled of baby poop. And when Papa came home angry, a teddy bear on the floor deserved a kick and a wet diaper earned Mama a mean, "*Sporca, sporca.*" A single note from the piano or a sound from Albert's violin earned snorts of contempt from Papa, evoking silent looks of "beware" between us kids.

On those rare occasions when Papa sat with us for minestrone, the kitchen became eerily quiet, and Mama seldom sat down to eat. If she asked for money, he said if she had any sense, she would stop trying to get water from a lake full of salt. If the boys fought over marbles or baseball cards, he would unbuckle his belt and whack their legs. When Agnes asked to sit on his lap, he would tell her to finish her soup.

Mama sulked about having to make do on five dollars a week. She spoke openly to Giulia about Papa having "gone down in the world," especially after the police confiscated one of his trucks as it crossed from New York into New Jersey, loaded with barrels of whiskey.

Papa and Mama yelled at each other constantly, louder and louder, day and night. They fought if he came home, they fought if he didn't come home. They fought on the phone. They fought if they were in the same room. They fought from different rooms.

Sometimes they both yelled at the same time. Other times one yelled and the other banged dishes or shoved chairs. They fought over the light bill or the mortgage or the cost of chicken feed.

Papa became more and more withdrawn. He would sit in his office for entire days and stare out the small window. Now, only two trucks were parked in the garage, and his big machinery was nowhere in sight. Occasionally he slept during the day, which frightened me, but I didn't ask why. He didn't keep his mustache trimmed, he didn't shave, and he seldom ate with us. He even stopped helping Agnes eat a "dippy egg."

Mid-winter Miriam left. We kids never got to say goodbye. On Friday, the week before Christmas, when Miriam went into Papa's office to get paid, he told her he couldn't afford to keep her, and it was her last day.

This infuriated Mama. She muttered, *"Cafone,"* under her breath and said the children didn't get to say goodbye. She would have given Miriam a fresh batch of gnocchi.

She phoned Miriam's son to apologize and asked him to tell Miriam that she knew nothing about Papa firing his mother.

She told him Miriam was the best help she ever had.

Mama's primary respite came from Giulia, who stopped complaining about the steep stairs and often sat quietly waiting for Mama to speak. Mama also took comfort in the weekly visits from Mrs. Gould, the public health nurse. If Mama was fond of someone, my sisters and I were fond of that person, too. When Mrs. Gould came, we greeted her with squeals of joy.

Still, Mrs. Gould made me feel ashamed—not unlike the way I'd felt at Middlehope School. Each time she came through the door, she would greet us cheerfully, then remove a clump of folded newspapers she carried tucked under her arm, and carefully place them on the floor before setting her black leather valise down atop them.

When I complained in private, Mama defended her. "It must be a public health rule Mrs. Gould has to follow. She's very responsible."

Yet every Thursday morning before Mrs. Gould arrived, Mama mopped the floor.

Now that Miriam was no longer with us, I took on extra chores. I routinely washed dishes, made baby bottles, minced garlic and parsley for Mama's meatballs, and put Evelyn to sleep. As I lay on the floor beneath the cradle, rocking it with my foot,

I closed my eyes and returned to the farm. I could imagine the glitter of fireflies that Mama said sparkled like her children's eyes. I missed all the space we'd had—the big barn with its huge hayloft, our storybook house with large walk-in closets, our big basement with nooks to hide in, and the huge attic where we could play Make-Believe whenever it rained.

But the hubbub of the city brought some consolation. The rag picker always came on Mondays before school started. Limping, he pushed his three-wheeled wooden cart slowly, steadily up the street, waking up the whole neighborhood with his loud chanting.

Mama said he sounded like a rabbi: "Rags for sale, Rags for sale."

From a tenement house window, women would cry out and wave an old blanket or a worn dress. He would stop, look up, and they would bargain. She would yell, "Twenty cents," and he would offer a dime.

She would respond with "Fifteen?"

"Eleven cents," he would reply and turn away, moving his cart up the block.

"Okay," she'd yell, and he would stop.

She would disappear from the window, then reappear on the doorstep below. If she didn't respond to his last offer, he would resume his trudging and slow chant and be on his way until the next week.

Mostly on warm days, but two or three times a week year round, we watched and waited for the Ice Man. As soon as he stopped his horse-drawn wagon, five or six kids would appear like magic from doorways or stoops. We would stand close by as he dropped the tailgate and tossed back the heavy oilcloth that protected his crystal-clear, icy load. We kids, awed by his skill but silenced by his terrifying tools, stood watching this performer like miniature theatre patrons.

The entire bed of his waterlogged wagon held a solid block of ice, clear as well water. He wielded a treacherous metal ice pick to chisel out chunks of different sizes. A foot square cube cost ten cents, larger chunks, fifteen. After he cut several blocks, he pushed them to the raised tailgate and flung a thick khaki-colored woolen blanket over the gleaming block in the cart. Almost tenderly, he smoothed a yellow oilcloth over the blanket, tucking in the ends like a father snuggling a blanket around his infant at bedtime.

Boys moved in closer, fascinated by a huge set of iron clamps the ice man exchanged for his pick. After padding his shoulder with a heavy hemp sack, he selected a cube of ice from the tailgate, hooked into it with the claws of his iron clamp, and tossed the giant ice cube up to his shoulder. He lumbered off and disappeared into one of the tenements or delivered it to Mama's new oak ice chest.

Most of the time he ignored us kids, but sometimes he'd smile at one of the big boys and say, "Watch my wagon" or "Don't touch the horse."

The minute he was out of view, all the onlookers from the block would scrounge and tussle for loose ice chips that had sprayed or fallen on the sidewalk or into the gutter under his wagon. Licking our precious ice pops, we'd scatter, the boys always bragging about theirs being the biggest, the girls letting the ice melt for a minute and checking for dirt.

Another regular source of excitement was the small planes that appeared in the sky shortly after Charles Lindbergh—the Lone Eagle—returned to America. They flew over the city trailing long rectangles of cloth with big, black letters advertising Lucky Strike Cigarettes or Wolf's Head Motor Oil.

The planes also flew over schoolyards during recess, dropping Tootsie Rolls and lollipops. Every now and then, small, pink-tipped white sugar cigarettes would float down from the sky, dangling on tiny Japanese parasols like gifts from heaven. On those days, the boys would scuffle to grab as many cigarettes as they could, shoving the girls aside and pretending not to notice if one of them fell to the ground.

I was less interested in the sugar cigarettes than the delicate little umbrellas that were smaller than an infant's hand. Each umbrella was made of thin, grayish tissue paper glued over tiny bamboo ribs. Attached to the delicately curved handle dangled a snowy white cigarette with a raspberry tip at one end. If a boy threw away a parasol, I'd run to grab it. Sometimes I traded cigarettes for parasols and brought home enough for my sisters so we could play Make-Believe Japanese princesses who caught their brother smoking a cigarette.

If the boys got too rowdy, there was a tall, handsome Irish policeman with blond hair and blue eyes to keep them in line. He seldom needed to say anything. He'd just walk toward them, rattling his billy club by dragging it along the wrought-iron fence that lined the school yard. Before he reached them, quiet had been restored.

At dusk, a troop of kids would trudge the streets behind the lamplighter. He wore a cap and knee-length jacket and carried a long rod. He would stop at each of the tall poles that lined the sidewalks, and like an experienced fisherman, swing the tip of his rod to light the gas wick inside a shiny glass lamp covered by a round metal hood.

Zing!

The ground below glowed with a bright, pale blue circle of light. We kids clapped and whooped until the lamplighter pinched the visor, raised his soft crinkled cap, and swung it across his chest in an exaggerated theatrical bow, bestowing a grandfatherly smile upon his small audience of tagalongs.

Maybe I didn't miss the country as much as I thought. Or maybe the interesting hubbub in the streets outside pushed away all the chaos inside.

CHAPTER TWENTY-ONE
—CHARLEY IS BORN

1930

My sense of calm and order didn't last. It was midday. A Saturday. We kids were eating lentil soup when we heard Papa's quick steps and he barged into the kitchen. Mama had been planning on leaving the house and had to step aside when he entered. Breathing hard, he told Mama two of Uncle Pete's trucks had been stopped by the police who put Uncle Pete in a jailhouse and dumped both truckloads of whiskey down a manhole in Newark. The police ransacked Uncle Pete's house and found too much cash, a dozen speakeasy addresses, and a stolen gun.

Mama smirked. "I told you this would happen. You never listen to me. I hope he stays in jail. At least he'll sober up."

"He's out on bail. Spent all his money on bail and lawyers."

Mama studied Papa. "So?" When Papa looked away, she added, "He's asking you?"

"Gave him all the cash I had. His lawyer said he needs more." Papa turned and stared out the kitchen window. "To keep from going to prison." Mama bit into her lip and tried to catch Papa's eyes, but he was staring across the rooftop when he said, "I'm going to mortgage the farm."

Francey and I gasped and looked at Mama, whose face flared a deep red. She stared at Papa's back with disgust. "You trade your children's summer home for a drunk who would be better off in prison."

Papa didn't budge. The younger children had stopped eating and were gazing from face to face, searching for answers. The kitchen became eerily quiet until Mama broke the silence, her voice commanding.

"Ask your sister Mary. She keeps a sock full of money under her mattress."

Papa turned to face her, yelled, *"La Strega,"* and stomped out of the kitchen, banging the door as he left.

Mama huffed several times, groaned, then turned to me. "Mind the little ones. I won't be long. Just down the block. Be good. I have to show my respects."

She had planned on attending the three-day wake for sixteen-year-old Patricia Maloney who had died of consumption just like her older sisters. Mama and Mrs. Ryan had planned to pay their respects to the Maloneys before they closed the casket. Giulia had reported that Patricia looked sound asleep, dressed as a bride, her hands holding a prayer book, and a veil covering her face. I wanted to see what she looked like, but Mama said no. I wasn't surprised because we kids were forbidden to go near her when she was alive—especially if we heard her cough. And consumption was catching and if you caught it, you died. It was worse than infantile paralysis.

When the little ones had finished eating, I took them outside and we waited on the stoop until Mama and Mrs. Ryan returned. As Mama came close, we overheard Papa tell Chenzi, his trusted driver, to move the almond truck from the garage to our farm upstate. Instantly, Mama started screaming at Papa. She said the farm was the only thing they had left, and Papa had spent more money on whores than on his family, and if he put that truck in the barn, she would burn it down.

Papa yelled, *"Strega! Strega!"* He shoved her hard and she fell to the ground. Papa kicked at her and disappeared inside the garage. Something sharp moved in my stomach. I pressed Evelyn close to my chest.

Mama cried out in pain and started to moan. Mrs. Ryan's face drained of color. She stooped down as if to lift Mama, but Chenzi was quicker. He bent over and picked Mama up from the cold sidewalk and very gently, as if she were his mother, helped her climb the three long flights of stairs to the kitchen. We kids followed in silence. Mama said she felt sick and went into her bedroom. She told me to keep the little ones inside and away from the stove.

At suppertime, when Papa entered the kitchen, I said, "Mama's resting in bed." He didn't go look. Instead, he turned to the stove and heated leftover minestrone. I set the table. Francey said he wasn't hungry. I said the same thing. Those who did eat left most of the minestrone in their bowls. Papa didn't eat. He went down to his garage. While I poured the leftovers back into the soup pot, I wished we had stayed on the farm.

The next day, Dr. Lupo came and told Mama to stay in bed. She should phone Miriam and ask her to work for a month or so and help with the kids until she stopped bleeding. Then, standing in the dining room, closer to Papa than ever before, his voice low, his expression stern, he spoke to Papa in Italian sounding like Father Alonzo. Papa dropped his gaze. I didn't understand a word Dr. Lupo said, but by the way Papa kept looking at the floor, I thought he needed to go to confession.

For weeks Mama rested. Papa seldom spoke, and we kids tried to be quiet, but outside in the streets, there was bedlam, people running and shouting, neighbors gathering in doorways, strangers sharing news of a great crash on the stock market. Newsboys screeched headlines about men jumping out of buildings, banks locking doors and refusing to allow entry. Mama muttered they were following their money down the drain on Wall Street. All the noise made me want to go to the farm.

Miriam never returned Mama's phone call for help. Her son said she had gone south, and Mama continued to spend most of her time in bed. Papa made our oatmeal for breakfast, then left for the day. Giulia usually came before we older kids went to school, and she left shortly after we returned home in the afternoon, saying she had to prepare dinner for Carlo. Francey and I took turns making minestrone, washing dishes, reminding three-year old Evelyn to go wee-wee so she wouldn't wet her bloomers, and making baby bottles for her and Genevieve.

Dr. Lupo said Mama needed to have her baby in the hospital because she had "complications," which Mrs. Gould explained wasn't catching.

In late January 1930, a week after my ninth birthday, Papa took Mama to the hospital in the middle of the night. She stayed for almost two weeks. When they walked in the door, Papa held our new baby brother Charley.

Mama looked pale and tired as we crowded around her. She sat in a kitchen chair, and we kids reached out to touch her arms and nudged each other to get close enough to rest a hand on her lap, embrace her neck, stroke her shiny black hair, savoring her presence as if she were an angel descended from heaven.

Mama's eyes filled with tears. Papa placed the baby in her lap. Leaning over, he kissed her cheek, close to her lips. She smiled and lowered her eyes. Her face grew rosy.

I would never see this again.

Charley was a beautiful blond boy with strange, squiggly things between his legs; he smiled when you touched his warm little pink hand, and he always looked surprised.

As the oldest girl—and having been identified by Louisa as "the best lilla Mama" when Genevieve was born—I perfected the role of second mother. I doted on Charley. He might have been brand-new, but I believed I had known him all my life. I decided he belonged to me. I wasn't alone.

Everyone considered him theirs. Giulia acted like he belonged to her, and Cousin Esther said he was her pet; my brothers said as a boy, he belonged to them; and my sisters scrapped about taking turns to hold him, to rock him to sleep, to make his bottle. Even baby Evelyn would stand near his crib and smooth his blond hair.

In contrast, Papa, rather than rejoicing over the new baby, fell into dark, angry moods. He argued with day workers, threatening one with a crowbar and chasing him off the property. Papa also fought with Uncle Pete, accusing him of making side deals with Business Partner. At one point, a driver said Papa had cheated him out of back pay. Papa punched him and when the driver fell, Papa kicked him in the groin. The man threatened to get the Mafia and left the garage.

Papa's wild mood swings led to constant arguments with Mama. They either yelled at each other or didn't talk at all. Mama stopped singing and was short-tempered with us kids. Then, Papa didn't come home for weeks. Mama said he was in the hospital with a "nerve problem in his back." Aunt Mary visited, bringing a pink box of Italian pastries. Mama said, "Thank you. Want coffee?" Aunt Mary shook her head sideways and both sat at the kitchen table but neither spoke. I thought they were both thinking about Papa being in the hospital with a hurt back. Shortly, Aunt Mary left, saying she had to get back to her pizzeria.

The weeks of chaos and confusion at home seemed contagious, for outside on street corners, angry men gathered. They stood on wooden crates and handed out pink sheets of paper, shouting and cursing Hoover. None of us asked questions, mostly out of fear of upsetting Mama and making things worse.

Except Gloria.

She faced Mama and asked, "Is Papa ever coming home?"

Instead of answering, Mama heaved a deep sigh, half smiled, and mumbled, *"shamastuette."* She followed this affectionate endearment with her usual comment, "Still water runs deep."

But Gloria's question must have sparked something in Mama, for later that afternoon she confided to Giulia, "As soon as school is out, I'm moving the children to the farm." She paused. "For good." As always, important decisions were made without any of us kids knowing why.

Shortly after school ended and while we kids sat on the stoop, a yellow cab pulled up. Out stepped Papa and Aunt Mary. She told Francey the nerves in Papa's back were fixed and he didn't need to stay in the hospital any longer. He could rest at home. We needed to be good and obey him. She stepped back into the cab and it drove off. I wondered why she didn't stay and visit.

Papa looked thin and pale, and his mustache was gone, but he was happy to see us. Agnes jumped into his arms; Gloria wanted to know why he cut off his mustache. He said the doctors wouldn't let him trim it. He would grow it back.

The next day Papa drove us to the farm but didn't spend the night.

In the weeks that followed, Mama looked more miserable than ever. She had no grown-ups to talk to, and I was certain she missed the daily visits from Giulia, her confidante. We kids asked each other about where Papa might be staying, but we didn't ask Mama. Not even outspoken Gloria. We comforted ourselves with comments like, "This will pass . . . they'll make up . . . Some Sunday morning Papa will be here."

The nearest neighbors in Middlehope lived half a mile away, and they were *Americanos*—too straight-faced for Mama's liking. Too slow to answer or too quick to smile, too shifty on their feet. They held their eyes too steady when they met hers, or they kept looking around our messy kitchen. For Mama, these traits proved them unworthy of her trust. I found myself studying them with Mama's eyes.

Locals said our farm was not a *real* farm. They called it a rich man's vacation home, too few acres to make a living, too fancy with the house bigger than the barn.

True, our house *was* the biggest, fanciest house in all Middlehope, sitting high on the hill above a landscaped lawn the size of a football field filled with imported trees and plants and shrubs.

I wondered what they would think if they heard Papa call Mama *La Strega* and saw Mama fling a pot lid at his feet.

Mama didn't respond to the neighbors' comments about the farm, but privately, in our kitchen, she worried about how she could hold on to it. She said Papa had bought the property when he made "more money than he knew what to do with." She said, "Like always, he spread his money too thin. He put only one hundred and fifty dollars down payment. He should have put more."

We learned from Aunt Mary that Papa, whom we hadn't seen for months, had been flailing about in his frenetic way, trying to regain an economic foothold. Yet, money or not, we always had tangerines and oranges, and every now and then boxes of persimmons or prickly pears would arrive from Florida where Papa had driven nonstop to "check out possibilities."

Aunt Mary also said he had rented a small house and bought a truck. No one asked, but I wondered if he would ever come home again.

CHAPTER TWENTY-TWO
—TOGETHER, APART

1930

For no reason I could imagine, in the autumn, Papa and Mama seemed to have declared a bewildering truce. Perhaps it was due to the sights and sounds of the crisp gold, burgundy, and bright yellow leaves that quilted the withered grass on the farm.

Papa returned from Florida and life became half and half. Both sides tame, yet family life split. Mama and the small kids stayed year-round in the country where Agnes started second grade, Gloria first, and Genevieve kindergarten. Papa moved back into our low-ceilinged flat over the two joined garages on Seventeenth Street. Francey, Albert, and I joined Papa and continued at P.S. 40 in Brooklyn.

I balked at this arrangement, but Mama reminded me, "You don't like Middlehope school and you love P.S. 40. Besides, schools in Brooklyn are better than three-room country schools." She said I did best at school, better than the boys, and she wanted me to have the best education so I could make something of myself in this world. We could try it for one school year. She added, "Miriam is back in Harlem. She'll come every day."

Miriam's return was pure joy. She had lunch ready every day and after school delicious treats. Acting like Mama, I sat opposite her at the kitchen table, and she answered my questions about the South as if I were Mama. Sometimes she had a pile of clean clothes to fold while we chatted. Occasionally, Giulia dropped by and held me on her lap. But I missed Mama and my sisters. I missed cuddling Charley and saw them only on weekends and holidays when Papa drove us to the farm.

At the end of the school year in 1932, Francey, Albert, and I rejoined Mama and our younger siblings on the farm. On the trip upstate, Papa was silent, and when we arrived, he dropped us off and drove away without coming inside. These silent visits, although unpredictable, had become routine, and after a quick exchange of looks, we kids pretended not to notice.

During breakfast the next morning, Mama stood at the stove, where a huge pot of milk simmered for her cheese-making. As she dipped her elbow into the milk, testing the temperature, she confided to Francey, Albert, and me, "You might be living here on the farm for good."

"For good?"

"All year long." She heaved a sigh. "Going back and forth to different schools isn't good." Another sigh, a quick glance. "The farm is the only thing that didn't get lost."

By this time, I had a clearer understanding of "lost." It meant we would never move into the quiet brownstone on Eighteenth Street with tall windows and a kitchen on the first floor. It meant I would never again see my friend Florence. And I'd never know, for sure, what happened to my little French flag from Lindy's celebration.

"Lost" also meant that summer vacations were no longer carefree. We stopped racing around catching fireflies, playing hide-and-seek behind hedges, and running zigzag atop the stone wall shouting, "I'm fastest" or "You're cheating." We stopped playing Romeo and Juliet in the stilted gazebo near the barn; we stopped poking fun at each other. Even Albert stopped making snide remarks at breakfast like, "Your bare feet smell like the dog's farts."

Sometimes Papa came home for a day to store something, like the Simplex limousine in the barn, or to pile all the empty fruit bushels from the shed into his truck. On those days we followed him around, seldom speaking, always on guard, watchful for the smallest signal that might lead to a nasty quarrel between our parents. Individually and collectively, we became self-appointed referees.

There were compensations. That winter, following a powdery snowfall, Mrs. Warren, who was active in the Balmville PTA and seemed to take a special interest in us kids, invited me and my sisters Agnes and Gloria to go skiing in the nearby Catskills. Unlike our schoolmates, who thought we were rich because we shared exotic fruits with them, owned a pony and a pony cart, and had hired help, grown-ups acted like we needed "extra curricula activities," because we never attended local events.

Delighted, Agnes, Gloria, and I searched the cedar chest for hand-me-downs and wool socks, which we hastily pulled over our heavy long johns. Under plaid skirts, we buttoned on leggings. We rummaged through closets for wool hats and found thick woolen gloves knitted by Aunt Tessie. Mama said we should put on an extra pair of bloomers. Outfitted to our satisfaction and reeking of mothballs, we trudged down the long lane to wait near the 9W Highway, our breath misty clouds.

Mrs. Warren, a tall, lean woman who had no children, drove a fancy Pierce-Arrow. She had pale, fine skin, as smooth and white as Greta Garbo's, whom we'd seen in the talkie *Anna Christie*. But her hair wasn't smooth and silky like Garbo's. It was short, blondish-gray, and dry, nothing like the long, shiny black manes that Mama and all my aunts wore in buns.

When Mrs. Warren stepped out of her big beige Pierce-Arrow, she stopped short and gazed at the three of us. Her eyes lowered, she cleared her throat and scanned the ground. Although Mama considered her *Americana,* we kids found Mrs. Warren warm and welcoming—but now, my sisters and I exchanged quick glances filled with flickers of doubt. Had she changed her mind? Perhaps she couldn't find words to soften our disappointment? She continued to search the snow-covered ground.

Finally, she spoke. "Where are your skis?" Relieved and without a moment's hesitation, all three of us pointed to the pair of skis I clutched to my chest and chorused in unison, "Here!" We siblings shared everything and thought nothing of having only one pair of skis, but Mrs. Warren seemed thrown off guard. She started to speak but said nothing. Instead, she turned and opened the car doors, then gestured toward the seats. We jumped up onto the Pierce-Arrow's running board and into the roomy interior and slid across the long, soft seats, raising the sweet scent of new leather. Settled in the back, Gloria and Agnes held the skis across their laps and started to play Guess Fingers, the winner deciding who would get to ski first. On the count of three each player calls a number, hoping to guess the total from one, two, or three fingers extended.

Sitting up front, I continued to sense something strange. I cast sidelong glances at Mrs. Warren's face, struggling to understand her shifting expression, all the while wondering why she had asked about our skis. Gradually, I watched her face change from a mixture of surprise and confusion to careful listening to my sisters' game.

Gloria cheered. "I won, but Eleanor can go first because she carried the skis the whole way down the lane to the highway." Mrs. Warren gave a quick look at my sisters, then turned to me and smiled. Her confusion was gone, and her skin had smoothed. I could see her eyes glistening the same way Mama's did when she read our report cards. I didn't know what we had done to earn that look. Whatever it was, it felt good.

That night, after the furnace died down, we five girls snuggled together for warmth, two in one bed, three in the other. We talked about the day, how most kids had skis of their own and didn't take turns. And how, on the way back from skiing, Mrs. Warren stopped and bought each of us a chocolate Charlotte Russe and hot cocoa.

Soon, as we did every night, we began to poke fun at skiers and other strangers we had seen, initially voicing brutal exaggerations, then jumping out of bed to elaborate with bodily distortions similar to those we routinely mocked—teachers, schoolmates, or neighbors.

Many nights, as a sequel to our merciless imitations before falling asleep, we unraveled or fueled grudges. Often, one or two of us remained silent, dwelling on some real or imagined transgression that Mama may have stuffed into the Bag.

Yet regardless of solitary secrets, temporary or ongoing feuds or alliances, our collective joys and burdens tethered us into one tight knot. Again and again, we acted as one, spontaneously answering in one voice or finishing each other's sentences.

Papa stayed in the city for weeks at a time. When he did come to the farm, he and Mama were not on speaking terms. We older kids became go-betweens, especially if both were in the same room.

"Tell your father the soup is ready."

"Let your mother know I'm leaving for Brooklyn."

"Ask your father to cut the bread."

"Tell your father to leave lunch money on the table before he goes to Brooklyn."

Although the family gathered for dinner, as soon as it was over, we kids would scatter, pretending important chores required our immediate attention. Albert would race outside to check on Billy the pony, and Francey would escape to the basement to bank the coals in the furnace. We girls would check the votive candle at the upper landing to the attic, take meticulous care sweeping the kitchen floor, or hurriedly wash and dry dishes as quietly as possible—anything to maintain the semblance of peace. Every moment, straining to catch every word, we struggled for invisibility.

One night, as Mama and Papa stood arguing with each other over five dollars, Mama sneered and tossed out a remark about

Papa and Josephine screwing around. Papa leapt forward and slapped Mama in the face, like he had before Charley was born. This time Francey, who was fourteen and almost as tall as Papa, jumped close and pushed him in the chest, shoving him away from Mama.

Papa fell backward, knocking several cups off the table as he toppled to the floor. His face turned ashen, and a strange, blank look darkened his eyes as he stared at Francey standing above him. When he started to rise, my sisters and I stepped back, giving him room. Francey, panic-stricken, didn't move. I was terrified. Would Papa strike Francey the way he had struck his worker?

But Papa didn't jump up. He turned over and crawled on hands and knees the short distance to the door, grabbed the knob, and pulled himself up. Without looking back, he left.

Francey and Mama started to cry. Soon we were all crying like the day I got lost in the Bronx Zoo and we caught the Police Station Crying Disease. Nobody said anything. The only sound above our sobs was the churning of pebbles as Papa's Packard drove away.

CHAPTER TWENTY-THREE
—MAKE-BELIEVE

1930

The next weekend Aunt Mary and Aunt Esther arrived and attempted to "patch things up." They were too late. During the week, Albert, Agnes, and I had gradually abandoned our human behaviors and took on the traits of domesticated animals. Our transformations were a spontaneous effort intended to lift Mama's spirits.

It began in the middle of the night. Albert woke as an unrestrained bull. He was snorting, cavorting, and stumbling, but mostly trotting wild-eyed through the bedrooms, bumping and banging into closed doors and closets. His bellows awakened everyone, causing the youngest ones to cry out in wonder and fear on and off until the roosters crowed.

Mama followed Albert around, pleading with him to calm down and go back to bed. Did he have a stomach ache? She would make him some hot cocoa. She held her hand to his forehead; did he have a fever? She never took her eyes off him.

Agnes, clearly envious of all the attention Albert received, was the next to transform. A few days after Albert's remarkable change, she began strutting around like a prize-winning Bantam hen, squawking to be noticed and seeking awards like bits of biscotti hand-fed to her mouth.

I, as the eldest girl, accepted my role as surrogate mother with quiet but excessive pride, staying up most of the night calming Charley, Evelyn, and Genevieve during the bull's initial rampage.

And I continued to do chores without complaining, secretly applauding myself for being able to climb trees and pick apples and perform other feats that Mama either couldn't do or chose not to do.

But inside myself, I simmered with imaginings about how I might outperform both Albert and Agnes, and within a day or so, I too made the change. I became a silky-haired llama.

Our animal transformations annoyed Aunt Mary and interfered with her attempts to appease Mama's anger and suppress our unmanageable behavior.

They were no match for our tyrannical triumvirate.

We knew it and they knew it.

We three, born within four years, were a renegade trio. I was ten, Agnes nine, Albert twelve. Once anchored on the farm, we romped around together, either as allies or foes. We finished chores, created mischief, brawled, built forbidden fires, and disappeared for hours at a time.

Mama played along with our new Make-Believe selves. I thought she silently enjoyed it when our antics infuriated Aunt Mary. Mama allowed us to come and go, occasionally—to Aunt Mary's displeasure—playing along by shooing Agnes out of her way as she would a chicken, or if I nuzzled her arm, acting like a sheep herder, picking up a rolling pin and waving it high, muttering, "Outside. Llamas stay outside."

But mostly she ignored our braying, clucking, and grunting. Sometimes she fed us at the kitchen table along with our siblings; other times, depending on the weather, she rang the cowbell and left food on the concrete bench outside the back door, pot lids covering wooden bowls or metal pie plates.

With the exception of Papa's older sister Aunt Mary, everyone else in the family took our animal antics in stride. Aunt Mary had always considered Mama *pazzo*—crazy. Now, when she visited, she grumbled at the way Mama lost her temper, threatened to throw a curse, held conversations with herself, practiced wizardry in the kitchen, and made dire predictions whenever she heard a storm overhead.

In the past, Aunt Mary had complained to Papa about Mama's extravagances—buying herself jewelry, giving the two older boys violin lessons, wasting money on tap-dancing lessons for Agnes and me, and buying a fancy Victrola so she could hear Caruso sing her favorite operas. For good measure, Aunt Mary always tossed in some snide remark about Mama's wild rages or the fierce vigilance with which she defended her children for any misbehavior outside our home—in contrast to her wild shouts or stuffing it in the Bag when we did the same transgression at home.

Hiding behind closed doors, we took secret delight in listening to Aunt Mary's complaints about Mama when she gossiped to Aunt Esther, Papa's youngest sister, who said it was a good thing Mama couldn't hear what she was saying. We smirked, secure in the knowledge that Mama knew what Aunt Mary was *thinking.* We never told Aunt Mary that Mama had invisible eyes in the back of her head and could hear through walls. And, since Truth was always in the room, Mama would know.

And when Aunt Mary asked when or why we became animals, we three changed the subject, not only because she refused to accept our new identities—choosing to treat us like disrespectful brats—but also because we relished keeping the secret of when and why we took flight from our human form.

Mama seemed to sense Aunt Mary's rejection of our Make-Believe and made deliberate efforts to demonstrate her acceptance of each of us, often scraping a carrot and holding it in her hand so the bull could grab it with his teeth and trot outdoors. To my way of thinking, Mama became excessively indulgent, overly attentive to the bull. She checked his forehead for signs of a fever. She beamed if he finished his soup and ignored the slivers of wood his clumsy hooves chiseled out of the wooden steps whenever he charged up the stairs to the bedroom that he shared with Francey.

Francey, our perpetually sad-eyed, lanky, long-faced fourteen-year-old brother, whined constantly about how Albert's fitful slumber and thrashing hooves tore the sheets on the bed they shared, and his noisy farts stunk up the room. One night, Francey grabbed a blanket from the cedar chest in Mama's bedroom and spent several nights sleeping in the hayloft above the cow stall.

Aunt Mary couldn't get over this. She scolded Mama repeatedly. "You letta the gooda sonna sleepa inna barna wi' da cows, an letta *animale* sleep inna bed." Mama paid her no heed.

Agnes reveled in her animal form. She outfitted herself with an array of ribbons and antics. This glossy-feathered, tiny Bantam hen—with her bright amber socks, skinny legs, and inscrutable beady brown eyes—was constantly scratching the table with a fork, ruffling and puffing up her taxi-yellow feathers, claiming entitlement to anything and everything she wanted the instant she wanted it. She flaunted her curly-feathered crown in rays of sunshine beaming through the windows. And if she received the slightest rebuff, she flew into a frenzy, her cackles and clucks interrupting anyone who might be talking, her beating wings raising flour from Mama's macaroni board, her bright yellow claws grazing the platter of freshly sauced gnocchi.

Although Mama played along, she had her limits. She'd shoo and shush and eventually grab a broom and whack Agnes' bottom. Agnes responded with squawks that sounded very much like Papa when he got mad and called Mama *"La Strega."*

Flaunting her disobedience, Agnes escaped by "flying" around the kitchen and roosting on top of the fridge or above the dish cabinet in the pantry—safely out of Mama's vengeful grasp.

When Aunt Mary railed at Papa (who had driven my aunts up to the farm) for letting Mama get away with raising a pack of wild animals, Papa ignored her comments. And Mama, who acted proud of raising feisty, part-human animals, would say in a contemptuous voice, speaking in Papa's direction, "Your sister doesn't know the difference between wild animals and domestic ones. Bulls, chickens, and llamas are not wild animals. They are domestic animals—they live with people.

Where had Mama learned this? She amazed me.

Shortly, my aunts left. Papa drove them to the city and he remained there.

But we kids continued our charade. Destined to be a beast of burden, I let the little ones climb on my back as I trotted around, giving them bouncy little rides, careful not to let them fall off. I licked the *pastina* off their chins while they giggled and dabbed more on their cheeks, and if they scraped their knees, I rubbed them with my soft coat to soothe the bruises and let them cry or wipe their runny noses on my furry haunch. However, like Mama, despite my maternal nature, I could be testy.

My siblings learned to be watchful and paid close attention to my brays. Even Albert acted wary of me. When he tried to make me pull his cart by knotting a rope around my torso while I was in the midst of hanging wash, I stiffened, locked my eyes on his, tossed my head high, took aim, opened my mouth, and spit.

Although unspoken, our animal antics were a desperate attempt to replace the ever-present gloom in the house with Make-Believe. Would Papa come home? Would he stay? Would he and Mama fight? If no relatives visited, Mama's sad moods and spells of silent withdrawal triggered a collective need to see her smile. Often, we found Mama standing motionless at the kitchen window, staring out. Other times, she moved about the room aimlessly, walking to the sink to wash a dish or two, adding coal to the stove, seemingly unaware of what was happening; sometimes she gave me or Francey a quiet nod of approval when we responded to one of the smaller children's requests to pour them some milk or peel a tangerine.

Gradually Mama began to treat Francey and me like grown-ups, saying we had to save electricity and not waste water and help her find ways to "keep food on the table." She said we had to think ahead, not just day to day, but for next month, next year.

We kids devoted ourselves to making her happy, or at least temporarily distract her from her sadness. Occasionally, if we begged, Mama would hum one of Miriam's laments. The lyrics sounded sad, but her beautiful soprano prompted Agnes and me to learn the tunes and sing along. Our singing with her made her smile, so we exaggerated our singing to loud crescendos, pretending to be performers on stage.

We took turns leaping from the stairwell and landing in the kitchen three steps below, Agnes flailing her skinny wings and flying out the door. Pretending to be an opera singer, I postured ridiculous imitations of imagined prima donnas. Mama would laugh and say we should both become actresses.

In many ways, with Papa gone, living in the country provided a peaceful respite. But I missed seeing him dressed up on Sundays, donning a silk shirt and polished shoes, taking us on outings after church. But without Papa home most weeks, there were fewer arguments. Mama no longer made dire predictions about Papa's "side business" trucking bootleg liquor, and when, as before, Papa did come home, he never talked defiantly about newspaper pictures of police raids on bootleggers. He stopped saying, "There's nothing in the Constitution about booze or forbidding stills" or "The Supreme Court is going to fix the problem." He never mentioned Prohibition or the stupid men who let themselves be fooled by a skinny Protestant lady who said drinking whiskey was a sin.

And he never hit Mama again.

When he did come home for a day or two, Papa was mostly quiet, busying himself in the basement, rearranging wine bottles or stacking wood for the furnace. Finally, he moved to Florida "for a while" and we periodically received boxes full of fruit —persimmons or prickly pears, pink grapefruit, huge oranges. Papa also sent ripe figs, Mama's favorite fruit. I doubted if she ever thanked him, but I never asked. Gradually, we kids got used to him not being around. And Mama didn't seem to mind.

Nicknaming was second nature to us. Cross-eye, Buck-tooth, Pigeon-toe, Four Eyes, and Fatso all became fixed substitutes for the given names of friends or foes. It was part of our sibling bond. We concocted strange words on a daily basis—a combination of invention and Italian slang. We had no idea how they were spelled.

"Gaga-zoot" would identify a timid schoolmate, someone so scared he could "poop in his pants."

"Stew-nod" meant stupid.

"Maadeeyool" meant a sneaky kid given to stealing.

These labels were spontaneous, and they stuck. Using them as prompts, we could spend hours rehearsing and escalating our caricatures into Make-Believe movies. This practice we inherited directly from Mama.

Keenly observant and ever vigilant, Mama was the quickest to single out some unique trait. Pooching out her lips and feigning a lisp, she might say, "If thsee were not thso bucktoothed, thsee'd be married by now." Or "His chin is too small. He'll never find a wife." Or if one of my older teenage cousins was close, she'd lower her voice and, half-laughing, say, "He's got a long nose; his wife is going to be satisfied."

Almost no one was off-limits. We nicknamed teachers, priests, farmers, chickens, and each other. Albert, Mama's favorite, was "Ruby," the prize jewel in her crown. Agnes, Papa's little princess, was dubbed "Spoiled" or "Selfish." I was "Gypsy" because I would disappear and find a quiet hiding place to read. Gloria was Shoomazoot for "Still Water Runs Deep." Genevieve, who stuttered, was Kaka Kaka Kaka, and hardheaded Evelyn we called Gabbadust. We had no idea if the Italian-sounding words were real or if they were a colloquialism from Mama's hometown of Chieti, Italy.

Only Charley was off-limits. He tended toward shyness and was so sweet and soft-spoken, none of us could bear to tease him —especially after the day Aunt Esther brought a suitcase full of Cousin Christina's hand-me-downs. We girls scrambled through the pile for favorites, trying on dresses, grabbing socks, bargaining, and making trades. Charley joined in the fracas. He found a delicate blue dress with a lace collar and pulled it on over his shirt.

Gloria yelled, "Everybody look at Sissy! Charley's a sissy wearing a girl's dress." Her voice carried such unfamiliar disdain, Charley broke into uncontrollable sobs.

Drawing him close, his tear-stained cheek wetting my throat, I imitated her, screeching, "Everybody look at Meanie. Meanie. Meanie."

While I continued to comfort Charley, Evelyn picked up where I had left off and kept repeating, "Meanie. Big Meanie. *Mean Meanie.*"

Gloria caught my eye, silently pleading forgiveness for her thoughtless mockery. Despite the tears filling her eyes, I joined the chorus and jabbed, "Mean. Mean. Mean."

Evelyn, Charley, and I left the room and sat on the front porch steps. Evelyn wiped his tears and soothed him by saying how cute he looked with a lace collar. Then we sat quietly. Charley sighed deeply. He looked at me, then turned to Evelyn: "When we grow up, we'll move away and get married."

Without skipping a beat, she said, "Okay. As soon as I turn sixteen. And we can both wear dresses." She looked up at me for approval. I smiled and hugged them close. They were not only my smallest siblings—they were my favorite children.

CHAPTER TWENTY-FOUR
—HOBO SOUP

1931

After supper, we kids liked to lounge on the not-yet-cool grass on the crest of our steep lawn, nudging for shaded spots. Eventually one of us would start our game of Counting Hobos. We'd yell numbers, with each player allowed one number. The point of the game was to guess how many hobos would walk past the far end of the grape vineyard that stretched below us before one stopped to examine the gnarled post that held up our mailbox. We seldom kept score.

Some nights we would count forty or fifty men, each walking slowly, always alone, head tilted down, searching the ground. I marveled at their clothes. Even in the hot summers of upstate New York, they all wore hats, mostly brown or herringbone woolen caps, or soft, smooth fedoras.

If one stopped at the mailbox, he would lift his hat and swipe it across his forehead before kneeling to read the symbol carved into the post. Mr. Pavone told Papa that seasoned hobos notched the posts that lined America's country highways to inform other hobos which houses would welcome them and which wouldn't.

The carvings on our mailbox post were two ovals, symbols for potatoes.

The stingy Shilos' post had a large X, which meant "nothing here."

The Felichellos' post, with a circle around the Xs, meant "pie."

The Mockos had a crude, menacing dog's face on theirs, which symbolized danger.

And the Palazzis had a hoe, which indicated work.

Near nightfall, if a man stopped and carefully checked our post, he'd always snag a few fresh weeds, tuck them at the base of the post, and hold them in place with a small rock before turning into the long driveway leading up the hill to our house. This was the hobos' way of telling anyone else who stopped, "This barn has been asked for."

When hoboes came to our back door, they always did two things: First they removed their hats before asking if they could sleep in the barn, and next they stared at the large tin vat in the corner of the back vestibule.

Mama would size each one up carefully before she spoke. If the hobo was young, she acted like his mother and made him promise not to smoke in the barn. With older men, she was more authoritative: "If you smoke, you can't sleep in the barn."

She would hold his gaze with a look that told him she knew he smoked, and he better not tell her otherwise.

These men were quick to confess they smoked but knew enough to smoke in the pasture, away from the barn. Some, eager to gain her approval or desperate for the potatoes, would elaborate on how much they knew about the dangers of smoking near hay. Once reassured, she would lift the lid and reach into the large tin vat and hand the hobo two raw potatoes.

Often, one or two of us would watch from a distance, peeking from behind trees to see how they prepared their meals. Some found a quiet spot under the hickory tree in the cow pasture. Others built fires too close to the barn for Mama's liking. Some picked a spot out in the open. Privately, I ranked the hobos according to their table manners. Mama and Papa considered good table manners important—especially "out in public." And Papa frequently reminded us that "good manners are necessary if you are going to be Supreme Court judges."

Some hobos washed the potatoes at the pump before they cooked them. A few just rubbed them on their trousers. Others peeled the potatoes and threw the skins under the hedge before putting the white part in a can. Most didn't peel the potatoes, just cut them up zigzag or in circles. A few carefully peeled the potato skins into long curls and added them later; I figured these men were making themselves a two-course meal.

Although we were forbidden to go close to the men or talk to them, we spied and learned how to make Hobo Soup. First, salvage an old tin coffee can and poke two holes opposite each other near the top rim (Francey did this). Fold a wire clothes hanger in half and bend the loose ends through the holes (finding the hanger was my job). Next, locate three strong saplings and tie them together at the top with a few strands of tough dandelion stems or a handful of fresh, long weeds—or, as some hobos did, twist and snap off a section of the wire clothes hanger and wrap it around the top of the sticks. Finally, snug this tripod into the ground.

For our Make-Believe Hobo Soup, we searched the sunny side of the pasture for several dry cow plops large as pizzas; then, mimicking the hobos, placed the plops over flat fieldstones and set them on fire. Last, we filled the coffee can with water from the pump near the dining room bay window and boiled our two potatoes without cutting them up. Unlike the hobos, we usually grew impatient and fed the half-cooked potatoes to the chickens.

Hobos took their time. While their soup simmered, they groomed themselves, using an assortment of knickknacks they carried—spoons, forks, pocketknives. From inside their breast pockets, some removed collapsible cups, either tin or celluloid. A shiny tin cup could be propped up between small branches of the apple tree and its round bottom became a tiny mirror. After moistening their fingers in the soup water, the men slathered their faces with bits of soap taken from one of their pockets, carefully wielded their knives or razor blades, and shaved. Every hobo's face gleamed pink and clean-shaven before he sat to eat his big meal of the day.

Sometimes the men removed their shirts, shook them hard, and put them back on. Other times, before or after they ate, they washed them in the rain barrel alongside the barn, wrung them hard, then stretched them across the hedge or over the large currant bushes to dry before morning.

When the potatoes were done, some hobos took off their caps and used them as pot holders to grab the hot wire hanger and carry the can over to one of the trees. Before sitting down, they removed a spoon like magic from a side or back pocket. The men settled down with their backs against the trunk, put the can between their legs, and slowly spooned the potatoes out of the can. Some drank the "soup" from a collapsible cup they dipped into the broth, while others lingered over their meals and stayed close to the makeshift fire, either stoking it absentmindedly or putting out the flames and spreading the ashes.

A few took out small books or old newspapers and read until dark. Many carried drawstring pouches filled with loose tobacco, which they shook into rectangles of white tissue paper. After pulling the drawstring tight with their teeth and letting the pouch fall into their laps, they would lick along the glue edge of the delicate paper and carefully roll it into a cigarette.

Although the men dressed differently—some carried heavy winter jackets throughout summer; others wore several layers of checkered flannel shirts and, occasionally, two pairs of pants —every man was bone-thin and they all shared the same look: confused, melancholy.

Once, Mama guessed that a tall, large-boned hobo over six feet tall looked like he weighed less than Francey, who weighed eighty pounds. She gave him an extra potato.

Many spoke with unfamiliar accents. Some looked scared, others angry. They would rest their stooped bodies against trees in the pasture or lean against the barn door, their eyes roving, as if to study their home for the night. But reading their eyes and faces, I knew they were imagining someplace far, far away.

Home.

One time, when I was alone in the house, one of these men to whom Mama had given two potatoes approached the house.

It was early evening. Aunt Tessie, whom Mama had taught to drive, had taken my four younger sisters and Charley to get ice cream cones, and my mother and the boys had gone to the peach orchard to check if the crop was ripe enough for picking. I stayed home to take a message if Papa phoned.

Being home alone and waiting for a phone call was one of my favorite chores. We had a party line, and although we kids were forbidden to answer when it wasn't our number (one long and two short rings), I took secret delight in disobeying. Instead, perfecting my skill, I would slowly lift the earpiece from its hook without making a sound so I could listen in on neighbors' gossip.

This particular evening, I watched from inside the open dining room window as the hobo, carrying a coffee can, approached the pump. He was very tall, much taller than my father and all my stocky Italian uncles. And he was also very, very thin. His trousers bunched together and tucked into folds at the sides and across the back. I wondered if factories made pants in only one size for very tall men.

The hobo held the can under the spout with his left hand and pumped the handle up and down two or three times with his right, then stopped. He seemed puzzled when no water gushed out of the curved spout. I called out, "You have to pump eleven times. Our well is very deep." I imitated Papa, who liked to boast about having the deepest well with the clearest water of any farm in the area.

The hobo started to pump again, and without pausing, he asked, "Does your mother have any salt?"

"My mother isn't home, but you can come in and get some from the shelf above the kitchen stove. It's too high for me to reach."

He stopped pumping, stared at the coffee pot for a few moments, then loosened his grip on the pump handle and watched it slowly drop. As he turned and approached the window, he reminded me of my mother's stories of George, her first love. The hobo's beautiful blue eyes searched mine. He held my gaze with a strange look. Leaning on the windowsill, close enough to touch me, he asked, "Are you alone?"

"Yes."

"Do you know where your mother went?"

"To the peach orchard to see if the peaches are ripe enough to pick."

"Will she be long?"

"I don't know."

We both stood still and stared at each other. At last he broke the silence. "How old are you?"

"Nine and a half."

After a few seconds, the hobo leaned in closer. His voice soft and low, he asked my name.

"Eleanor."

He cleared his throat. "Eleanor, I have a little girl who's about your age. Her name is Ingrid. When I was living at home, I taught her that she must never, never ask a stranger into the house. Never. Especially if her mother is not at home."

When Mama and the boys came back from the orchard, I told her about the salt and what the hobo had said. Mama's eyes turned dark and woolen, the way they did when something mattered a lot; she seemed to be reasoning inside herself. Biting into the side of her lower lip, she moved across the kitchen. She tore a thin sheet of paper from the Sears catalogue we kept near the stove for kindling, then reached into the salt bowl and dropped a small handful into the paper, twirled it shut, and called, "Francey, take this to the hobo."

As Francey started out the kitchen door, she stopped him. "Wait."

Mama turned back to the stove. She lifted the lid from the simmering pasta sauce, ladled out three warm meatballs, wrapped them in a large lettuce leaf, and handed them to Francey. As he headed out the door, she said, "Ask the hobo to stop by the back door in the morning."

"Why isn't the hobo home with his daughter?" I asked.

She carefully slid the tomato sauce to the back of the stove. "Maybe his family is living with his wife's mother." More to herself than to me, she added, "He's ashamed. He has no job. He can't support them. He's one less mouth to feed."

The next morning as the hobo pumped water and rinsed the coffee can, Mama went outside and spoke to him. "I talked to my husband. He said if you wanted work, you could help out in the orchard until all the peaches are picked. It might be work for a week or two." She paused, held his gaze. "It's a dollar a day."

The hobo didn't stir. He looked at the ground, then reached his long, thin arm around his back and removed his flattened, pie-shaped fedora from under his belt. He took a long time to answer. We kids had formed a semicircle around him and watched in silence as he unfolded the hat, smoothed it open, creased it, and then lowered it across his chest. "I'd be much obliged." Then, fixing his eyes so they met Mama's straight on, almost stumbling over the words, he said, "Would it be possible to get paid a little something on the first day?" I was puzzled. A little something? A dime? A quarter?

Mama didn't seem puzzled. She nodded. "I'll have a dollar ready for you at the end of the day." Her tone sounded soft and gentle, seeming to imply she understood why he took so long to answer. They smiled at each other like old friends. Then she turned to Francey and told him to show the hobo where the empty wooden pecks were stacked and to take him to the peach orchard.

The following morning, before the hobo went to the orchard, I saw him put a letter in the mailbox and lift the red metal flag, alerting the postman to check inside. After the hobo crossed the 9W Highway and disappeared into the peach orchard, I ran down to the mailbox, peeked inside, and saw an envelope with dark creases outlining where it had been folded. It was addressed to Ingrid Clark, care of Anders and Hanna Bjordstrup, Stillwater, Minnesota. A red two-cent stamp decorated the top on the right. On the left, our address: DeVito, Sunny Ridge Fruit Farm, Middlehope, New York.

Drawn on the back of the envelope were four hearts. Inside the largest, he had written "Ingrid." In gradually smaller and smaller hearts, he had written, "Little Ingrid," "Jens," and "Erik."

That night, sitting around the dining room table, I supervised a new project. We cut wrinkled paper bags and folded them into envelopes, gluing the sides together with homemade flour-and-water paste. On the front right-hand corners, we drew profiles of George Washington stamps with red crayons and "mailed" them to imaginary people, schoolmates, or each other. I addressed mine to Tia Marietta, Mama's sister in Italy whom we had never met. Agnes addressed hers to George, Chieti, Italy. Albert addressed his to The Boss, Sing Sing Prison.

Well into the first week, as Mama gave the hobo his day's pay, she asked—no, not asked—she said, "You must be a teacher. You speak such good English." Always striving to perfect her speech, she paid special attention to how people spoke. Like Papa, she believed good English was important. She often boasted about having enrolled in night school within three months of landing on Ellis Island. "The same week I got a job sewing," she would say. Sometimes she added, "Not like Aunt Mary, who went to grade school in this country but still can't speak proper English."

But this was one of the rare times Mama guessed wrong. He wasn't a teacher; he "kept books."

During the next two weeks, while we older kids worked alongside him, brushing peach fuzz off peaches, grading them for size and ripeness before putting them into different containers, we learned to call the hobo Mister Clark.

He told us that in Minnesota, where he was born and raised, there were many Indians. But they didn't wear headgear with feathers or live in tents or ride bareback. They worked in the wheat mill just like everybody else, and just like everybody else, they lost their jobs after the Wall Street crash. And, he said, like the Poles or Irish, they were given to heavy drinking.

Mr. Clark said he never rode the freight cars because if you did, the railroad men would hit you with billy clubs. Also, down-and-out drifters would steal your shoes while you slept if you took them off. "Even if you tied them around your neck or through your belt, they'd simply cut the shoelaces."

He told us he had left home early that spring, and, as Mama had correctly surmised, his family lived with his wife's parents. Mr. Clark described how he walked all the way from Minnesota, avoiding large cities where he knew there was no work for people who kept books, and told us he didn't have the stomach to join the angry men who preached and bad-mouthed the government, tossing pink sheets of paper, urging protests and marches. He avoided hobo camps where fights broke out between those who wanted America to change into a communist or socialist nation and those who didn't.

Days later, near the end of the peach season, I pondered a question over and over. It had been easy for me to picture Mr. Clark with his family, teaching his son how to write numbers and, like Noel Coward in the movies, beaming at his wife, who sang in the church choir. But I didn't know where he "kept his books." Were they in his mother-in-law's house? When I asked, he took a long time to answer.

"Kept books at St. Paul Bank of Minnesota for twelve years." Smiling, he added, "Sorta like school, mostly adding and subtracting, taking time to get the right answer." That cleared up a lot of things. "Last year, the bank failed."

"Failed?" I asked, confused, wondering how banks took tests.

He smiled again. "The bank ran out of money. It closed for good. It wasn't just me who lost his job. Everyone who worked there lost his job. Even the president." He sounded like he felt sorry for the president. I knew Papa didn't like President Hoover because he had caused the Great Depression, so I stopped asking questions.

After the peaches were all picked, packed, and sent to market, Mr. Clark stayed on for the rest of the summer.

He lived in the quarters on one side of the barn over the storage area, where caretakers had lived in earlier years when we spent winters in the city and only vacationed in the country during summertime. He helped pick the concord grapes that ripened after the peaches. But once all the grapes had been harvested, Papa couldn't afford to keep him on. It was time for Mr. Clark to leave.

The last morning, Mama handed Mr. Clark a meatball sandwich wrapped in wax paper, and several of us stood at the back door waving goodbye as he tipped his hat, that beautiful, soft gray fedora, and headed down the driveway to the highway. As he disappeared around the stone wall, Mama said he looked homesick, and my sisters and I wondered aloud if he would ever tell his Little Ingrid about us.

My sisters and I ran out to the lane, waved to his back, and watched him walk down the long driveway. When he reached the 9W Highway, he hesitated. Instead of turning northeast, the way he had been walking when we first saw him, he headed west. Mama said that was the direction of his family in Minnesota.

As he passed the mailbox, he dropped an envelope inside. This time when I peeked, the envelope had no return address.

CHAPTER TWENTY-FIVE—LIFE AND DEATH ON THE FARM

Whether by accident or design, growing up on the farm taught us kids much about the cycles of life and death. We incubated eggs into fluffy chicks, then, when they were full-grown hens, we felt their death spasms as we held them between our knees to keep them from spattering blood all over the yard when Mama slit their throats for chicken soup. We had seen Papa glow with pride when he erected the pole and raised the flag, then felt his shame as he crawled to the door after Francey shoved him for hitting Mama. We had planted hundreds of tomato plants only to see them ground to pulp by icy hailstones.

We learned to trust and respect Henry Brown, who replaced the former caretaker—a man who said Bessie the cow hated women, and who quit because he thought we kids were too unruly.

Henry Brown gave us our first lesson when he summed up the Bessie problem: "Ain't women. It be loose skirts." One day he told me to put on a pair of my brother's pants and walk up to Bessie, who ignored me.

Henry Brown would become the closest we kids would ever come to having a grandfather.

Papa said Mama hired Henry Brown, but that's not quite right. Henry Brown just showed up one day. Standing at the back door, Mama sized him up. He stood straight and tall with long, thin arms, dark navy blue-black skin, and a short, tight cap of light gray hair. He began to point out things he could do around the farm: "Milk the cow, feed the horse, plow, plant, pick, pack—whatever needs doin'."

Mama told him she seldom had money enough to pay anyone on a regular basis, but if he wanted a place to live, there were living quarters on one side of the barn. She added, "Whenever I can afford to pay you something, I will." The two of them faced each other for a few seconds.

"You seem like a mighty fair woman," Henry said. "I'd be much obliged."

The way they looked at each other—Mama smiled and Henry Brown nodded his head—I felt certain both would keep their bargain. And they did.

Henry Brown settled in. After a year or so, his friend Christina moved in with him. Unlike the men in our family, Henry was slow-moving and never raised his voice in anger. We learned to love his soft-spoken praise or reprimands, his calm and steady work habits, and above all his loyalty to Mama.

During this time, Mama ran the farm by herself because mostly we didn't know where Papa was living. Henry Brown helped. He knew when to plant, where to buy feed for the livestock, and how much to feed the animals. And he really helped when we got bedbugs. Mama said Albert brought them in after he came home with a cap he found at the Cameo movie theatre. Luckily, Henry Brown knew exactly what to do.

He said, "First thing you drag all the mattresses outside to the lawn. Then you douse them good."

We watched as he emptied gallons of kerosene on the corners and along the seams of all the cotton mattresses, the entire time warning us not to light a match anywhere near them, "'Less you want to set da whole fahm on fire. Just leave 'em in the sun to bake dry."

He showed us how to toss and turn them every day or two, eventually leaning them against the hedge to "aih out da stench."

Meanwhile, Henry Brown borrowed a blowtorch from one of
his friends, and when he carried it upstairs to the bedrooms, we
followed and helped him move the beds away from the walls.
He allowed us to take one look to satisfy our curiosity while he
began to torch the bedsprings.

Then he said, "Mind yo' Mama an leave da house."

It worked. The bedbugs vanished. But the kerosene smell
never, ever fully left.

Gloria threatened, "When school starts, I'm going to take
clean blankets and sleep on the dining room table. I don't want
to stink up the whole school."

In response, Mama gradually replaced the mattresses one
by one—mostly, I thought, because she agreed with Gloria and
didn't want to send us to school smelling like kerosene.

While the poisoning and broiling of the bedbugs went on
upstairs, we kids, having been shooed outdoors, started creating our own bedrooms on the porch. We fashioned single cots,
some from thick pillows carefully checked for vermin that we
tossed over wooden crates, some improvised hammocks, and a
few made from piles of folded blankets tied to a row of chairs. We
tucked the eight makeshift cots against the wall and under the
high windows that lined the wraparound porch. It must have
looked to outsiders like a hastily constructed emergency ward
for skinny, wayward children.

But that's not how it seemed to us. We loved everything about
it—breathing in the fragrance from the huge lilac hedge that
flanked the curved driveway just yards away, taking deep snuffs
of the delicate, exotic aroma of distant skunk spray, watching
glittering fireflies beneath the Big Dipper, and feeling the still,
dark air cool our skin.

From then on, we spent all warm summer nights sleeping
out on the porch. My two older brothers slept on one side of the
porch in their underwear. We girls lay around the corner on the
longest side, our young chests flat as wallpaper, wearing nothing but cotton bloomers as we stretched out, staring up at the
stars.

Before bedding down, all eight of us would chase wildly around the moist lawn, grasping the flickering fireflies that we called lightning bugs. Albert and Francey, perpetually engaged in competitive squabbles, launched unending verbal battles over whose "lantern" was fullest or who filled his up first. They used glass Kerr or Mason jars as lanterns to snare their prey, holding the tiny, flickering beetles captive by pressing their palms across the openings.

Albert, always besting Francey, would slowly permit his bounty to escape, only to quickly smear the escaping luminescent prisoners up and down his bare arms, mashing them to death. Then he'd romp around, elbows flapping, yelling just as he had on our very first night on the farm, "I'm King of the Lightning Bugs."

Eventually, we would settle down for the night. Petty fights occasionally erupted over stolen pillows, recent put-downs or long-standing grudges. More often, we'd start humming tunes from Mama's Caruso recordings on the Victrola. During moments of silence, the boys would start their imitations of hoot owls.

Being the eldest girl, I sometimes let my teaching impulse take over. I'd point out the seven stars of the Big Dipper, counting aloud for the younger kids. Sometimes I refereed as they competed to spy the brightest star.

CHAPTER TWENTY-SIX—
STEALING CHICKENS

One humid summer night Mama woke me by pressing her fingers into my cheek. "Quick," she said, leaning close to my ear and speaking, as always, in short, imperative sentences. "Quick," she repeated in a hushed voice, holding a finger over her sealed mouth, signaling me not to awaken my four younger sisters as they slept on the porch. Certain I would obey, Mama gestured to Albert, and they disappeared into the house.

"Come," Mama scolded impatiently from inside. Roused from my dreamy state, I followed them upstairs. Mama, gripping a large flashlight, speaking in hushed tones, handed Albert the rifle from her bedroom closet. With several short nods of her head, she silently directed us to proceed down the stairs. In total darkness, we made our way toward the kitchen, maneuvered past the long table, avoiding the benches, and left the house by the back door.

"Stay on the grass," Mama whispered. The dark air was laden with moisture, and underfoot, the grass felt cool and slippery. Mama was wearing her housedress. Albert and I, barefoot, were in our underwear. Bozo, our German shepherd, ever obedient to Mama, loped alongside her. As we crossed the side lawn, I heard the chickens squawking erratically. Mama hushed Bozo. Keeping close, we walked around the gazebo and crept down the soft slope, across Mama's vegetable garden, then up the hill alongside the barn in the direction of the two coops, not yet visible but emitting the familiar stench of chicken manure.

The squawking grew louder and more frantic. Mama, putting

her fingers to her lips, again signaled absolute silence. Our pace slowed as we continued up the hill, trying to remain hidden under the lowest branches of the cherry trees. The wire-fenced chicken yard was now visible. With exquisite delicacy, Mama silently unfastened the metal latch and carefully opened the small wrought-iron gate. Inside, and following her lead, Albert and I stayed hidden in the shadow of the heavy, low-hung branches of the lone McIntosh apple tree shading the larger chicken coop.

From the shadows, I made out the shapes of two men, both scrambling close to the open door of the chicken coop, each frantically snatching the air in attempts to catch a chicken. One dark-skinned man was swirling a long stick with a hooked wire clothes hanger attached at its tip end. The other, fair-haired and much younger, was grabbing erratically with his bare hands. Moving about lower to the ground, he grunted as he lost his grip on a clawing chicken. The dark-skinned man kept thrusting his hook.

Without warning, the men were captured inside the bright beam of Mama's flashlight. "Shoot!" she screamed.

Albert obeyed.

Instantly, as the blast went off, Paura clutched my chest. Encased within a mesh cocoon of brilliant, blue-white light, I staggered with nausea and struggled to breathe.

"Oh God," the white man moaned.

Pointing to the ground, Mama shrieked, "You want chickens. Take chickens!"

Through the blue-white mesh, I saw two statues framed in the yellow circle of the flashlight. One was frozen in a stooped position. The older man was on his knees, leaning backwards, hands held high and mouth wide open. In the beam of the flashlight, the color of his face changed, slowly becoming an ashen blue-black. Again, piercing the terrifying silence, Mama, her voice an unfamiliar animal-like, long wail, repeated her command, "Take them! Take them!" Wailing louder and waving the light furiously about the ground around their feet, she shrieked, "Take them! Now!"

The men didn't stir. But chickens were swirling—four flailing, bloody hens, their shiny amber feathers flying and floating skyward. They thrashed about mindlessly, toppling into each other like drunks, one without a head, its neck dangling, flinging blood, dirt, droppings, and dead grass in weird semicircles, tattooing us, the ground, and the coop with thin streams of gooey blood. The light caught little pebbles that glittered like shiny fireflies as they were flung into the air and pitter-pattered against the dry, wood siding of the coop. Panic-stricken, dozens of White Leghorns and Rhode Island Reds scattered out the open coop windows. Squawking frantically, they half-leapt, half-flew off their perches into the light cast by Mama's flashlight, then disappeared into the black space beyond. The whole time, Bozo, hunched low on his hindquarters, was barking furiously.

What seemed an eternity, but must have been only seconds later, I heard Mama once again. This time, her long shriek was more menacing, followed by yet another savage-sounding wail. "TAKE THEM. NOW!"

Trapped in my cocoon, the blue-white light began to fade into dark gray. I felt the air grow icy cold. Now I could see the men more clearly. Both were thin as boys, and their faces revealed— even to my twelve-year-old eyes—an unmistakable mixture of fear, shame, and submission.

Breathing hard, eyes wide and fixed on my mother, they lowered themselves to the ground and obeyed with groping cowardice. Each man, hands dirty and splotched with blood, grabbed a dying chicken and dragged it to his belly, then turned and fled. They scrambled, half-falling, over the waist-high, stone wall that formed the western border of the chicken yard and disappeared toward the Hudson River.

Once they were out of sight, Mama, using one hand, picked up two dying chickens, one by a claw, the headless one by its neck, then turned off the flashlight. Albert reloaded the rifle. I vomited.

When I stopped heaving, Mama, trying to comfort me, said, "Tomorrow I'll make you chicken soup with pastina"—she considered this her best medicine. In silence, the three of us and Bozo took the shortest route back to the house. As we approached the back door, Mama predicted, above the noise of my chattering teeth, "That's the end of stealing chickens." And it was.

Under Henry Brown's guidance, we helped sow hundreds of tomato seeds, then watched them sprout and bear fruit. We learned to suppress complaints and fatigue as we hurried to pick ripe tomatoes under a sweltering sun, pack them, and send them to Wallabout Market before nightfall. At season's end we watched the plants wither, then mounted Mamie, our huge draft horse, and rode backward while talking to Henry Brown as he and Mamie plowed the dry stalks back into the soil.

Gradually, sometimes in casual and sometimes in confusing or traumatic ways, we also learned about copulation and procreation. We saw roosters impulsively fly skyward and topple helter-skelter on the backs of indifferent hens. We cried as Henry Brown slaughtered a bleating baby lamb. We counted each newly laid blue robin egg in the nest that miraculously stayed anchored year round, high in the sycamore tree just outside the small attic window.

As evenings wore on and one by one we went to bed and fell asleep, a gentle quiet would settle in, occasionally broken by the rasp of a heavy truck that rumbled along the 9 W Highway in the distance.

One evening, however, Bessie ruptured the quiet. The young cow began bellowing in long, loud, insistent moos. Over and over again, *mmmmooooooo*.

We older kids knew what the moos meant. Earlier that morning, Agnes and I had overheard Mama talking on the phone to Mrs. Shilo, who owned the only breeding Guernsey bull in the county. We knew Mama didn't have the five dollars she needed to breed Bessie. We also knew that today or tomorrow was the third and last possible time for Bessie to be bred this year.

Henry Brown had taught us that each year, cows come into heat only three times—once a week for three weeks, and each time for only eighteen hours.

We shared the gnawing fear that slid across Mama's face as she slammed the heavy earpiece into its metal stirrup, her thumb tapping against the cuplike mouthpiece. As she plunked the phone down on the hall table, she muttered, *"Avarizia. Avarizia,"* her voice disdainful.

Mama bit into the side of her lower lip as she always did when she was troubled or didn't get her way.

Sharing her feelings aloud, she said, "If Bessie doesn't get bred today or tomorrow, she won't come in heat for another nine months," and repeated, *"Avarizia."*

On this night, the mournful bellowing crowded out all other sounds. Agnes, lying on her stomach, sighed repeatedly in frustration, and blew between her lips, sounding like the neighing of a horse. She reached an arm over her head and tugged at my hair. "I can't sleep."

"Neither can I. Bessie sounds so sad."

"Sad? To me she sounds mad." After a moment or two of silence, she raised her head. "Let's take Bessie to Mrs. Shilo's."

"We can't. Mama doesn't have five dollars," I reminded her, with a holier-than-thou tone.

"So?"

"We can't disobey Mama." There. I had settled the argument.

Agnes was silent for a moment, then blurted, "Mama didn't tell us *not* to." She let that sink in, then added, "If Bessie doesn't get bred, she won't have a calf and if she doesn't have a calf, she won't come fresh and we won't have enough milk or butter for Mama to make any cheese or rice pudding."

I marveled at Agnes' logic. Even though I was older and labeled the smart one, at that moment I thought Agnes was brilliant. I sat upright. "Let's do it."

Without making a sound and avoiding the long row of cots between us and the stairs, Agnes and I climbed over the sturdy white railing beside our makeshift porch beds. Barefoot, we dropped to the ground and dashed around the lilac hedge, heading for the cow pasture, stopping first at the barn to pick up the heavy leather halter.

Bessie let me snap the halter on her head gear without a fuss. Agnes and I led her out of our pasture, through the gate, and toward the opening in the stone wall that separated our farm from the next. Soon Bessie stopped her bellowing and picked up her pace. I figured she knew where she was going.

Agnes held one side of Bessie's head gear and I held the leather lead. We took a shortcut through Mr. Shad's property to Mrs. Shilo's, trying to avoid the rough hay stubble that scratched the soles of our bare feet.

As we approached Mrs. Shilo's pasture, we heard the bull snort and stomp around in his pen, raising the earthy smell of fresh manure. Now Bessie took the lead and sped up. We struggled to keep pace with her. We could hear the bull's rapid snorts quicken, his pawing at the ground growing louder and louder. At the pen, I struggled to lift the iron rod that held the gate shut. It weighed more than a bushel of peaches and was thick as a crowbar. Agnes struggled to unhitch the halter from Bessie, who began tossing her head up and down, compounding the task. Bessie kept pushing the gate in from the outside, the bull kept butting against it from the inside, and Agnes kept trying to unsnap the halter, all three making my job of lifting the crowbar almost impossible.

Suddenly Bessie stopped pushing. She raised her head high and bellowed—one thunderous, prolonged moo, giving me time to get the gate open and Agnes time to unhitch the halter and reins. Bessie shoved the gate open, knocking Agnes down as it swung wide. The bull gave several explosive snorts from where he pranced, stomping the ground in the far corner of the pen. He braced, arched his neck, and charged toward Bessie to begin a short, rough courtship ritual of rasping snorts and grunts, butting Bessie's flanks, almost knocking her over, nuzzling her nostrils and pawing at the soft ground. He looked like the gallant, ponderous bull in a Spanish bullfight I had once viewed on

Movietone News.

Bessie stopped moving, every muscle taut. Standing stark still, she raised herself tippy-toe on her hooves, her rear legs straddled stiffly apart, solid as a statue, waiting to be mounted.

Without warning, a light flashed on in Mrs. Shilo's upstairs window and cast a glow toward the pen. Agnes and I glanced at each other. Another light went on in her downstairs hall. Without a word, we bolted. As we dashed out, I picked up the halter Agnes had dropped when she fell. We raced toward home, not stopping until we were safely back in our makeshift beds. Still clutching the leather head gear, I slid it under my cot.

I could not remember if I had closed the gate. But for sure I wasn't going back to check.

As my hard breathing slowly returned to normal, a new fear startled me. Had we sinned? Mortal or venial? No—nobody had been murdered, no mortal sin. And nothing was stolen, so no— no venial sin. Adultery? I figured adultery didn't apply to animals because they never got married. I sighed in relief. Neither Agnes nor I needed to go to confession. We hadn't sinned.

Early the next morning, the phone rang. It was Mrs. Shilo, who demanded to know how our cow ended up in her bull pen.

Mama, genuinely puzzled, simply answered, "How should I know?" Piqued with Mrs. Shilo, she snapped, "I'll send the boys over to get her," and hung up the phone.

Immediately, I volunteered to get the halter and ran out of the kitchen. I noticed Agnes concentrating extra hard on her oatmeal.

While the boys were still within earshot, Mama yelled, "Bring Bessie to the house and tie her to the pump. She might be thirsty." When they returned, Mama, standing in the back door, eyed Bessie. A smile began to trace her face, and, talking mostly to herself, she muttered, "Good. She looks satisfied."

Nine months later, Bessie bore a calf with deep amber markings exactly like Mrs. Shilo's bull. Mama's eyes scanned ours with a wise and knowing look. "Notice. Notice, the apple never falls far from the tree."

Silently I imagined a mock christening and named the new calf Apple.

Bessie's swollen udder held gallons of fresh, rich milk for custards and cocoa and cream for whipping and churning into butter. Mama spent hours making three or four different types of cheeses. As warm curds formed and floated in the huge blue enamel kettle, she tenderly scooped them up with her long-handled blue strainer and let the whey drain back into the pot. When most of the liquid had drained, she dropped the curds into several different-sized handwoven, low-rimmed baskets she had purchased in Little Italy.

My job was to press the curds flat, using a dinner plate to remove all the whey that oozed into the baking tray under the basket and form decorative rings of sweet, delicate cheese. Others she salted, wrapped in cheesecloth, and stored in a heavy crock in the basement to "ripen."

Surveying my work, she smoothed the surface of the cheese in the largest basket, gave a final press with both palms to remove the last few drops of whey, and said, "Take this one to Mrs. Shilo. It's my biggest."

I could tell from the way Mama lifted her head high with her chin stuck out that she felt proud.

"I should get Agnes to come with me."

"You *should?*"

I lowered my eyes but not before I glimpsed her wise, knowing look.

"Ehhh." She paused, looking at me without blinking. "Tell Mrs. Shilo if she wants another fresh cheese, Agnes can take her turn to deliver it."

As I picked up the cheese and headed out the door, she lectured, "Never take anything for nothing. And bring back my basket."

CHAPTER TWENTY-SEVEN
—PO LOCK JOE

1931

N ot all the hobos were like Mr. Clark, whom Mama called "respectable and 'umble." Since the "h" in Italian is always silent, she never learned to pronounce it in English. It was the only word she ever mispronounced, and she seldom used it, either out of pride because she knew it sounded wrong, or due to the exquisite care she took in doling out praise for the genuinely humble. She admired humility almost as much as courage.

Most hobos who asked to sleep in the barn were reserved and withdrawn. They looked at the ground and hid inside themselves, hard to read. They came at dusk and were gone by daybreak.

The few who slipped into the barn without asking permission, Mama disdained outright.

When our dog Bozo's barks alerted her, her eyes would flash like fireflies and she would bite or gnaw the side of her lip, her body stiffened.

We were forbidden to talk to these men or go near them. "Not one word, not one look. They're sneaks. Don't go close. Not arm's length. Not ten feet. Not a hundred."

Mama's primal instincts and pointed warnings held tremendous power. Once flung, they were terrifying projectiles no one could dodge. I knew never to disobey these warnings.

And for good reason.

One man in particular, hired temporarily by Papa during the fall harvest of concord grapes, was thrust into that category. Fueled by Mama's scorn, we kids nicknamed him Po Lock Joe and took delight in merciless imitations of how he walked, talked, and smelled. Although he was Polish, his nickname had little to do with his nationality; it was a combination of the first part of his name followed by Lock because he had a habit of locking the cow stall, fearing the young calf might escape.

Sometimes we had gibberish conversations, exaggerating his Polish accent. We blackened a front tooth with charcoal or stomped wobbly-legged around Mama as she moved about the kitchen. Having sensed his lecherous tendency, we teased by touching her, then jumped back, avoiding a spontaneous angry pinch. If anything, Mama disliked Po Lock Joe more than we did, so deeply she couldn't bear to see him as the source of so much fun.

"Stop, stop," she shrieked.

Mama refused to allow him to stay in the caretaker's quarters. He was a "drifter," exactly the opposite of "respectable men like Mr. Clark."

Po Lock Joe had several rotten teeth and smelled like barn stalls, dried pee, and old sweat. When he stood in one place, he kept shifting his short, bowed legs side to side. And he stood too close, cheating on your space.

On her own, Mama never would have hired him, but Po Lock Joe had asked Papa if he could stay on and help in the vineyard before winter set in. Papa had agreed to provide shelter and a meal until all the vines had been trimmed and tied. This was a tedious task. We kids helped after school, but time was of the essence, and the bulk of the work needed to be done by hired hands before a heavy freeze. Also, the animals had to be fed mash to supplement their meager grazing in frost-covered fields.

Po Lock Joe slept in the hayloft, and Mama grudgingly prepared his evening meals, which he ate alone at the kitchen table either before or after we kids ate, providing a perfect setting for one or two of us to waddle through the kitchen talking gibberish to each other.

One evening, during one of the cold snaps, Mama was preparing a slab of salt pork, something Po Lock Joe had asked for but which we ourselves never ate. She heard him stomping dirt off his boots in the back vestibule and called, "Your food is cooked. Are you ready?"

He entered and with a queer, dirty-toothed smile, thrusting his hips back and forth, said, "I was ready forty-five years ago," followed by a rude and overly familiar guttural laugh. He danced in his wobbly fashion toward Mama, trying to catch her eye. She quickly turned toward the stove, kept her back to him, and bit into her lower lip. Hard. I could see she tried to hold back words. She tossed the salt pork, a baked potato and cooked greens on a plate, put it down on the kitchen table, and left the room, saying, "Kids. Come upstairs."

Later that week, Francey, returning from feeding the animals, told Mama that the young calf wouldn't rise and eat. Mama phoned Dr. Allott, the veterinarian who periodically came to help deliver a calf or check Mamie.

Mama told Dr. Allott the young calf had foundered. "She's off her feed and too sick to stand. Can you come and take a look?"

Dr. Allott drove up in his old car, parked it outside the barn door, and went inside. We kids adored Dr. Allott almost as much as Dr. Banks, the country doctor. Whenever either came, before they left, they would always snap open similar black leather satchels and dole out identical little pink pills that looked and tasted like candy.

Shortly, Dr. Allott walked back to the house, his head lowered. He took Mama aside and asked who was taking care of the calf and had she hired any strangers. Mama's face clouded. She nodded yes.

"Get rid of the man. You don't want him around the barn, and you don't want him around the children." Dr. Allott beckoned Mama aside and dropped his voice to a whisper. Sensing we were not supposed to go close, we kids became silent as stones and listened extra hard.

Between us we put together the snatches: ". . . rectum . . . violated . . . insides ripped up . . . have to put her down . . . easiest way . . ."

When Dr. Allott headed toward the barn we kids began to follow. Mama stopped us, saying we couldn't watch.

Initially, Mama's eyes teared up, then she began to carry on like a crazy woman. She banged pots and flung a cup across the kitchen. It ricocheted off the coal stove and shattered. She whacked the screen door with her broom until she tore a gash in it. She grabbed the uncooked chunk of salt pork and, threw it into the dirt outside the kitchen door, where she beat it until it was a black pulp. She bit into the neckline of her dress and ripped the front open.

Paura stood behind Mama, making the air behind her turn dark and fill with flashing blue lights. My chest hurt. I couldn't breathe until I shut my eyes and turned away.

Even though it was midweek, within hours Papa's car swung into the driveway—so fast it churned up gravel pebbles before he came to a stop outside the kitchen door.

Before he took a step, Mama screamed from the doorway, her voice shrill and filled with contempt, "You. It's your fault." Then, screaming louder, some words in English, others in Italian, "*Bruto . . . animale . . .* work for cheap? Make me cook for a stinking bastard that screws innocent animals."

Then her most ominous cry, "I curse him."

Her voice, a crescendo of shrill rage, filled the entire back yard. Staring straight at Papa, her face flushed and growing deep, dark red, she pointed toward the barn, the timbre of her voice suddenly low, almost a groan. "He'll be found in the dirt. His balls cut off. A feast for the worms. My curse."

Papa cowered, speechless. He knew Mama wouldn't stop. She might get worse. His silence and his bent head convinced me that Mama was justified. Perhaps in a futile attempt to curb her mounting fury, he turned toward the barn. Grabbing a knife,

Mama screamed to Papa's back, "Find him. Don't let him go. Bring him here. I'll cut it off!" Paura's shadow clung to Mama. I felt sick to my stomach.

But Po Lock Joe was gone. We never saw him again.

Later that winter, we heard rumors that a drifter had been found in a ditch near Latintown Road. The *Newburgh Daily News* reported that "body parts had been mutilated."

When Mama read it, she set the newspaper on the table and, looking like a judge, her face a mixture of smirk and smile, almost jubilant, handed down a verdict with absolute certainty: "Po Lock Joe. My curse."

CHAPTER TWENTY-EIGHT
—WHO'S THE BEST

1932

We all competed for Mama's attention in our own ways, but hard as he tried, Francey could never win her praise. She treated Francey as if he were all grown up. She said as the oldest, she expected him to do more. Unlike Giulia, who babied Francey and snuck sugar-titties to him, Mama often told Francey that if he didn't stop "touching himself," he would go blind and end up *stupido* with no brains.

It wasn't as if Mama didn't notice that Francey was also the kindest and the most thoughtful, eager to help inside the house or around the farm. She simply took everything he did for granted. If Henry Brown or I commented on how much he helped, she said, "He's the oldest. He's supposed to do more than the rest."

Years later in high school, Mrs. Miller, the algebra teacher, told Mama Francey was the brightest student in the class. I figured his touching himself hadn't hurt his brains. I also thought Mrs. Miller, like Giulia, would have loved him as a son.

Francey actually did do more than the rest of us, and he was the most sensitive, constantly caring for a sibling or a kitten, ever watchful of Mama's moods. He, more than anyone, seemed to understand everybody and everything. He always noticed when Mama said something in anger that he thought she would regret or when Agnes didn't get her way and said something mean. He noticed when Albert taunted and accused one of us of snooping into everybody's business: "With such a big nose you'll never find a husband."

Francey would find where you had gone to be by yourself; maybe you were up in the attic or under the mulberry tree. He would not come too soon—he would always give you enough time to figure out all alone how you felt. When you were no longer crying, but while your throat still felt so tight it hurt, he would say, "If Albert would put his head inside a history book, he would know that all the beautiful women in the world have big noses."

Sitting beside one of us, he would open his European history book, point to Catherine the Great, and say, "Here's proof. And she had three husbands. Your profile is just like the lady on the silver dollar. Who would trade that for a pug nose?" Then he would poke fun and press his little pinky to the tip of his nose, scrunching it as high as he could to make a pug nose out of his long nose. And we would laugh.

I couldn't understand why Mama didn't appreciate these things about Francey. What puzzled me most was that she never noticed that her tall, gentle son—who never interrupted, who found things in books, and who spoke softly—resembled George.

As for Francey, his sole source of joy was the sweet awakening of first love with Cousin Esther. We girls recognized the glow. Even Mama, yielding to her romanticism, would sing an aria from "La Boheme" while they rode the horses or picked cherries or teased each other playfully. Inevitably, Aunt Mary, fearful of a full blossoming of adolescent passion, forbade Esther to visit us or see Francey, and the light in Francey's eyes disappeared.

I helped around the farm a great deal too, but unlike Francey, Mama praised me daily. She praised me for doing things without being asked. She praised me for never whining. She praised me for creating skirt and culotte patterns out of newspapers. She praised me for sewing. She praised me for only taking time off from being her helper to study for tests. She praised me for getting the best report card.

I thrived on her praise, and when Gloria bragged, "Mama says I'm the best," I knew better. I could prove her wrong.

She and I sat opposite each other under the grapevines picking currants to send to market, each of us having shifted the stones beneath our bottoms until they had all been rolled aside or pressed flat into the soft earth. Both of us were fast pickers, but Gloria was fussier, so I always filled my wooden tray first.

When I settled my last quart container into the tray before she did and selected another empty one, Gloria, miffed—showing exaggerated care—tossed a stray leaf out of her container, leaving only shiny clusters of red currants. Glaring at my tray dotted with curly green leaves and stray twigs, she said, "Mama says I'm always the best."

I knew better.

As soon as we finished picking our row of currant bushes, we set the trays down for Henry Brown to collect and headed to the kitchen to find Mama and settle the issue.

We faced her and challenged in unison, "Who's the best?"

Mama eyed both of us briefly, her expression dismissive. "You're both the best."

"We can't be," I said.

"Only one can be the best." Gloria spoke at the same time.

"Gloria's the best at being neat," Mama said. "She rolls her socks and folds her bloomers and keeps them in a row in her drawer."

Mama was right, but she didn't mention that Gloria could throw a fit and give you dirty looks for hours if any of your stuff happened to get on her side of the drawer.

Mama continued, "And Eleanor's the best at school and sewing. So, you're both the best."

That settled it for me.

Gloria, still dissatisfied, probed. "Then what's Agnes the best at?"

"Fighting."

Mama always spoke the truth.

"And the rest of us?" I asked.

"Genevieve always obeys. She's never going to get in trouble . . ." Mama looked like she didn't have anything else to add, then said, "The little ones are too young."

I prodded, "Francey and Albert? They're big."

"That's enough about the best." Mama turned back to working her macaroni dough. Raising her voice, she added, "When I light a second candle it doesn't dim the first one."

After that sunk in, Gloria said, "We know you think Albert's the best. He's your favorite."

I nodded in agreement. Mama never punished us for saying what we thought.

Mama laughed and said we didn't have it right.

"You call him your ruby," I said.

Mama kept smiling and said she loved how his eyes flashed like fireflies when he got a notion to do something.

"Such as?"

"Looping a rope to a high branch and yanking on it to make all the ripe plums drop to the ground so I can make jam."

Saying we didn't have it right didn't matter. We knew in her heart Albert was the Best of the Best. She took joy in his feistiness, laughed at his antics, and didn't seem to notice when he bullied Agnes. She always let them fight it out themselves.

Once, when they fought the entire time we ate bread pudding, Aunt Tessie begged Mama to stop them. Mama looked at Agnes and Albert as they tried to out-yell each other.

She turned to Aunt Tessie with a sigh. "They're only screeching, not hitting. Listen. They're learning how to win an argument." Then, sighing again, she added, "With those two, nobody wins."

Mama had her standards, however. She did intervene the time

Albert created an electric chair and tried to electrocute Agnes.

Albert had found an old armchair in the attic and hammered metal strips on its arms and legs. He added copper loops for the ankles and nailed a copper headband to the top. It looked like a twin to the one that had been readied for a man to be executed at Sing Sing Prison, located about twenty miles away across the Hudson River.

Radio announcers talked about the execution, and every day newspapers carried stories featuring photos of Ruth Snyder, who had murdered her husband and was the first woman to be electrocuted a few years earlier.

Mama kept sighing over the sadness the man's mother must be feeling.

I asked Mama why—with some people saying the electrocution was wrong and others saying the man was a murderer and was getting what he deserved—they didn't forgive him, like Jesus would do.

Mama wiped her hands on her apron and removed it. She smoothed her new paisley housedress with short, pleated sleeves. Then she looked at me with one of her wise looks, her eyes neither sparkling with fireflies nor dark like woolen buttons. "Jesus, yes. But in this world only a mother can forgive her child if he takes a life."

"Only mothers?"

"Every mother. Completely. Forgive completely."

Albert interrupted us. He had finished his project. Beaming with satisfaction, he called Agnes, showed her the newspaper photo, and persuaded her to act like Ruth Snyder. Both dashed up to the attic.

My sisters and I followed.

Agnes climbed into Albert's chair. She wriggled and twitched as if she were in her death throes. Albert told her to stop moving and began to shackle her head. When she realized what he was doing, she started to struggle for real and screamed, "Mama! Albert's electrocuting me. Albert's electrocuting me."

By now, Albert was trying to attach the makeshift extension

cord to the plug in the overhead light fixture.

Mama came running up the stairs, yelling, "Stop. Stop." Arriving breathless, seconds after Agnes had unshackled herself, she looked relieved to see Agnes threatening Albert with "getting even."

She gave Albert a token rebuke, but as she headed back down the attic steps, I could see she was proud of Albert and his "invention."

I wondered if his metal strips and makeshift electric extension cord would really have jolted Agnes. We never found out because Mama yanked the cord free and carried it with her when she left to go downstairs.

CHAPTER TWENTY-NINE —ACCIDENT ON 9W

1932

E xactly as he had left, Papa abruptly returned from exploring wholesale fruit marketing opportunities in Florida. We girls were delighted to see him. The boys were guarded. Mama greeted him with a series of cool glares.

He said he planned to return to Florida, hoped to move the family when everything was settled. He had made connections and would be sending money, but he knew the trees in our peach orchard were ripe, and he wanted to help get the peaches picked and off to market while he was home.

Picking peaches in the orchard, Papa, acted like the movie star Charlie Chaplin. He yelled to the boys and pretended to toss a peach at Albert, then sent it flying to Francey. He tossed his cap to little Charley and told the youngest girls to make their skirts into sacks, and one by one, he dropped peaches into them from his perch in the tree. He talked about Miami's palm trees and blue moons and blazing orange trees in mid-winter.

I wished Mama were here to listen. Maybe she would change her mind about refusing to move, which caused me to imagine other possibilities. Maybe Papa would change his mind and stay. But no. He told the boys they could take the train and visit him during school vacation. He would send train fare. He was looking for a small house. Gloria wanted to know if he planned to live in Florida "for good." He repeated something barely audible about Mama not wanting to leave the farm. His comment about

Mama, and the fact that we were almost finished picking, made me realize I needed to return to the house and help Mama make dinner. I left as everyone finished carrying the peaches out of the orchard to load into the old pickup parked near the highway.

On the way to the house, I splashed in the brook, swirling dirt off my sandals. Once inside the kitchen I kicked them off and stepped on the cool linoleum floor. A loud thud from the highway made Mama stiffen. Paura darkened the room, triggering dread in me. Without looking at Mama, I bolted from the kitchen and took a shortcut down the sloping lawn, through the vineyard, and across the brook. I headed straight for the two-lane 9 W Highway, following the scent of gasoline, peaches, and tar from the hot asphalt road. I scrambled up the slope. Dozens of cars from both directions had stopped, their headlights beaming on a shiny new black car, its front end mangled and wedged into our pickup, now tilted sideways, a front wheel off the ground.

People were stepping out of cars, leaving doors open, gathering in clusters.

I overheard one man talking to another. "The girls say the car stalled gettin' 'cross the road. They was inside the cab with their dad. Brothers outside on the runnin' board of that old pickup."

Dashing past the strangers, I skirted broken wooden crates, my bare feet sloshing through patches of peach pulp that smelled like cooked jam. Charley ran to me and rubbed his face against my neck, his skin dusted with bits of glass. Several people circled Albert, his big black eyes blank, staring like a blind man, seeing nothing.

He sat upright in a puddle of blood that oozed from under his flattened right trouser leg. Sickened, I turned my head. A few feet away, lying in the road, a detached middle toe dangled from a flap of a section of a foot. Holding Charley aside, I retched. Across the road, my four younger sisters clumped together crying uncontrollably, Genevieve doubled over, heaving. Three women stood shoulder to shoulder, creating a barrier between the girls and Albert.

Paura stalked erratically, her shadow casting fear in everyone's eyes. One terrified woman grabbed her youngster's arm and dragged him back to their car.

A man murmured, nodding in the direction of a tall man in a pinstriped jacket. "That's the guy what hit 'em. Too drunk to stop."

Another man took off his belt, then buckled it and turned to a woman standing close. "Give me your scarf. I'll try a tourniquet."

As he bent over Albert, Mama appeared. She dropped to her knees, the red puddle splattering her housedress with clots of blood.

Covering her mouth but unable to stifle her cry, she lifted her head toward the dark sky and moaned, "*Gesu, perché? Perché, Gesu? Perché?*" Why, Jesus, why?

Francey moved toward her, his bloody hand partially hiding an open gash down the side of his left cheek. Hidden in the shadows, Papa, bent over and rocking back and forth, the palms of both hands covering his eyes, howled like a wounded animal, crying, "*Figlio mio, Figlio mio.*" My son, my son.

Slowly, the large man in the pinstriped jacket wove unsteadily through the crowd encircling Albert and walked toward the mangled car wedged into the pickup. He opened the back door and leaned inside, one arm bracing his face against the door frame and the other, outstretched, pounded the black roof. Each time his big hand hit the metal, he sobbed convulsively, coughing up deep, wet groans. "Oh God, oh God, oh God."

Mama, overcome with grief and aflame with rage, kept repeating, "Reckless. Reckless. *Pazzo.*" Papa shriveled under her attacks and retreated to Brooklyn. He left in the middle of the night shortly after he and Mama returned from the hospital, where the doctors had amputated Albert's right leg below his knee.

From our bedroom above the kitchen, we girls heard Mama's screams. "Get out of my sight. You crippled my son. Leave. Leave. I never want to see you again."

Papa never said a word.

Mama sobbed day and night. She spent days sleeping in her housedress, her back to the door, her forearm covering her eyes. She didn't eat. She didn't comb her hair. She didn't remove her slippers. She looked lifeless. We took turns staring at her, reassuring each other that she still breathed. I cooked breakfast oatmeal and *pastina* with butter for dinner. We brought a cot for Charley into the girls' room to keep him close.

But when we visited the hospital, the boys seemed to be having a great time. The slash across Francey's face healed quickly and left no disfiguring scar. He could have come home, but the hospital let him stay to keep Albert out of trouble.

Late one afternoon the phone rang, and the nurse asked Mama to come to the hospital. Albert's temperature had suddenly risen to one hundred and six degrees. Terrified, all seven of us packed into the Ford and drove to the hospital. Breathless, we tumbled into the room helter-skelter and were met by Albert's cheers and several nurses laughing hysterically. He had taken the thermometer out of his mouth, placed it inside his baked potato, and when he heard the nurses approaching, put it back in his mouth and pretended to be comatose.

Indeed, Albert, whether out of a desire to lessen Mama's grief or from his own zest for life, seemed undaunted by the loss of his lower limb. I marveled at his bravado and wished I could feel the same way. But I couldn't. Like Mama, I grieved over the loss of his leg.

CHAPTER THIRTY—CONSPIRATORS

1932

That autumn, when I was about twelve, Agnes barged into the kitchen, and I overheard her talking to Mama. She said Louis Martin, a schoolmate in Albert's shop class, told her that Mr. Shad, our neighbor—who always yelled at the boys to keep off his property—got two hundred dollars from Budweiser Beer Company for the sign that recently went up in his pasture at the edge of our grape vineyard.

Agnes thought maybe we could get Budweiser to put another sign on the opposite edge of our property and get paid, too. She added, "Eleanor could write the letter."

As always, Mama, who never said no to anything we wanted to do so long as it didn't violate her "Three Rules," gave us the go-ahead. "Write. Write."

Agnes and I dashed into the dining room, cleared a space between the piles of clean clothes, and began composing the letter, becoming more and more inventive with each draft. I suggested a sign across the road in our peach orchard facing the opposite direction. Agnes said that wouldn't work as it faced away from town. She thought a sign next to our lane at the north end of our property would be better. I said no, that would compete with our small sign advertising "Fresh Fruit" near the fruit stand. Finally we agreed on what to say to Mr. Budweiser to catch his attention.

We asked Albert to ask Louis Martin—who smelled of beer even though he was a teenager—if he knew the names of different beer companies.

I avoided talking to Louis directly because he never took his eyes off the two little knobs emerging through my dress.

Agnes added, "Once we get the names, we can write Mr. Budweiser and say those companies want to put up a sign on our property in front of his Budweiser sign."

"But that's not true." I sounded like Mama.

"It *could* be true."

"How could it be true?"

"When Louis gives Albert the names and Albert gives them to you, you can write those companies and ask if they would consider placing a sign on our property."

That sounded close enough to the truth.

While I tore a page out of a lined notebook and snipped off the ripped edge, Agnes found a pen with blue ink. We sat at the dining room table rehearsing what to include. Albert swung by and said we had to straight out ask for two hundred dollars. I disagreed. Agnes said he was right. Finally, pen in hand, Agnes standing over me, I wrote,

Dear Mr. Budweiser,

I regret having to write this letter. Another beer company has offered me $200 to install a sign in our grape vineyard. The 9W highway curves at that spot and their sign will block your sign from view.

Times are hard. I have eight children to feed. I wanted you to know the truth be fourhand.

Mrs. Elvira DeVito

I drew several barely visible pencil lines on the front of the envelope to make sure the address would be straight: *Attention. Mr. Budweiser, Budweiser Beer Company, St. Louis, Missouri.*

On the back I copied the words from the small sign near our fruit stand: *Sunny Ridge Fruit Farm, 9W Highway, Middlehope, New York.*

Agnes was ready with the two-cent stamp she took from the silverware drawer. Before sealing the envelope, we showed the letter to Mama, who praised my neat handwriting but puzzled over the address on the front of the envelope. She doubted it would find him.

"I'll pray to St. Christopher and ask him to watch over the letter until it lands on Mr. Budweiser's desk."

To reassure her, I said, "Budweiser is famous. Louis Martin said now that Prohibition is done for, Budweiser Beer is known throughout America—every mailman in St. Louis knows him." I added, "It's the same as sending a Christmas card to Pope Pius XI in Italy. You know it would go straight to the Vatican in Rome."

Agnes nodded in approval.

Mama said she would still pray to St. Christopher.

Agnes and I beamed at each other. We had done our part to help make ends meet.

Stealing electricity was more difficult.

Louis Martin spent most afternoons at our house. He was an only child and Henry Brown said, "He know everything 'bout workin' under the hood of the Ford but spends too much time peekin' at the oldest girls."

Henry Brown missed nothing.

Louis showed my brothers how to jump the meter using a thick copper wire he'd swiped from shop class. He said we could save hundreds of dollars a year on our electric bill.

Mama was furious. Furious at Louis for teaching my brothers this trick, furious with my brothers for letting him practice stealing on our meter, furious with me and Agnes for saying it was a good way to save money and help put food on the table. Mama told them to go outside and find something better to do. No way was she going to steal.

However, when a cutoff notice came in the mail from Mid-Hudson Electric, Mama sat for a long time at the kitchen table looking out the window, folding and refolding a napkin into smaller and smaller squares. Soon, all my sisters and brothers were in the kitchen, quietly watching Mama. After a while, her chest heaved and she started to weep. She gulped a few times and then addressed all of us, two streams of tears wetting her housedress. "We have to do it. But if I die before I can pay back what I owe, you have to do it for me. No matter how long it takes. Promise."

My siblings and I chorused like opera stars in a grand finale. "We promise."

I had no idea how we could keep this promise, and I prayed she wouldn't die, but I was glad we would have electricity so I could do homework and iron the clothes we wore to school.

Writing to the Budweiser Beer Company held no real threat; jumping the electric meter did. As the boys fiddled with wires, Agnes and I watched from the top basement steps.

Francey warned, "If you ever touch the copper wire you will be electrocuted and drop dead on the spot. And if the meter reader ever finds out what we're doing, the whole family will end up in jail."

Agnes and I swore secrecy.

A month or two later Mama and I were sorting apples at our makeshift fruit stand adjacent to the 9W highway when we saw the Mid-Hudson Electric meter reader's car exit Mr. Shad's driveway. He would soon turn into our lane to check the monthly meter reading. Mama barely suppressed a scream. "Quick. Run. Don't let him in. The jumper is hooked up!"

I dashed into the grape vineyard, across the brook, up the lawn, into the house by the front door, and through the vestibule. As I jumped up the few steps to the landing that led to the kitchen, panic struck. We didn't have a key to the basement door.

We didn't have any keys. Not to the back door, not to the front door, not to the basement door. How could I lock any of them? The meter reader's car rolled onto the pebbled driveway, circled the house, and stopped near the back door. Petrified, I grabbed one of the heavy kitchen benches, pressed it against the back door and sat on top, feeling trapped and helpless. My chest began to tighten; the room darkened. Paura arrived.

"I'm here to read the meter."

The voice came from just outside the back door. Did he know I was in the kitchen?

"Missus not home. You cain't go in." Henry Brown!

"It'll take me just a few minutes."

"Ifn' the Missus not home, nobody go inside."

"But—"

"Them's my orders. Cain't disobey the Missus." Henry Brown's voice sounded even closer. Was he standing with his back to the door? "Come later. Tomorrow."

"But I'm just checking the meter."

"Ain't nobody go inside if the Missus not home. Nobody." The way Henry Brown spoke, it was clear he wasn't about to budge.

Was that Paura in the shadow above the basement door? I refused to look. Instead, I kept my eyes on the kitchen door and pictured Henry Brown. Was he standing on the stone step towering above the meter reader, his back to the door.?

A car door slammed, an engine started, and I heard the sound of tires as they rolled away. I waited until the noise of churning pebbles disappeared before I moved the bench and opened the back door.

Henry Brown smiled. "Hmm. You inside the whole time? Knowin' you, if he hadda knocked, you woulda fibbed and said the basement door locked." Henry Brown gave me more credit than I deserved. At that moment I felt Henry Brown was like a grandfather, and I told him so. He smiled. "Much obliged."

A few weeks later, a letter arrived from Anheuser Busch Company. We kids squealed and crowded around. Agnes tried to grasp it as Mama tore it open. It contained a check for two hundred dollars clipped to a bunch of papers including a return envelope with a two-cent stamp.

Francey was the first to read the cover letter; next was Mama. Then I took over. Albert said I should read it aloud. It said Mama had to take the documents to her bank and notarize the form stating she accepted the two hundred dollars in exchange for pledging not to place a sign blocking the Budweiser sign in perpetuity.

Albert said Mama shouldn't sign. We didn't know what perpetuity meant.

Per-pet-u-i-ty—a long word I hummed under my breath.

Francey said it meant forever. Mama murmured *perpetua* in Italian and said Francey was right. She would go to Marlboro Bank and sign.

Like worker bees skittering around their queen, we circled Mama as she reread the letter. Albert warned her to read the small print again—there might be other strange words.

Agnes wanted to examine the check. I examined the return address on the stamped envelope. Mama asked Gloria to get her pocketbook and we would all go to Marlboro Bank.

I reread the form and directed Mama to keep her signature between the lines.

Gloria said we should all shut up and leave Mama alone. "She knows exactly what to do."

Mama gave her a warm look and told everybody to get in the Ford. All nine squeezed in, the boys and Mama in front and the five girls and Charley in back. The two littlest sat on laps.

After the usual lurches, we were on our way. As we passed our mailbox Agnes said after Mama signed the paper she would mail it since it was her idea.

Albert said *he* should mail it. Louis Martin was *his* friend and that's how we learned about the two hundred dollars. I thought the banker should mail it.

Agnes and Albert began shouting over each other. Mama ignored both. Studying her face and the way she bent over the steering wheel I could tell Mama had a plan. When we arrived at Marlboro Bank, Mama told Francey to keep everybody in the car and wait while she signed the paper and deposited the check. While she was gone, we played Subtracting Backwards. Albert said it wasn't fair because the three little kids didn't know numbers. He was right, but I also knew he objected because he would have trouble with the game.

Looking pleased when she returned, Mama gave each of us ten cents. She said we were going to the movies and afterward, on the way home, we would stop at the drugstore and get ice cream cones.

This was the last Friday of the month when the fancy Broadway Cinema was half-price for first-run movies. That day it featured Shirley Temple in *Runt Page*. The boys said they wanted to go to the second-run Cameo Theatre because it had a double feature—one with Tom Mix, the other with Hoot Gibson. It always cost ten cents.

On the way home, licking our ice cream cones, we girls vied for attention with our imitations of Shirley Temple's pouty voice.

Mama, pensive, took a deep breath, scanned my sisters and me with clouded eyes and mumbled, "No three-year-old child could do all those things. Shirley Temple must be a midget."

Despite the Budweiser check, Mama persisted in carefully watching how she spent money. Living on the farm helped. We kids had everything we needed: we had chickens for soup, eggs for eggnogs and custards, vegetables for dinner, and a cow for milk, cheese, whipped cream, and butter. Indeed, our schoolmates said we were rich because we lived in the biggest Victorian home in the area, had a pony and a carriage, and ate exotic fruits Papa sent from Florida. The only thing we lacked was a steady supply of money.

Thus, when Mr. Westlake phoned Mama to tell her that our pony Billy had trampled all his daffodils after he spent two dollars on them, and she owed him two dollars, Mama fumed. We heard her say she would be right over with the money. She hung up the phone, took two dollars from under her pillow, and told Francey and me to grab a few small garden tools. Within minutes she drove us to Mr. Westlake's, where he and his daughter Marion waited.

Mama stepped out and before she'd closed the car door,

she handed Mr. Westlake two dollars, then turned to me and Francey. "Quick, quick! Pull up all the bulbs. I paid for them."

Mr. Westlake and Marion watched in surprise, shame, and confusion as Francey and I, heads down, moved along the side of their house, digging. As we unearthed the bulbs one by one, Mama took the plants and shook them hard, causing dirt to scatter on the ground. Without looking at Mr. Westlake, she said, "I'm leaving all your dirt here."

CHAPTER THIRTY-ONE—
THE HARDEST OF TIMES

1932

It was mid-November and bitter cold, every tree in upstate New York naked, gray frost everywhere. My four younger sisters and I bounced off the school bus like jackrabbits and headed for the shortcut through Mr. Shad's pasture. Our German shepherd Bozo waited, primed to greet us, seated tall on the waist high fieldstone wall that separated our farm from our neighbor's.

We raced toward him. Genevieve stopped briefly to give him a friendly hug while the rest of us, fighting for the lead, jockeyed toward the house where Mama would have mugs of hot cocoa topped with hats of whipped cream ready for us.

As we crossed the side lawn, we saw Papa's Packard parked outside the back door. He must have returned from Florida. Agnes took the lead. But as we crossed the side lawn we heard Mama and Papa yelling at each other.

At the back door, we hesitated. Should we go inside or stand in the cold, watching each other's foggy breath? All eyes on me sought the signal to act.

Mama screamed. "How can I feed the children on five dollars a week? It's not enough for a day."

A thud—something flung down hard on the table. Was Mama hitting the table with a dish towel or a pot holder like she did when she lost her temper? Or did Papa hit her again?

The thudding continued. Papa's voice rose over the noise.

"You worry about five dollars. You should be worrying about Rusk. He refused to extend the mortgage. He's foreclosing on the farm."

Mama gasped. The thudding stopped. After a few moments, her voice returned, low and menacing. "You have to stop him. It's all we have." Then, her voice thick with mockery, she said, "Call your *friends* in Florida."

Papa's voice grew angrier. "If I try to reach them, I'll get in trouble with the cops. The stupid bastards got picked up."

"Stupid bastards? Who's a stupid bastard? You! You let them talk you into risking everything. And they left you holding the bag. You should have listened to me." Her voice, now shrill with contempt, ricocheted through the door. "I warned you. I warned you."

Outdoors, my sisters and I stared at each other in silence. Gloria and Agnes shivered. Genevieve, hugging Bozo, began to cry and looked at me, eyes pleading. Evelyn, the youngest, clung to my coat. I didn't move. We stared at the back door, darkened by Paura's shadow. My chest froze.

Mama continued in a commanding tone, "You have to do something. *Something.* You can't let them take our home." Her voice became a low moan. "It's all we have."

"Do something!" she screamed as the thudding started again and quickened.

"You think it's so easy to get blood out of a stone? *You* do something."

We heard a bang, then the back door from the kitchen flung open. Papa leapt between us. Agnes stepped toward him with her arms raised, anticipating her usual twirl in the air.

Papa ignored her, tossed his head toward the kitchen, and wailed, *"La Strega. La Strega."* Racing to the driveway, he jerked open the Packard's door, leapt inside, revved the engine, and took off, wheels churning the frozen pebbles. Bozo bolted inside and we followed in silence.

Although the warmth from the coal stove felt comforting, Mama had begun to cry, upsetting Evelyn, who tugged at my coat. The best I could do was draw her close.

Mama, seated at one end of the long table bench, kept pounding her clenched fist on a crumpled towel. She struggled to stifle the sounds welling up in her throat. Without looking up, she sobbed, "Change your school clothes." Then, catching my eye, she added, "Make the cocoa. The cream is in the window box." The window box was an add-on to one side of the back vestibule, used as a freezer in winter.

That evening, Mama stood at one corner of the big coal stove preparing stuffed cabbage. I set the table, tearing pages from an old Sears catalogue for napkins. Agnes appeared on the landing above the kitchen for the second time. Looking down at Mama, she asked when dinner would be ready. Mama had already told her to keep busy upstairs where the house was warmer while she finished making cabbage rolls.

"Not ready yet? I'm tired of waiting," Agnes complained.

"Almost ready. You have to wait."

"You told me to wait an hour ago." Agnes' voice sounded mean. And she exaggerated the time.

Glancing up, hoping to deflect a contest of wills between them, I cautioned, "Wait. Mama will call when supper's ready. Go back upstairs."

Mama's voice was a low murmur. "You can't be that hungry. You had two cups of cocoa. I'm almost done."

Using two forks, she lifted hot cabbage leaves from the boiling water and placed them in a baking dish. When they were cool enough to handle, she filled each leaf with a concoction of day-old bread that had been soaked in milk and beaten eggs mixed with bits of leftover chicken, rice, celery, onion, and a small handful of raisins.

Agnes prodded, her voice now a taunt, "You said you were almost done before."

"Well, I'm not done. I'm almost ready. They have to bake. You have to wait."

"I'm tired of waiting. You keep saying, 'Almost done. Almost done.' I'm tired of waiting."

Mama shouted, "Wait!"

"You should have started earlier. If you had, they would be ready by now."

Mama's face flushed. "I'm almost done. I told you to wait. Wait. Whatever I do, you're never satisfied. Just like your father, you expect me to obey you. I'm your mother—*you* obey *me!*"

Agnes' back straightened. My warning glance missed its target. Like an opera star, her head tilted sideways, chin high, she strutted down the three steps, stopped at the bottom, and confronted Mama across the room. In mock imitation of Mama, her voice a high soprano, she chanted, "I'm almost done. I'm almost done." Changing her voice, sounding savage, she went on, "You're not almost done. Papa's right, he—"

Mama's face flared deep red, her eyes wild and glassy, her voice a rising crescendo. "You want to eat right away? Here. Eat. *Eat!*" A clump of boiling hot cabbage flew across the room. I gasped in horror as Agnes turned away, but not soon enough. Several chunks of the boiling hot cabbage stuck to the back of her floral dress and blotted into a thick, dark stream. Agnes lunged forward, bent over, and screeched in pain.

She bolted up the three steps to the landing and turned toward Mama. "You burned me. You burned me on purpose. I'm going to tell Papa." Wailing in pain, she disappeared upstairs.

Mama appeared dumbstruck, her eyes still wild but her face darkened with a mixture of fear and shame. She drew in her breath with a sudden, deep gasp, her chest rising sharply. Her hand covering her mouth, her eyes sought mine in a bewildering appeal as if I were her judge and jury. Voice shaking, she said, "They push me too far. They only think of themselves. They never understand. They never understand."

By *they*, I knew she meant Papa and Agnes. I stared at her trembling chin, huge tears wetting her face as she shook her head from side to side and whispered to herself, "She pushed me too far. She pushed me too far."

From the kitchen, we could hear Agnes screaming and the younger girls all talking at once, asking questions, trying to grasp what had happened.

Mama took one long, deep breath, sighed a low moan, and walked to the dumbwaiter where she kept medicines. Lifting the tin of Unguentine, she turned to me. "Get a clean towel from the pile." Between sobs, she added, "Find a soft one."

I left the kitchen, rummaged through the clean clothes piled helter-skelter on the dining room table waiting to be ironed, found a well-worn flannel cloth, and brought it to Mama. Handing it to her, I wanted to say that what she did was wrong, and I wished she hadn't done it. I also wanted to say Agnes was wrong and I felt sorry for both. I wanted to say Papa was wrong for calling Mama *witch, witch,* and he was wrong for not twirling Agnes in the air. But he had looked so scared, I felt sorry for Papa, too.

Most of all, I wished I could say I understood. But my throat hurt too much. And words swirled in my mind, but I couldn't find any to match my feelings. I watched in silence as Mama mounted the stairs to the landing and disappeared behind the wall.

After a few minutes, I followed.

Agnes lay face-down and crosswise on the bed she and I shared with Evelyn. Her dress had been pulled up, covering her head. My three younger sisters stood at the foot of the bed, hands on the round brass railing, watching in silence.

Mama sat on the mattress next to Agnes, her hand moving lightly, tenderly, smoothing the amber ointment across Agnes' upper back. Both wept. Soon, one by one, we all wept in silence. The room seemed eerily quiet except for the thin, harsh scratching of an errant branch of the sycamore tree trailing back and forth across the dark bedroom window, moved by the cold winter wind.

Weeks later, while eating lentil soup, outspoken Gloria asked Mama if Papa might come home for Christmas. We had no idea where he had been sleeping or eating, or if he lived in Brooklyn or had returned to Florida. Mama shifted her eyes away from the table, paying too much attention to the floor. She said Aunt Mary had phoned. Papa was in the hospital again with a nerve condition in his back. He needed to rest for a few weeks. Mama's voice sounded strange, as if she was pretending Truth wasn't in the room.

Later that day, Mama phoned Mr. Pavone, the former owner of our farm. She said if he still wanted the Simplex limousine Papa had stored in the barn, he could have it for fifty dollars. She said it was worth more. The headlamps were pure nickel. Not many made. Mr. Pavone offered forty dollars and came to pick it up that afternoon. As he drove off, my sisters and I exchanged forlorn looks. No more pretending we were dressed in fancy gowns with a chauffeur driving us to the debutante's ball.

After school and all day on weekends, we kids took turns monitoring the fruit stand. Using the little money that Papa sent, the small but steady income from the fruit stand (paying Henry Brown whatever she could whenever she could), and owing almost nothing for electricity since we jumped the meter, Mama began paying off what she considered her debts.

Whenever she made a payment to Mr. Rusk at Marlboro Bank, she always took two or three of us with her. Starting the car, she would raise her chin and tell us, "Little by little, I'm paying off our debt. Remember, no such thing as an unpaid debt. *Somebody* pays every debt. If you owe it, you pay it. Then you can always hold your head high."

After the lurching stopped and we drove steadily down the road, she would praise herself. "I'm keeping my word."

"I look for the day I pay back Mid-Hudson Electric." Mama prided herself on never taking anything for nothing. Homemade noodles in exchange for garlic starts, cheese in exchange for Mrs. Goodman's matzoh balls. Always something in exchange.

Papa didn't come home for Christmas, and just before New Year's a letter arrived from the Marlboro Bank. When Mama opened it, her face blanched, but within moments she phoned Mr. Rusk.

"I need to see you as soon as possible." Settling the earpiece in its hook, she turned to me. "Go to the attic and get the Box. We're going to Mr. Rusk."

Francey had hidden the Box in the crawl space of the eaves shortly after we moved to the farm. He had tucked it between two studs in the attic. The Box was a dark gray metal Hershey's Cocoa container that held Mama's precious jewels. Jewels she had purchased years earlier when Papa was making money hand over fist, trucking bootleg whiskey. The box held diamond rings, gold lockets, bracelets, and a handful of five-dollar gold pieces, one for each girl. It also held mysterious gold charms shaped like hot peppers and little fists with pinkies and index fingers pointing straight up like horns. All children of Italian immigrants wore these pinned to baby clothes or underwear to ward off the evil eye.

Mama changed into a fancy, light-gray church dress with a large off-white satin collar. She told me to put on a clean dress and school shoes, then take the Box to the car and wait. The leather seat felt ice cold.

As usual, when she started the old Ford, it stalled and lurched a few times before it moved forward. Mama drove the way she always did, looking straight ahead and moving so slowly, young men often yelled, "Get a horse!" and older men called, "Get off the road and back to the kitchen where you belong." Mama took no notice, kept her eyes on the road, and drove in focused silence.

Mr. Rusk met us at the door of the one-story, brown brick building and ushered us into a warm room with green shades, half-drawn. Two men in brown business suits sat at one side of a long table. They rose when we entered and sat down as soon as Mama and I took the seats opposite them. Mr. Rusk, seated at the head of the table, opened a green folder.

While he shuffled papers, Mama unbuttoned her coat, took the Box from me, pried it open, and slid it across the shiny, polished table toward Mr. Rusk, making the room smell like linseed oil. Before he could speak, she said, "You have to take these for now and . . ."

Mr. Rusk interrupted. "Mrs. DeVi—"

"The dinner ring has a yellow diamond. It's platinum."

"But there's been no payment in more than four years, I—"

"You have to take them." Mama sounded like a West Point general.

Mr. Rusk glanced at the two men, who both looked puzzled. They shifted uncomfortably. He tried again: "But—"

Mama wouldn't let him say another word. She stiffened her back and looked at the three men, her dark eyes moving back and forth from one to the next. "You cannot take my home from my children."

Mr. Rusk's expression changed. He looked embarrassed. The two men looked at each other as if they had been caught stealing.

"Mrs. DeVi—"

Mama ignored him. Her voice began to tremble, but she still managed to sound threatening. "You cannot take my home from my children." Tears filled her eyes. I began to cry.

Mama's head turned to me. "Don't cry," she commanded, even as she struggled to hold back her own tears. I swallowed hard. Mama's eyes shifted back to the men. Staring at them, her voice rose higher and louder. "You cannot take my home from my children." Now tears slid down her face and dropped from her chin, making dark spots on the wide satin collar. Instead of wiping them away, she lifted her head higher, her voice screeching, "You cannot take my home from my children."

Mr. Rusk's forehead glistened. He looked confused. Ashamed? He stopped trying to get a word in. The two men across the table sunk lower in their chairs. Mama kept demanding, "You cannot take my home from my children."

She reached toward her ring finger. Mr. Rusk and both men drew in short gasps as she removed her wedding band and dropped it into the Hershey Cocoa box. Her voice rose higher. "It's 24 karats."

She moved the tin box closer to Mr. Rusk, her voice breaking. "Take them." Holding his gaze, she repeated, "You cannot take my home from my children."

Mr. Rusk locked eyes with the two men and cleared his throat. He raised his hand like Father Joseppi from St. Mary's Church, as though to calm Mama. "All right, Mrs. DeVito."

It sounded like an apology. He looked at the two men again. "I'll carry the mortgage for . . . for . . ."

Without a moment's delay, Mama broke in, her cheeks wet, her chin high. "Two years. Two years. Until we're back on our feet. You have my word. You have my word."

It sounded like a promise she would never, ever break.

Mr. Rusk must have thought so, too. He looked at the two men again. They looked back at him, reminding me of how we kids talked to each other without using words, a language more eloquent, more meaningful than English or Italian or Overheard. More important than the gibberish we invented to confuse strangers while we waited in line at stores or the movies. Studying the men as they looked at each other, I felt at home. They, too, had a language of looks.

Banker's looks.

Mr. Rusk turned to Mama, closed the ledger, and murmured, "All right, two years." Then, gently, very gently, he slid the Hershey's Cocoa box back to Mama.

Without a word, Mama lifted the box, snapped the lid in place, and handed it to me. Turning, she grabbed my other hand and tugged me out the door.

On the ride home she heaved long, half-choked sighs. When they softened, I asked, almost reprimanding her for breaking one of her own rules of etiquette, "Mama, why didn't you say thank you to Mr. Rusk?"

Her response was immediate. "My pride was too hurt." After a moment, she added, "Mr. Rusk understood. He understood my pride was too hurt."

I stared up at her, convinced beyond doubt that Mama could read minds. The late afternoon sun shone through her side of the car, warming us. I held the box close and imagined telling my sisters how Mama saved our home. Mama glanced at me and smiled. I was sure she had read my mind.

But Mama wasn't finished.

Before we got home, she slowed down and turned in at the Palatine Inn, which sat with its windows boarded up. With few or no customers, the inn had gone out of business. Close to the highway, the owners had placed a sign advertising the sale of its golf shed for forty dollars. Mama circled around the main building and stopped the car. Before stepping outside, she told me to hold on to the box and cover it with my skirt. Then she disappeared inside.

Shortly after, she came out with a man I recognized as the owner. They walked to the golf shed, and the owner fiddled with a ring of keys, opening a fancy door with a separate top and bottom. I thought it would make a wonderful stage set; you could make speeches from the open top and pretend to be a devil in hell peeking out from the bottom. The owner held the door open for Mama to step inside. When they came out, they shook hands, and Mama returned to the car.

"We made a deal," she said. "I bought it for twenty-five dollars, and he is going to move it to our property for two dollars. Now we can store the fruit inside the shed instead of dragging it in and out from the grape orchard every night." She drove in silence for a few moments, then looked at me. "I promised to pay him as soon as I could. With the first money we get from selling fruit on the highway."

CHAPTER THIRTY-TWO—BOZO

1932

One day after school, we kids knew something was wrong when we didn't see Bozo, our faithful German shepherd, sitting on the stone wall, haunches braced, waiting for the school bus. As soon as the driver pulled off the 9W and stopped, all six of us, the last of the passengers, jumped, pushed, or pummeled each other to get out the door first.

Mama often said that if all the clocks in the world stopped, she could reset them by Bozo. At three-forty on the dot, he scratched at the kitchen door to get out. He headed across the lawn, disappeared behind the barn, and raced across Mrs. Henningson's pasture to wait in welcome.

This day, Bozo was not in his accustomed place, nor anywhere to be seen. Our roughhousing stopped and we did what we usually did in a crisis: We became silent, communicating our fear in a series of glances, the three youngest seeking answers from reading the expressions of the three eldest, who exchanged telling gazes with each other before glancing at the perplexed faces of the younger ones, unable to explain or reassure.

Our attention shifted. For a moment, we all gazed at the empty stone wall in silence, our eyes scanning left and right. Without exchanging a word, my siblings and I raced across Mrs. Henningson's field, crunching dry hay stubble and crisp autumn leaves. We skirted the swampy area that became a skating rink in midwinter, scaled the uneven stone wall, and climbed up the steep slope.

As we moved through our pasture, we called, voices growing louder and louder, "Bozo, Bozo, Bozo!"

No Bozo.

We argued about what might have happened. Maybe Mama accidentally locked him in the cellar. But then he would have barked. Maybe his collar got caught on a branch, since Henry Brown was trimming trees.

"Maybe," Albert muttered, "there's a bitch in heat."

"No," Agnes corrected, "it's the wrong time of year."

Albert, first through the door, yelled, "Mama, have you seen Bozo?"

"No," Mama replied, "and he didn't come home last night. His dish is still full. Change out of your school clothes." Then, sounding uncertain, she said, "Go look near the highway. Stay off the road."

Hours later, one by one, we straggled home. We had walked both sides of the highway half a mile in each direction. We had looked under the chicken coops and in the Filiberti's shed. We even crawled through the large oval tube under the driveway, now empty of brook water.

At dusk Bozo was still nowhere to be found.

Several days went by without a sign of Bozo. We kids trudged through the entire vineyard row by row, walked to the Hudson River and along the railroad tracks, and searched under the mulberry tree, calling continuously. Each evening, as we drank our frothy cocoa before going to bed, Mama said she would light a candle for Bozo and pray to St. Anthony, the patron saint of lost items.

Mama's prayers worked.

Three days later, after school, we bolted through the back door and found Bozo on the kitchen floor in the corner near the dumbwaiter. The room became a circus of shouts and squeals. We were elated.

"Where did you find him?"

"Did he come home by himself?"

"Why is he on that blanket?"

Genevieve leaned close to Bozo's ear and asked him directly, "Where were you hiding?"

Bozo didn't answer, but Genevieve acted like he had and continued her conversation with him. She didn't seem to notice his stench.

Henry Brown had found Bozo lying under some brush at the far end of the peach orchard on the other side of the 9W Highway and had walked back home to tell Mama where Bozo lay, "mostly dead . . ."

"But still alive?"

When Henry nodded yes, Mama didn't hesitate. She started the old Tin Lizzie and drove around the back road to get close enough for Henry to place Bozo on a blanket and put him in the back seat. Henry was sure Bozo would die before they got back to the house.

Now, tending to the dying dog who lay huddled on a blanket in the kitchen with unseeing eyes and a drooling mouth, Henry had not changed his view. "None uh dis gonna help. But what yo Mama say do, ahm doin' it," he said while carefully tucking hay under the blanket near Bozo's head.

Gloria, turning away from Bozo with a disgusted snort, said, "I can't stand it. The whole room stinks." She opened the kitchen door, stomped through the vestibule, and flung open the back door, the entire time saying she knew the fresh air would not reduce the strange and putrid stench coming from Bozo's wounds.

Silently, I agreed. Bozo's hind leg was covered with dried blood, dirty dead grass, and small butter-colored, lumpy, wriggly clumps of maggots.

Henry stood up and muttered, "She right." He moved toward the kitchen door, eager to leave. Clearly, this was not a task to his liking.

And we kids didn't make it any easier. Everyone spoke at the same time. We were curious for all the details and kept repeating our questions, interrupting each other, telling each other to shut up and listen, shoving to get closer to Henry.

"Where was he?"

"Did you call for a long time?"

"Do you know how it happened?"

"Was he heavy to carry?"

"How did you get him to the car?"

Henry said it wasn't calling or listening, it was "smellin.'" He bobbed his head sideways toward the outside door, then back to Mama, trying to catch her eye, subtly asking if his job was done, asking to leave. Lowering his voice, he added, "He home but he not gonna live. That leg got gangrene."

Although we didn't know for certain what gangrene was, we knew Henry Brown was never wrong, and if Henry said Bozo was going to die, it meant Bozo was going to die. This collective realization started a contagion of five girls wailing. The boys kept staring at Bozo.

Albert began to outline a proposal for the proper burial plot. Should it be where Bozo was found? In the peach orchard? Near the house out front where the driveway turned, and we could place a gravestone? Yes, Albert decided. A big one from the stone wall, and a memorial service.

First, he would chisel Bozo's name on the thick slate slab by hammering the letters using an oversized nail. He headed out the door to find a headstone for his project.

Mama told us all to stop bawling and preparing for a funeral. "We have to take Bozo to Dr. Allott. He's not dead yet."

When we got there, Dr. Allott took Bozo into a back room and came out shortly after.

"Mrs. DeVito, the leg is too far gone for him to ever use it again. He's got gangrene and these maggots are down to the bone. Caring for him here could take weeks." He paused, and they stared at each other. I interpreted the somber expressions that he and Mama exchanged as silent calculations of the potential debt.

Mama kept silent, ignoring Genevieve's pleas to "get an X-ray, get an X-ray."

Speaking softly and avoiding eye contact with any of us, Dr. Allott said, "It's best if we put him to sleep. It won't cost."

I wasn't sure about gangrene, but I had seen maggots blanketing a possum by the side of the road, and that possum was very dead. And everyone understood what *put him to sleep* meant. This verdict created an explosion of wails and tears until Mama told us to be quiet or go outside and wait. Everyone tried to stifle sobs. Nobody moved.

Mama stood quietly for a few more moments, then said, "Well, if Bozo's going to die, he can die at home." Without a moment's hesitation and already primed for action, Albert and Francey went behind the counter and followed Dr. Allott into the back room. They picked up the four corners of the blanket they had placed him in before leaving home and carried Bozo toward the car.

Some of us raced to open Dr. Allott's exit door while others held open the back door of the old Ford. The boys hoisted Bozo up and put him on the back seat as we piled in around him, holding our noses.

Mama spent a few minutes talking to Dr. Allott. When she came out, we waited for her to start the engine, automatically bracing ourselves for the inevitable series of stalls followed by a sudden lurch as we got underway. Bozo looked less in pain than confused and ashamed. None of us said anything, mostly because we began to feel nauseous from the stench of the rotting flesh.

Mama didn't drive straight home. She stopped at Mr. Thomas's drugstore, parked, reached inside her brassiere, and took out two dollars, which she handed to Francey. "Buy the biggest bottle of Lysol and the thickest roll of cotton. And if Mr. Thomas has a leech, buy it too." Francey came out with a large brown bottle, a plump roll of soft white cotton coiled like a jelly roll in crinkled royal-blue tissue paper, and a small Mason jar with a slimy-looking, reddish-brown leech stuck to the inside. On the way home, Mama said we would make a corner of the kitchen into a hospital. Sanitized by Lysol. And we would practice being veterinarians.

Periodically during the five-mile drive, she elaborated on her standards for care. She began with what she considered the all-important underlying philosophy: "Good doctors work day and night." Next, she outlined the diagnosis, the treatment regimen, and the routine schedule, talking as much to herself as to us.

"The maggots are eating his flesh. We need to kill the maggots. The maggots can't live in Lysol. But the Lysol will kill the leech. If the solution is too strong, it will destroy the good flesh. So, for today we use the leech and see what it does. Then if we keep his leg wet with the Lysol, the maggot eggs will die. If the maggot eggs die, Bozo will live. Our job is set."

We understood. The message was clear. One by one, we began to see ourselves as Miracle Workers fully capable of performing all medical strategies and procedures. Silently, each of us pledged to dedicate ourselves to whatever menial or surgical tasks would be assigned.

Buoyed by hope and vague, exhilarating expectations of success, we stood aside—almost at attention—as Albert and Francey carefully lifted Bozo out of the car.

Mama headed straight for the cast-iron coal stove and kindled the fire. "We have to keep the kitchen warm," she said. Normally in cool or cold weather, the fire in the kitchen stove was well stoked but allowed to die during the night. If we had a cold snap during autumn days like this, the kitchen could be bitterly cold in the morning. "The fire has to go all night," Mama warned. "We'll take turns. Eleanor, you put in extra coal when everybody is ready for bed. I'll come down twice in the middle of the night. Francey, you get up early and come down first to add fresh coal. Albert, you empty the ashes before you go to bed. We have to keep the room warm."

Mama then turned to Bozo. Although she wore her floral housedress, when she kneeled and examined Bozo's leg with all the confidence of a professional diagnostician entering the operating room, she could have been a doctor with a white jacket.

"Watch," she instructed. Eight residents-in-training closed in and looked on. Francey checked to see if the bedding, a former oilcloth table covering placed under the blanket to protect the floor from being drenched, was securely in place before he handed her the little jar with the leech stuck to the side of the glass.

Mama looked at the leech, paused, and said, "We're not using the leech."

Her last-minute change in plans unnerved us, but before we could react or question, Mama said, "I just remembered. Leeches suck blood. Bozo is too weak to lose any more blood." Relieved and reassured by her fleet assessment under pressure, we felt even more confident of her brilliant diagnostic skills.

While I certainly did not want Bozo to be leeched to death, I felt disappointed about not being exposed to the full range of surgical techniques. I really wanted to see the leech in action. Instead, I watched as Mama poured fresh water from the well into a white enamel basin and heated it on the stove. It was drinking water, not the rainwater collected in the attic cistern which we used for bathing or washing clothes.

After a few minutes, she tested the temperature with her elbow. Satisfied, she measured out a half cup of Lysol and poured it into the basin of tepid water. Pointing to the roll of cotton I was holding, she told me to unroll it and tear off a large wad about the size of man's fist. She drenched it in the amber liquid, lifted it, and gently squeezed out some of the excess liquid. Cupping one hand under the wad to catch the drips, she moved closer to Bozo and told Albert and Francey to hold him still while she swabbed the crawling maggots away from the shank of his lower limb.

Bozo squirmed and whimpered but didn't try to get up. Mama twisted the cotton, scooping up a handful of maggots within the fold; she then squeezed the cotton so that the liquid drenched the wound that enveloped his entire right rear leg.

Not quite satisfied with her "surgery," Mama took another dab at the leg and scooped up a few more maggots before standing and walking to the stove. Clutching the wad in one hand and grasping the coiled handle of the lifter in the other, she raised the stove lid and dropped the cotton swab into the flames, releasing a sizzling burst of steam as the moist wad hit the hot coals. The kitchen, already reeking with rotting flesh, worsened from the added foul smell of burning maggots and cotton.

"I'll do it three or four times before we go to bed," she muttered, speaking more to herself than to any of us.

Only then did she turn from the "surgical field" and go to the sink to wash her hands.

Genevieve and I went outside and threw up.

For the next several days, Mama swabbed away the maggots and burned the cotton swabs. She phoned Papa in the city and told him when he came home on the weekend to bring a fresh bottle of Lysol and another roll of cotton.

Gradually, the odor of Lysol and burnt cotton replaced the putrid stench in the kitchen. Through it all, like dedicated interns, we maintained our vigil, taking turns at dawn, after school, and during the night. We kept the kitchen warm and Bozo's leg moist, and we competed against each with our superior skills.

Each of us smugly described in exaggerated detail an unscheduled midnight shift we'd undertaken. Or we would flaunt our newly acquired skills with a great show of expertise: heating the water, testing it with an elbow, adding a tablespoon or two of Lysol, tearing a fistful of cotton, swirling it in the basin, removing just enough of the solution to keep it from dribbling on the blanket, then confidently squeezing it over the entire length of Bozo's wounded hind leg.

Then we would gloat, "And I did it without Bozo flinching."

Genevieve stopped crying, and Mama no longer supervised Bozo's care. She had trained her resident staff well, and the ritual become routine.

As predicted, the maggots died. After several weeks, the raw flesh began to heal and form a scab that covered the exposed bone and sinew. Albert finally gave up on his search for a large, flat fieldstone. Mama made a lemon custard cake to celebrate the day Bozo got up by himself, hobbled on three legs to the back door, whined to go outside, and did his business with newly restored pride.

CHAPTER THIRTY-THREE—STORMS

1932-33

Despite Mama's storehouse of skills, sudden storms of any kind threw her into a frenzy of fear. Dark clouds, icy hailstorms, lightning, thunder, sleet, or snow pitched her into what we kids called a fit.

During a fit, Mama's eyes would get wild, she would scream, she would bite the heel of her thumb, she would look over her shoulder and mutter, "Paura. Paura." If we didn't obey her immediately, she would throw pots or break cups. Privately, we kids considered her fits during storms a form of temporary insanity. For us, storms mostly gave rise to squeals of excitement along with shudders of fear.

We knew the fit would pass as soon as the storm subsided.

One midsummer day, Agnes and I, standing high up on two limbs in the cherry tree, picking, eating, and saving the pits until we had a mouthful, started a "pit fight." As we pelted each other until the last pit had been spit, clouds gathered and thunder rumbled. Scrambling down, we called to Gloria, Genevieve, and Evelyn out on the lawn. They were dangling earrings made of two cherries joined by the stems—doubles—which Agnes and I had dropped to the ground. They braided the cherries into necklaces. Evelyn made earrings for Charley, who wanted a necklace, too.

The girls stopped, tossed stray cherries into their laps, then gathered their dress hems into small bundles. Lifting the bundles to their belly buttons, they headed for the house.

As the next thunderclap hit, Mama, leaning against the screened back door, screamed multiple orders. "Francey, get everybody inside. Inside. Come. Quick. Bring Charley. *Inside.* Right now. Now. *Now!*"

As we scrambled toward the back door, she barked more orders.

"Agnes, go upstairs. Turn off all the lights. Eleanora. Quick, quick. Take the wash off the line."

She couldn't see Albert or Francey and kept screaming their names and yelling at the rest of us.

"Go. Run. Find them. Now. Quick. Shut the upstairs windows. *Quick!*"

Mama kept insisting that we simultaneously come inside that instant and run outside to find the boys.

Somehow, we did.

Our highly developed individual and collective knowledge of teamwork, all unspoken, vaulted each of us on a self-appointed mission. The explosive flashes of lightning that ignited hysteria in Mama always sparked a streak of spontaneous defiance in us kids. Our delight came from both our mischievous bravado against Mama's threats and our imagined triumph over the lightning bolts that Mama warned would strike us dead.

Best of all, the mixture of nature's ferocity, Mama's paralyzing fear, and our outrageous disregard of both were always a prelude to Make-Believe story time and hot cocoa in the kitchen.

I grabbed the sheets and towels from the clothesline, hollered for the boys, then buried my face in the sweet, fresh scent of cool summer air locked into their rumpled folds. Tucking and clutching loose ends, I dashed inside and tossed the bundle on the kitchen table just as Agnes jumped down the three steps into the kitchen and announced, with mock servility, "I turned off all the upstairs lights. What's next?"

Without saying a word, our eyes met. Within seconds, Agnes and I began dragging the long benches away from the table to set the stage for Make-Believe story time.

Halfway through our rearranging, we noticed Albert and

Francey on the lawn jumping up and down, heads upturned, gulping hail pellets. Agnes and I dashed around Mama and out the back door. Another brilliant flash of lightning momentarily blazoned the sky.

Mama, too slow-footed to stop us and too terrified to leave the house, screeched, "Stop. *Obey me.* Come inside. Now. Get out of the rain. Come inside. Now. *Now, now!*"

Gloria, Genevieve, Evelyn, and Charley obeyed, but we four older kids pretended the thunderclap had deafened us to her screams as we raced recklessly around the large summer gazebo on the side lawn, deliberately keeping our backs toward her, tongues outstretched, swallowing frozen hail pellets and getting drenched.

Her wails that Billy, our pony, would be struck dead if he didn't get put in the barn went unheeded. She threatened that the next bolt could strike the electric wire that hung through the trees from our house to the barn, and that it would kill me, my brothers, and Agnes. She tossed in, "And burn down the house like the Polizzi barn."

She kept it up, helpless and furious, fully aware that we were faking deafness. "Wait till you get inside. I know you hear me. I'm putting it in the Bag."

When the storm began to subside, my brothers, Agnes, and I, gloating with devilishness, dripping wet, and exhausted, disappeared from Mama's view by circling the house and sneaking inside through the front door. We tiptoed through the front vestibule into the kitchen from the stairwell. In silence, we seated ourselves on the kitchen benches and exchanged smirks, our eyes glued to the back of Mama's head as she peered out the kitchen door yelling at the top of her voice. The sudden quiet may have alerted her. She turned and faced us.

Without missing a beat, the four of us saluted like stiff, obedient soldiers and squealed in unison, "We're here!"

Relieved to find us safely corralled and within her reach, she, like a benevolent dictator, conceded victory. Besides, we knew any show of courage on our part—including defiance—made her extra proud. With an exaggerated look of resignation, she shook her head toward the ceiling, gave thanks to Jesus, and tossed dry towels at us from the pile on the table.

"If you get pneumonia," she warned, "it's what you deserve. Go. Check everything again. Move the wash to the dining room table. I'll make cocoa."

I searched Mama's face, wondering if she had put our scheming in the Bag or if our fearlessness had made her feel so proud, she forgot.

Grabbing towels and drying ourselves, we scattered, feigning contrition, racing upstairs, and overdoing everything, pretending another storm was on its way. We slammed windows shut, secured shutters that didn't need securing, faked panic, and yelled for Bozo to hurry in, the whole time imitating Mama and shouting orders to each other with wild screams. We took special delight in yelling orders Mama had overlooked from her repertoire.

"Check the attic window. See if any water leaked into the basement."

"Be sure the candle under the Virgin is still lit."

"Find the cat. The *caaaat*."

"Lights out. All lights *out*."

Breathless, we returned to the kitchen, pretending extreme exhaustion. Albert dropped to the floor as though dead. Mama, now over her fit, used the heel of her shoe to nudge him out from underfoot and grunted, her face distorted with a mixture of disdain, relief, and spent anger.

She set down the last of our odd assortment of mugs, each filled with hot cocoa topped with thick whipped cream. Agnes, whose tone had been especially mean-spirited during our charade, got a quick slap on the back of her head as she sat down.

Was Mama emptying Agnes' Bag?

Slowly, sipping and slurping, mostly having forgotten the pinches and slaps, we kids eased into a quiet mood. Halfway through cocoa, Albert sang, "Mama is a scaredy-cat, afraid of rain, and that's that."

Unable to resist his charm, Mama smiled. "Your voice is strong, but you can't carry a tune." Looking hard at the rest of us, her mood grew solemn. "You don't know what nature can do. Nature has no religion. She has no mercy." Moving her head side to side, her face somber, she continued. "That crossing. That crossing." We knew she was thinking of her ocean voyage to America. "The storm almost sank the ship. The storm lasted three days and three nights. I'll never get over the fear."

Gloria, ever eager for a semblance of order, urged her on. "Tell us about how the ship almost sank, about the three days and nights."

"You've heard it."

"Tell us again."

There was a chorus of requests, one voice over the other.

"Tell us about Ellis Island, and the streets of New York."

"No, start with how the storm became captain of the ship."

"More about *Pa-ooo-ra*," said Albert, sounding spooky, trying to frighten us.

Our pleading and prompting loosened Mama's lips into a half-smile as her body relaxed. She took a deep breath, sat down on the end of one of the long benches, and sighed.

We kids, slurping and sniffing the sweet cocoa, covertly competing via eye contact for the biggest white mustache, straddled the benches, huddled for warmth, and waited.

Mama reached across the long table toward a pile of fresh unshelled peas. Picking them up one by one, she carefully pinched them open, ran her thumb in the groove, and dropped the peas into a blue enamel bowl. Periodically, she gazed out the darkened wet window.

"Paura. *Pa-ooo-ra*," she mouthed in Italian, so low we could barely hear, much less fully understand her meaning of the word. Did she whisper because she feared Papa's rule prohibiting her from speaking Italian? Or did she whisper because she was afraid Paura might be in the room?

Mama cleared her voice, but she remained silent. Even the storm grew silent. The only sound in the kitchen was that of crisp peas dropping into the bowl.

I checked out the half-open back door. Was Paura lurking close by? Listening?

"Talk like Paura," I begged. She shook her head as if to say she didn't know how Paura spoke.

Mama's eyes scanned ours, each pair asking her to begin. She put the peas aside, dropped her hands to her lap, smoothed her housedress over her knees, and began.

Mama spoke as though to an invisible stranger. "When we landed—three days before Christmas—there was nothing but rain to greet us. No candles in any windows of the tall buildings, no red decorations or holy crosses in doorways, no children racing around selling necklaces of roasted chickpeas, no musicians with accordions, no choir boys singing 'Ave Maria.' Nothing to celebrate. Nothing to celebrate."

In little bursts and pauses, she recalled everything she saw that rainy night in lower Manhattan. Everything was wet or gray or dirty: the dark, gray sky; the gray cobblestone streets; the wet and muddy pavement; the slabs of wet gray newspaper stuck to railings on fire escapes; the black clumps of dirt on unpaved streets; the dark hats that men wore; the trash that littered the gutters; the foul smell of burning garbage; the stench of horse manure and urine swirling in puddles; the gruff sounds of foreign voices; the pushing and shoving, everyone looking down, watching their feet, fearful of where they stepped. Mama, sighing deeply, said it was an ominous sign.

"Nothing golden. Nothing golden." She gnawed the side of her lower lip. "I let myself be deceived." Her chest heaved, and we sighed with her, even Evelyn, who usually seemed lost in her own thoughts. Charley searched our faces trying to understand. I snuggled him close.

"I vowed never again to believe anyone without questioning. Without questioning hard." Her voice quivered and her eyes roved, locking on ours. "What you hear, question hard. Question. Always question."

"If I could have forgotten my fear . . . if I could have forgotten the waves crashing against the side of the ship, waves so high they took the two masts under, I would have taken the next boat back to sunny Chieti." She paused, and we waited. "During the fourteen-day crossing, everything I ate came back up. When we landed on Ellis Island, my dress hung off my shoulders like a loose sheet. The ocean taught me about the force, the treachery of nature. And the ship, the *Prinzess Irene*—she taught me a lesson . . . about the struggle to survive. Throughout the crossing, I prayed for the ship. I prayed for it to hold up against the heavy blows. So loud they hurt my ears. I prayed for quiet. I prayed for my life."

Mama told how she covered her ears with a woolen coat, trying to muffle the roar of the ocean, but also the constant moans of ailing passengers who lay in long rows in the cavernous hold of steerage, stacked like animals in tier after tier of bunks that ran the entire length and breadth of the ship.

Silences were followed by thunderous crashes against the hull, heightening the yowls of babies and screams of terrified children. All hours of the night and day, men cursed and women prayed, every voice a different dialect. Mama's hands turned white and stiff with cramps from clutching the metal bunk rails for hours and hours. The force of the storm that battered the hull heaved the weak passengers into each other's bunks. Those who tumbled out, unable to hang on to the metal pipes that served as guardrails, fell into the narrow aisles and smeared their clothes and bare arms with slimy straw—straw that was soaked with urine, diarrhea, and vomit—and cloaked them with a sickening stench.

"For three long days and nights, Paura was captain. She trapped everyone's breath. No one breathed in fear the ship would go under as it rose and fell hundreds of feet. Three days black as night. Ehhh . . ."

Mama's voice trailed into a whisper. "Paura. Paura. She stayed with us the whole time. More than a thousand passengers scared day and night. Paura never left. Never. The storm delayed the ship three days. Three days late to land on Ellis Island. Three days before Christmas and nothing but icy cold rain to greet us." As if she were reliving the trip, she repeated, "No holy crosses in the windows, no old men selling roasted chestnuts, no altar boys singing 'Ava Maria'." Mama sighed, her lips trembled, and she began to weep softly.

We sat in silence, exchanging looks of fear and wonder, sighing in unison, and as always, when tears welled in Mama's eyes, Agnes, Gloria, Genevieve, and I wept with her. Even Francey.

Charley looked at Evelyn who, like Albert, never cried. But when Charley saw the rest of us crying, he cried, too.

Mama's storytelling held us captive. She transported us with recollections of her homeland, her mother, her terrifying crossing. During storms at the farm, when electric lines fell, we would sit huddled around the black, cast-iron coal stove in the kitchen, waiting for the lights to come back on, and Mama would tell and retell stories about her childhood in Italy, her sister Tia Marietta, her mother—who failed to keep the teachings of the Catholic nuns—and about *las maestras* and the two old peasant women whose milk and cheese gave Mama her strong white teeth. She told stories about her dreams of coming to America and making something of herself, and stories about George, the tall, fair-haired, blue-eyed suitor who had promised to follow her to America.

As long as the rain continued and the lights failed to come back on, we pleaded with her to retell her stories over and over. And she did. If she forgot a detail, one of us would remind her and fill in what she had left out. We memorized each variation, and we elaborated at will, improvising scene after scene: Mama threatening to kill herself if her mother didn't sign the legal papers allowing her to come to America; Mama stealing milk behind the tree; Mama waving goodbye to George in the traditional

Italian way, not side to side with palm facing out, but instead stretching her arm then repeatedly curling her hand back toward her heart, beckoning.

Often, we played Make-Believe, creating theatrical performances to cheer her up. We would find Mama sitting in the kitchen, staring out the window, neither cooking nor singing, alone in a world of her own. Was she thinking about her friend Giulia in Brooklyn? Or Mrs. Gould? Or George? Was she holding a grudge against Papa for leaving us? Or was she sensing Paura's presence?

Ever eager to lift her sadness, we would cluster around her with prompts to sing a particular aria or prods about her life in Italy.

"Did you miss your mother?"

"I missed *las maestras*."

"Did you miss George?" She didn't answer.

"Why did you come to America?"

"To make something of myself. Depending on others is hard on your pride."

Raising her head, Mama would study us with one of her many wise looks and preach. "Keeping your pride is everything." I wasn't sure what keeping my pride meant, other than if you kept it, you could lift your head high and hold your chin stuck out the way she did. I practiced imitating her in the bedroom mirror and liked the way I looked. I felt like Mama.

Proud.

Other times, when my sisters and I were alone with Mama and wanted to play Make-Believe, we begged, "Tell us again about George." This request always made her voice grow soft and her eyelids lower.

Mama never spoke of George if Papa or our older brothers were in the room. That made George extra special. We girls shared a secret the boys and Papa never learned.

And when Charley begged to be told, we gave in and swore

him to secrecy.

"Does that make me a girl?" he asked.

"No," Evelyn said. "It makes you, *you*."

It didn't seem at all strange to me or my younger siblings to hear Mama reminisce about her lost love. It was just part of Make-Believe, another story. Talking about George made her eyes sparkle. It gave us an early glimpse into the romantic heart she kept hidden from grown-ups like Aunt Mary or Aunt Esther. Maybe even Papa.

Mama still yearned for George; I could tell by the tenderness in her voice when she mentioned his name. I believed she felt more love for him than for Papa. I believed I knew George better than I knew Uncle Tony or Uncle Pete or Uncle Frank. Maybe I knew George better than I knew Papa.

George was fair-haired and had large blue eyes Mama described as looking like the northern sky. She said his family came from Tuscany. "Blue, blue eyes, light hair. He didn't speak loud and common. He never interrupted women. Always a book under his arm. Tall, not like your father."

Gloria once asked Mama why she hadn't stayed in Italy and married him. "I believed he would follow me. When I told him that I had saved enough money to go to America and make something of myself, he took my left hand and promised to come later. I believed him. I believed him."

Her expression would change as her mouth tightened. "His mother wanted him to become a priest. He was her only son. It was the custom." She would grow quiet. "I should have known better. I should have known. I waited four years. He never wrote."

For a few moments, she became lost in thought. She heaved a long, deep breath. We sighed with her. Hearing us, she straightened her back and met our eyes. Mama was back in America. Back in our kitchen. Make-Believe was over. She ended it as she so often did—with a warning. "Question promises. Question promises. Don't take them for granted. Question hard."

CHAPTER THIRTY-FOUR—
MAKING ENDS MEET

1934

When I was in my early teens, Mama taught me about my first period. One morning I entered the kitchen telling Mama that I must have hurt myself because I was bleeding.

"No," she said, "that's a sign." She smiled, came close, spit on her thumbs, and smoothed my eyebrows. "Go upstairs and get the sewing basket. I'll make the *seckla*"—a strip of soft diaper folded and refolded into a two-inch wide strip. She rummaged through the sewing basket, took out a strip of elastic, put it around my waist, cut it to size, and said, "Go sew the ends together and put it over your belly." As I stood before before her, she tucked the neatly folded strip of soft diaper between my legs, draped the ends over the elastic, snugged the *seckla* between my legs, and pinned it in place over the elastic front and back. "There. Make yourself three or four *secklas.* You need to change them often. Before you go to bed, wash them. Let them air dry."

"Do I wear these for the rest of my life?"

She laughed. "No. Once a month for three or four days. This happens to all girls when they turn thirteen or fourteen, like you. Go. Cut up the rest of the diaper and fold them the way you like. I'm going to bake a chocolate cake with poppy seeds for tonight to celebrate."

It was springtime in 1933 when Mama barged through the door, yelling, "Quick, quick," and setting a big cardboard box on the kitchen table.

We gathered around while she showed us its contents—several dozen eggs, each one wrapped inside a crumpled page torn from an old Sears catalogue. She said we were going to hatch them.

"Hatch them?" we chorused.

We would use the dining room for a breeding coop. First, we needed to turn the table into a big nest to "incubate" the eggs. *Incubate* was a fancy word Mama must have learned at the feed store. I liked the sound of it and started humming, "ink-u-bate, ink-u-bate," while clearing a large pile of clean but wrinkled clothes from the table and dumping it into an armchair.

Pretty soon we were all singing, "Ink-u-bate baby chickens, Ink-u-bate like the dickens," to the tune of "Celeste Aida." Our singing grew louder and louder. Albert turned on the Victrola and pretty soon Enrico Caruso sang along with us.

Singing didn't interfere with our project. We covered the large table with oilcloth to protect its shiny mahogany surface, collected old newspapers and Sears catalogues, and—imitating Mama—tore the paper into shreds. We competed to see who tore the most into the smallest shreds.

Once mounds of shredded paper littered the table, Mama opened the drawer to the sideboard, took out several tablecloths, and began rolling them into logs. "Go. Run upstairs. Get some clean bed sheets. Roll them up around the edge of the table. We have to fence them in."

I wondered if Mama had learned how to incubate chickens in Italy when she learned to milk a cow and make cheese, but she seemed too intent on getting the coop set up to answer questions. Instead, I helped finish making the fence.

That task done, we imitated Mama in picking up an egg and carefully hiding it in the shredded paper. Mama reminded Francey that he would have to keep the furnace going for the next three weeks to be sure the eggs stayed warm during the chilly spring nights. To the rest of us she said we would act like mother hens and shuffle the eggs once or twice a day, rolling them around under the paper.

After twenty-one days, just as Mama had predicted, the shredded paper began to jiggle. One by one, the hatchlings began to peep. Mama set a bowl full of water in the middle of the table. Francey tucked small stones inside the rolled linen logs to anchor the fence and keep the chicks from falling off the table. Albert put a handful of his marbles inside the bowl of water to keep it from getting knocked over.

Soon the dining room reeked from the stench of baby chicks' droppings. Soon the kitchen and the vestibule smelled just as bad until eventually the fluffy chicks stank up the whole house. Gloria wouldn't go near the dining room and screamed if anyone left the door to the girls' bedroom open. She complained constantly about our house being filthy and said, "If we did this in the city, the Public Health Nurse would report us. Even Mrs. Gould." Eyeing the ceiling above Mama's head with a dirty look, she added, "And she should."

Gloria threatened to sleep on the cold porch. "If I get diphtheria again . . ."

She didn't finish her threats, just nagged and nagged. Mama let Gloria carry on without getting in the least upset, until she couldn't take it anymore and announced it was time to move the chicks into the chicken coop as the days were getting warmer.

From the moment Mama relented, Gloria took charge and oversaw the entire transition. Acting like a sergeant from West Point, she ordered the boys to make a fresh paper nest in the sunniest area of the coop. Then she demonstrated how we girls should lift our skirts, tuck the hem into a tight knot near our belly buttons, and gently cuddle five or six chicks into these sacks. Marching like a soldier, she led us out of the house and into the chicken coop where she deposited her despised possessions.

After the chicks were moved, sheets washed, and the dining room cleaned up, Gloria said moving them didn't help. The house still stank. Through all of Gloria's grunts and groans of disgust, even her threats to sleep outside, Mama acted like she never heard them. Out of earshot, however, Mama would affectionately whisper, "Schoomazoot," for Gloria was the neatest and most orderly, and like Mama, the most outspoken. And Mama said Gloria resembled Tia Marietta, Mama's sister.

When asked why Mama never got mad at Gloria, she said, "She always speaks the truth." And Mama obediently followed Gloria's orders to keep the dining room windows open day and night for more than a week.

With the chicks settled into their new nest, Mama started buying bags filled with stale baked goods to supplement the expensive chicken feed. We kids got first pickings. Mama let us dig through the stash for Twinkies before giving the rest to the chickens, which she said would lay eggs and provide meat for minestrone. Mama said we were taking steps in learning how to plan ahead.

Perhaps it was the heightened awareness of the need to plan ahead or salvage and save which caused six-year-old Evelyn to cry with fear when she tripped and tore her dress. I told her to stop crying. I would make her a new one if she helped me gather dry clothes on the line.

Once inside, I rummaged through the freshly laundered pile of clothes until I found a floral-print feed bag slated to be cut up as dish towels or turned into a pillowcase. I ironed it and spread it out on the dining room table, then asked Evelyn to climb up and lie on top of it. One end came to just below her knees, the other under her chin. I asked her to spread her arms to keep them away from the scissors. I felt like a grown-up dressmaker. Like Mama.

Starting from the bottom, I cut up the sides until I got to her armpits. Stumped, I asked her to roll over, first to one side, then to the other. But now what? I had no idea how to proceed.

I ran upstairs and found one of Evelyn's sleeveless summer hand-me-downs. Back in the dining room, I told Evelyn to get up. I needed to trace the curved arm opening and round neckline. An hour later, I had stitched the sides and shoulders together, and Evelyn sported a new dress—with two pockets so she could tell front from back. Nobody seemed to notice the too-large neckline that allowed Evelyn's head to fit through.

Mama seemed dazzled. "When you grow up, you will be famous. Like Schiaparelli, the Italian designer." I had no idea who she was talking about. But I felt proud.

From that day on, once homework and ironing were out of the way, I spent most of my time after school sewing. In winter I sewed school skirts for myself and my sisters. In summer I sewed halter tops and culottes. At Penny's department store we could buy scraps big enough to make triangular halter tops that covered our flat chests but were bare in back.

Years later, when the boy who would later become her husband invited Gloria to her first school prom, she and I knew Mama couldn't afford to buy a fancy dress. I remembered the scene in *Gone with the Wind* during which Scarlett O'Hara ripped down the drapes to make a dress. Although Mama demanded obedience to her requests, she never said no to anything any one of us wanted to do. I asked if I could cut two strips from the heavy turquoise satin drapes in the parlor. They were so heavily tucked, nobody would ever notice what I removed.

Mama gave me the go-ahead and I made a pleated skirt topped with a fitted bodice. Gloria, taller and slimmer than the rest of us, looked radiant. But I knew how to make it even more stunning—if only I could use the hand-embroidered, silver metallic scarf atop the bureau in Mama's bedroom.

It was one of the few items Mama had brought from Italy when she came to America. It had been for her trousseau. The fabric was half a yard wide and a foot and a half long. I wanted to overlay the bodice of Gloria's prom dress with this delicately embroidered runner.

"Cut. Cut," said Mama.

Gloria looked like the belle of the ball.

Genevieve wore it to her school proms, and Evelyn wore it to Genevieve's wedding.

CHAPTER THIRTY-FIVE—
ROSETON BEACH

1936

A s soon as the door closed behind a newcomer who might be a salesman, someone seeking a job, or a religious Evangelist, Mama, speaking to no one in particular, would comment upon or imitate a specific trait or shortcoming, and her caricatures would end up in our collective repertoire of merciless imitations. It could be a similarity to a movie star or a mild lisp or twitch, an affectation, anything that caught her fancy to mock in jest or pique. We kids immediately (but mostly to best her) imitated or amplified her caricature.

She might say, "Her eyes bulge like Joan Crawford, but she looks more like a frog." Or she might caution, "He smiles too quick. Not honest." Or "His eyes are too shifty. Can't trust him." Sometimes, after taking a few moments to reflect, she might add, mouth taut and nodding resolutely to herself as though bringing closure to an inner debate, "He's a whoremaster."

One day our neighbor Mrs. Talbert dropped by to pick up some ripe Alberta peaches to can for the winter. This simple woman became the unfortunate object of our delight. She had already been branded—Mrs. T. Who Talks a Lot and Says Nothing—and her infrequent visits brought out outrageous behind-her-back competitions. She spoke by elongating her vowels in a peculiar crescendo. The minute she started talking, one, two, or three of us took positions behind her back, facing Mama. As Mrs. T. talked—almost nonstop—we kids would make comical grimaces.

Each time she used a vowel, we rolled our eyes, twirled our heads, and swayed our bodies, crouching low and slowly sliding to tiptoe in slow-moving arabesques, silently mouthing "tooo" or "gooo" or "paaay" or "eeeeat."

Mama, forced to control her temper, avoided eye contact with each of us and pretended not to notice. We took extra delight in this momentary tyranny, and our theatrics became more and more daring and exuberant. Taking turns, one of us moved and stood alongside Mama, facing Mrs. Talbert, and ever so subtly raised our eyebrows, open and closed our mouths in "Os," and slowly wobbled our heads in mock attentiveness.

As soon as Mrs. Talbert left and was out of earshot, Mama, laughing at our antics, began to waddle back and forth across the kitchen like a drunken duck. "And how come you didn't notice she walks like this?"

Exploding with joy and squealing with laughter, we started imitating Mama imitating Mrs. Talbert. Each of us, Mama included, improvised, shifting between imitations of Mrs. Talbert's walk and the *toooing, goooing, caaaning,* and *eeeeating,* until Francey, coming into the kitchen, yelled over the din, "Who wants to go swimming?"

Francey had recently obtained his driver's license and took every opportunity to get behind the wheel of Mama's Ford. He announced that he and Albert—finished with carrying crates to the tomato field—had put on their bathing trunks and were ready to leave. Like fireflies, the rest of us darted about; some grabbed bathing suits helter-skelter from the clothesline on the side lawn, others sorted through the pile on the dining room table, and within minutes everyone landed in the car, three in front, four in back.

Mama told us to be gone no more than an hour or so. The day laborers would be bringing in tomatoes for us to help sort and pack for market.

She caught my attention, held my gaze, and said, "Be careful. Watch Charley. You know he can't swim."

As we headed toward the Hudson River, I hugged our six-year-old on my lap and started to play "counting backward one-by-one from ten."

Before Francey got his license, we often took a shortcut to the beach through neighbors' orchards and pastures, sipping water from the spring at the Westlakes' farm on the way. Our pace always picked up as we got close to the swimming hole.

Showing off, we'd race down the short, steep slope of the bluff that rose above the railroad tracks, each grabbing a branch of the young sapling to steady our slippery slides. When we hit solid ground we raced toward a dead end from the county road that was used as a parking lot.

Adjacent to the makeshift parking lot, local handiwork had carefully fashioned a large opening in the barbed wire fence, all the sharp, cut ends turned back, allowing easy access across the railroad tracks to the beach. Locals had nicknamed this cove in the Hudson River the Roseton Beach after its township name.

Once Francey got his license, we seldom walked. Francey always drove, parking close to the barbed wire opening.

"Last one in has a double chin," we screamed as we tumbled out of the old Ford.

Climbing through the opening, everyone but Albert leapt over the railroad tracks and ran across the dry stubble and wild grasses down the path to the water. Taking cover behind bushes and towels, we quickly changed into our bathing suits. Albert took the longest to undress, leaving his artificial leg inside his trousers under a bush before hopping on one leg into the water. It pained me to see him hop across the sand and belly flop into the water. He, however, splashed and swam, had water fights, and chatted with other swimmers. But he didn't sunbathe.

When I realized we had stayed too long, I changed into dry clothes under a towel and yelled, "We have to leave. Hurry."

Everyone else dawdled, but I headed toward the car, yelling that we would get in trouble if they weren't quick. No one followed. After a few minutes, I pounded on the horn and held it loud and long. Looking up, I saw Charley on the far side of the second row of tracks. He turned his head toward the roar of a train on his right, then started to leap across the far tracks and run toward the car.

"Wait! Wait!" I screamed. He looked panicked but sped toward me, trying to outrun the train. My wild cries were muffled by the deafening roar of churning black wheels that blotted the sunlight.

Out of the swirling bits of flying debris and the roar of the passing freight cars, Paura appeared and clutched me in a suffocating, swirling cocoon of blue-white light and black air. As the roar diminished, I peered through the blurry haze. Shrieking like a crazed beast, I searched the horizon.

Charley was gone.

He must have run back to the beach.

Soon, everyone on the beach, young and old, searched for my baby brother. Holding hands, people made a long human net and waded through the water. Several young priests from Oblate House, a nearby seminary descended the hillside from their sanctuary.

I couldn't move, my eyes fixed on the airless space where I had last seen Charley, racing in his small blue trunks, one knee raised high.

Paura was everywhere, darkening the sun, her robe taunting me. I fought to breathe.

One of the men in a small group near a clump of brush about fifty feet down the track raised both his arms to shield Genevieve from approaching. She ducked under his arms, screamed, covered her eyes, turned away, doubled over, and vomited. So, too, did I.

Strangers appeared from nowhere, their mouths moving soundlessly. I could hear nothing but the roar of the train. A sheriff's car arrived. Then another police car. One of the priests shepherded my three sisters toward the car where I stood. He called my brothers and motioned for all of us to get inside, then slid into the driver's seat. He drove us home, stiff, shrunken, and silent. Paura's shadow blanketed me in icy cold black silence.

As we entered the driveway, sound returned. First the pebbles churning under the car, then Mama's voice from the back doorway. Catching sight of the priest, Mama wailed like a primal beast before anyone said a word. "My baby. My baby."

Within an hour, Papa arrived from the city with Agnes, who had been visiting Aunt Mary. His car screeched to a halt outside the back door, and he rushed inside, leaving the car door swinging back and forth like a large broken black wing.

Three days later, everything in the parlor was icy cold and unreal, everything and every mourner encased in a glassy haze. The Victrola, the piano, the turquoise draperies—everything was covered with floral-scented frozen air. Paura hovered above the casket, barely visible, yet tangible enough to cast a shadow over the crucifix of white carnations mounted above the small white coffin. Her shadow moved, raising the scent of carnations.

Paura turned toward me, and I saw someone who looked like me, standing in a wrinkled lavender dress in the distant corner of the dining room, far from the wide opening into the parlor, the heavy oak pocket doors out of sight. Paura snatched the *girl's* breath and held it, then drifted closer to my younger sisters and brothers, forcing them to sigh and gasp for air. She didn't go near Mama.

Mr. Toohey, the broad-shouldered, thick-chested Irish undertaker, assumed the role of official greeter. His enormous frame, strong and solid, cut through the haze that blurred my vision. He strode about with studied courtesy—almost cheerful—welcoming visitors or bidding them goodbye in his robust baritone. His rosy cheeks, his overly pleasant smile, his bigger-than-life bulk sickened me and twisted a jagged black bone into the lining of my stomach.

Paura floated toward me. A sudden swirling cocoon of blazing light enveloped my body and thrusted me from the dining room, into the front vestibule, away from everyone. For the remainder of the two-day wake, day and night, outside, I swayed back and forth on the old wooden glider on the small side of the front porch, unseen.

A steady stream of neighbors, aunts, uncles, cousins—even strangers—came and went like ghosts, many through the back door. Others—Italian farmers we hardly knew, teachers past and present, the Phelps family, including all six of their children, Mr. Rusk from Marlboro Bank, the veterinarian, Dr. Allott, even the pastor from the Protestant church—all drove slowly up the lane, left their cars, and tiptoed quietly through the wide front door into the dim vestibule, walking past the life-size Carrara marble statue of a Victorian child reprimanding a cat for having killed a fledgling bird lying dead at her feet.

As cars lined up behind the hearse and mourners began to leave for St. Joseph's Catholic Church in Marlboro, Francey searched for me. He looked frantic. His watery eyes met mine.

Without a word, he took my arm, eased me up from the glider, and guided me into the vestibule. As we neared the door to the adjoining parlor, I hesitated. Papa sat slumped over on the edge of the kitchen bench against the wall next to the casket, his slight, thin body folded in half. He looked like a puppet rocking back and forth, his eyes dull and unseeing, repeating a low wail, *"Piu bello figlio. Piu bello figlio."* Most beautiful son.

Mr. Toohey walked to the corner of the adjacent dining room. He stood over Mama, whose back was toward the parlor. His hand rested on her shoulder as he gently urged her to rise from the armchair. She wore her black Sunday dress and sobbed uncontrollably. My four younger sisters, also dressed for church, huddled around her, sobbing in unison. Cousin Esther stood behind them, looking like a stranger, and stared out the bay window toward the heavy hedge that framed the lawn.

For the first two days of the wake, Mama lay on her bed in her housedress, her back to the bedroom door, one arm covering her eyes. Francey pleaded with her repeatedly to go downstairs and grant visitors a few moments of consolation, but she would not stir. She refused to enter the parlor. She would not look inside the casket. Now, as last-minute mourners approached her stooped frame, they struggled to find words of comfort. None succeeded.

Deaf to their mumblings, she repeated over and over, her voice a long, low sigh of blame, self-pity, and rage, *"Gesu, perché? Perché?* Why? Thirteen years ago—*el primo bambino.* And now my last. My baby. *Ma non pecare.* Why punish me? *Se no ono, ma duo. Duo. Perché?"* She paused. Turning toward Father Joseph, who had given last rites, she mumbled, almost inaudible and directed at the wall, "I would curse Him. Curse Him. But He has no mercy. He would take a third."

Father Joseph lowered his head and left the room.

Francey nudged me. "They're going to close the casket. Come. You have to say goodbye." My feet were stone. I could not move. He pleaded, "I'll go with you." He pushed against my back and guided me close to the coffin. We knelt. Charley lay on shimmering, white satin.

Stunned, I almost cried out, *It's a trick. It's Make-Believe. He isn't dead. There's only a small scratch on his forehead. The train didn't kill him.*

I looked with disbelief at Francey, who read my thoughts. Carefully, tenderly, he raised my wrist and placed my hand over Charley's small fingers, which curled around Mama's lavender rosary beads. I muffled a gasp and pulled away from the cold marble beneath my palm.

Not Make-Believe.

Mr. Toohey, towering above the short, stocky Italian men in the room, moved closer to the casket. He touched my shoulder lightly, then reached toward the lid.

Wait. Don't. Charley's only wearing his long-sleeved white cotton shirt. He's cold. I'll get him his sweater.

The lid slammed shut.

Uncle Pete, Uncle Frank, and Aunt Angelina's grown sons, Justin and Sol, placed the cross of flowers on the closed casket and lifted it awkwardly. They carried it into the vestibule and out the wide front door.

The rooms, almost devoid of people, felt twice their normal size. Hollow. Mama rose like a sleepwalker and followed the coffin. She never looked inside. As she walked toward the door, she turned and beckoned my sisters and Cousin Esther, her hand curling toward her heart with the same gesture she used to wave goodbye.

She whispered, *"Veni. Veni."* Come. Come.

As they filed out, Francey took a step toward Mama, but she turned away. Her eyelids dropped, closing contact with me and Francey. The last two in the room, we remained still. Mr. Toohey, his frame filling the entire doorway, turned to face us. He smiled broadly. "Perhaps the next time we meet, it'll be at a clam bake."

The jagged black bone pierced my gut. I wanted to hit him. Hard. Hard. *Hard.*

During the next few weeks, our home changed into a silent tomb. No one mentioned Charley's name. No one spoke. We avoided each other's eyes, never using our language of looks. To do so would cause heartbreaking sobs. Instead, we shrouded ourselves in separate silences.

Mama's grief magnified and complicated our own. She stayed in bed day and night, her face turned away, her back to the bedroom door, her forearm over her eyes. She didn't brush her hair or pin up her heavy black braid, and she refused food. She slept in her housedress, and when she did rise—to check the little votive candle in the alcove on the landing to the attic, keeping it lit day and night—her wrinkled dress hung on her like a loose shawl. Her strong, sturdy frame looked shrunken and bent.

Papa stayed home at first, preoccupied and unsure about whether he should remain on the farm, stay with Aunt Mary in Brooklyn, or return to Florida.

In contrast to the guarded behavior and heavy silence of our collective sorrow, Papa needed noise. And he never slept. He disappeared into the basement and rattled things around in the middle of the night. Early the next morning, after slamming the back door, he revved up the engine of his Packard and drove down the lane to arrange and rearrange the setup of our small fruit stand near the highway, where each continued to take turns, finding respite in solitude while we waited for people to stop and buy fruit.

After a week, Papa wasn't around when we woke up, and he stayed in the city for longer and longer spells.

Then he stopped coming home.

CHAPTER THIRTY-SIX—GRIEF

L eft to ourselves, we kids felt a new, unbidden tenderness rise among us. No snide slurs, no endless arguments over who was right or wrong, or best, or first or last. No merciless, vulgar caricatures or imitations of anyone or anything. No loud, competitive strivings. Each, lost and alone, wandered in a foreign land, treading aimlessly, desperate to ease each other's pain.

We set the table without a sound, each bowl placed with cautious gentleness on the bare oak tabletop. No one smacked at flies or jumped down the stairs. No doors slammed. My sisters and I busied ourselves by endlessly sweeping the halls, cleaning the medicine cabinet, polishing banisters, rearranging dishes in the pantry closet, and nesting forks and spoons in the wide silverware drawer. The boys invented problems with spark plugs and battery cables, doing and undoing tasks to start the car or stop it.

At night, after supper, we gathered on the wide front porch. Some of us sat on the railing of the long section of the U-shaped porch, while others sat on the shortest side We sat side-by-side or alone, not stirring the glider, pretending interest in the fireflies. No one tried to catch any, nor did my brothers try to hoard them or smear their arms and act like they were flying streaks of lightning. We listened to the frogs and crickets and hoped Mama found solace in sleep.

Evelyn was the quietest of all. She was the most withdrawn; she never cried, never stared out a window to follow the flight of a bird or noticed the splatter of rain on a windowsill. She moved through each day like a marionette, her face fixed, her eyes turned inward, mysteriously connected to some universe far, far away.

Often, I found her standing in front of the votive candle that burned day and night. Her lips moved in a silent prayer. Just as often, she left the house and stood waiting in the driveway, motionless, looking toward the Hudson River. To me, she looked smaller than before. Paler. Now she was the baby in the family—a role I knew she didn't want.

One night I heard her slip out from under the sheets at the bottom of the bed she shared with Agnes and me. Without a sound, she walked to the closet, found one of Charley's white shirts, slipped it on, then walked to the narrow bed where Charley had slept and climbed in. She lay on her back with her eyes closed, holding very still, her arms crossed with one hand over the other holding her white prayer book. From then on, each night she moved from our bed to Charley's.

Not long afterward, on a cold September evening, I glimpsed Evelyn from the kitchen window, kneeling outside by the high stone wall next to the lane that led to the Hudson River. She was on her knees, praying before a small alter she created out of round white stones she had gathered each day on her way home from school.

Inside, the kitchen felt warm from the fire Francey had built in the coal stove. Outside, the chilled air was frosty, and Evelyn, wearing a thin cotton dress, looked cold. I searched for a sweater, went outside, and cautiously put it around her shoulders. She didn't seem to notice. Her hands were clasped in prayer.

I recalled hearing Mrs. Hamilton, the gentle Balmville schoolteacher, tell Mama, her voice wistful, as though she wished it weren't true, "Evelyn is different from your other girls."

Unlike the rest of us, Evelyn never poked fun, she didn't mock, she didn't pretend she was a foreigner who never spoke an intelligible language the way we older girls did when we went shopping. Instead, she spent her time playing with Charley.

Had Charley kept her anchored in this world?

Standing close, I wanted to stroke her uncombed hair but couldn't move. The little nine-year-old I had helped nurture from infancy was gone. Her eyes were unreadable. She hadn't noticed the sweater over her shoulders. She had traveled elsewhere, out of reach. The child I mothered was gone. Forever lost in a reality of her making.

Over time, Mama began to come downstairs, briefly at first during the middle of the night, then for longer periods of time during the day. We kids became more alert, more vigilant, desperate to anticipate her needs, eager to do her bidding. She never spoke and often burst out in uncontrollable sobs. She appeared unaware of our presence, moving about, preparing a meal absentmindedly, then disappearing upstairs to her bedroom.

As for Papa, Aunt Mary phoned to tell Mama he had turned his face to the wall and wouldn't get out of bed.

"When I bring him soup, he tella me he eat later. An when I coma back, he no touch a drop."

Because Mama and the rest of us had stopped talking, nobody asked questions of Aunt Mary.

One morning I heard Mama moving around upstairs. She spoke to Agnes. "Maybe if you had been with them, Charley would still be here."

Agnes started to cry.

Mama sobbed, and in a strange, hoarse voice, she said, "Come. Let's go to the cemetery."

I waited out of sight in the pantry. Footsteps went out the door to the car. From the big kitchen window, I watched the car lurch and disappear behind the fieldstone wall at the end of the driveway. I leaned my head against the cool glass and kept it there for a long time, not moving. No one was nearby. I could weep in privacy.

But I was wrong. Francey stood next to me, his hand sweeping aside droplets of tears from the windowsill. I didn't know if they were his or mine.

The only one who continued with his normal routine was Henry Brown. Every morning, he milked the cow, put the big animals out to pasture, cleaned their stalls, and fed the chickens. He stopped whistling, but now and then, picking the right moment, in his soft voice he would urge one or another of us, "Perk up. Life go on."

One morning, after tap-tap-tapping, he shuffled his lean frame through the back door. His eyes lit up as he caught a rare glimpse of Mama at the stove stirring oatmeal.

Standing with the bucket of milk and talking to her back, Henry Brown reminded her of our annual ritual. "Time to take the young 'uns shoppin' for new shoes?"

It sounded like a question, but Mama didn't respond. He continued, his voice softer, "School be startin' soon."

Mama kept stirring the oatmeal, staring at the wooden spoon going around and around in the pot.

Henry waited in the doorway for a moment, then proceeded into the kitchen and carefully poured the milk through the strainer into the big white pitcher the way Mama usually did. I wasn't sure if Mama had heard a word.

But the next morning, Mama put on a clean church dress and called, "Wash up and get in the car. It's time to get new shoes. School starts in a couple of weeks."

But before school started, two men drove into the driveway and parked outside the back door, where Mama absentmindedly swept the stone step. They wore suits and ties and one asked politely, "Mrs. DeVito?"

When she nodded, he said they needed her signature on some documents. Mama looked puzzled but invited them into the dining room, where they sat facing her across the table. Several of us kids stood around, waiting and watching in silence.

One of the men unclasped a large alligator-leather case and took out several long sheets of paper. The other man held a yellow legal pad. They introduced themselves, saying they were from the Union Railroad Company, and they had completed the investigation and wanted to propose a settlement.

"Settlement? Settlement?" Distrust rose in Mama's voice.

One of them handed her a sheet of paper.

"We're here to offer eleven thousand dollars, in settlement for the death of your son, Charles DeVito. Your signature—"

Mama raised her hand, her face ashen, and Francey and I exchanged looks of panic.

Mama exploded in a wild rage. "You are offering me money for my baby's life. Money in exchange for my baby's life? Bastards. American bastards." Her voice became an odd shriek. Trembling, eyes blazing, she stood up, knocking over her chair. Towering above them, she pointed to the door. "Get out of my house. Go, go before I get a knife. Out. Go. Go now. Now. *Now. Now!*"

Confused and terrified, the men swept up their papers, mumbled feeble apologies that went unheeded by everyone, and quickly withdrew. They slid past Mama where she stood pointing to the door, fiercely waving her arm. Eyes darting, they retreated from the dining room, through the kitchen and out the way they had come. Mama followed them into the kitchen, her rage consuming the air.

Francey stopped by the knife drawer and stood in front of it.

As the car backed out of the driveway, Mama's face grew purple with rage. Her eyes streaming with tears, she turned toward me. "They would never have come if you had obeyed me. I told you to watch him. You killed my baby. You killed my baby. And they come offering money for my baby's life."

I fled.

Outside, I followed the strangers' car as it rounded the driveway toward the highway, but I ran in the opposite direction toward the river. Convulsed with remorse and shame, I raced up the lane, zigzagged through the apple trees in the Westlake orchard, went through the wide pasture and past the spring, and headed toward the bluff overlooking the train tracks.

Without warning, Francey wrenched my shoulder and gripped my arm, yanking me toward him. Weeping openly, he grabbed me close, his lips pressed momentarily against my forehead, his face wet with tears. Wiping his runny nose against his sleeve, he demanded, "Why didn't you stop? I kept calling you."

I hadn't heard a sound. I had a plan for atonement.

Wrenching free, I stumbled on. Francey jerked me back. "Stop! Mama sent me. She told me not to come home without you."

"Let me go!"

Sensing my resolve, he tightened his grip. "Then I'm going with you. I can't go home without you. Mama said not to come back without you."

His large, light amber eyes, perpetually sad, reminded me of how hopelessly he competed with Albert for Mama's affection. His chin quivered. He looked sadder and more vulnerable than ever. Struggling against his vise-like grip, knowing I could not take him with me, I pleaded. "Let go of me. Leave me alone. I don't want to go home. I don't want to be here anymore."

His fingers dug into my shoulders and he drew me closer to his chest. "I'm not letting you go. Mama needs you. We all need you. Come home." Sobbing, he repeated, "Mama told me not to come home without you."

Off in the distance, I heard the long, slow toot of a train approaching Roseton. I stirred, and Francey's grip dug deeper into my arm. The roar of the train grew louder.

Paura appeared. Darkness and flashing lights exploded. I couldn't breathe but I stopped wrestling. In a flash, a clear but transparent image of myself dressed in my homemade tan culottes and blue blouse appeared. *She* stood, enveloped in Paura's black shroud. Both climbed to the top of the bluff. She grabbed the lowest branch of the sapling, slid down the short, steep incline, separated the loose strands of barbed wire, and stepped out onto the tracks. She stood there, Paura at her side, facing the approaching train.

When the train passed, she and Paura were gone. The air grew silent.

I began to breathe. I felt strange. Different. Even my clothing had changed. Now I was wearing a new paisley housedress, identical to the one Mama had worn the day we talked about the Sing Sing execution. The day Mama had said, "Only a mother can forgive completely." Had I become Mama?

I turned to Francey and heard a voice that sounded familiar. Mine. "You can let go. I'll go home with you."

As we neared the house from the lane, my sisters, waiting for us in hiding, disappeared behind the high fieldstone wall. As Francey and I entered the driveway, they stood in silence, like sentinels. Warily, the girls came to greet us, but no one spoke. I glimpsed Mama turning hastily from the kitchen window. As we entered the kitchen, Mama, standing at the stove with her back to the table, called out in an unsteady voice, "Everybody wash up. It's time to eat."

She paused. "I made Eleanor's favorite lentil soup."

PART THREE—MOVING ON

CHAPTER THIRTY-SEVEN—
RETURNING TO HIGH SCHOOL

1936

Autumn brought a quick frost and sharp winds which turned upstate New York into a flying circus of color. Crisp leaves flew helter-skelter skyward and swirled down against car hoods and windows, and sun burnt lawns until the ground became a quilt of blazing orange, ruby red, and golden yellow. The random elegance compounded our collective sorrow.

In past years, the crisp air and brilliant autumn leaves of yellow, red, and plum had sparked an annual ritual of outrageous hilarity. We kids raked, swept, kicked, tossed, and blew the crunchy leaves into huge mounds, competing with the wind, with each other, and with ourselves.

Even Bozo joined in the fun by racing into the mounds while we screeched, "Mine's the fattest," or "I've got the mostest," or "You stole my batch."

We raked and piled until we decided to play hide-and-seek and one person hid while the others looked away.

Charley, the smallest, was always the hardest to find; we girls would fake-poke into the pile, yelling, "Nobody's here. Nobody's here. Let's go look in Gloria's pile." We would feign shock when he jumped out and yelled, "I'm here, I'm here."

That fall, nobody raked leaves. Mostly we looked out separate windows and watched the branches grow bare and lose their vibrant glory.

Only Evelyn noticed the leaves. One cold September evening as the day grew dark, she went outside and gathered up an armful of leaves. She brought them to her face and breathed deeply, deeply, deeply, her head rising and falling with each long breath. Then, holding them close, she walked to the small white stone marker she had placed on the side of the lane that led to the river and carefully mounded the leaves over it. She knelt and moved her lips in silent prayer.

I began my senior year of high school in a stupor. Unlike my first three years, during which I had excelled, my last became a year of relentless confusion. I could not remove the images of the train, the wake, the casket. And on the first day of school, seeing all the young boys wearing well-pressed long white shirts, I was thrust back into the parlor viewing the open casket.

The entire school—the entrance, the halls, the classrooms—appeared filled with boys wearing white shirts. My eyes lingered on those who wore checkered sweaters or woolen jackets over their white shirts. Throughout the day, I sought out soft, warm plaids, heavy tan woolens, jackets that draped in gentle folds over the moving bodies of my classmates. One by one, I placed them in the casket to warm Charley's cold body.

When the bell rang for first period, I walked into Miss MacDonald's classroom. Like a marionette with a puppet master controlling the strings, I took my front row seat on the window side of the room. After she welcomed us to English class, she passed out sheets of blue-lined composition paper.

"Write a short essay on 'My Summer Vacation.' Write about your happiest adventure."

I stared at the blue lines and blank spaces, unable to reach for my pen. Sounds of shifting paper and scrawling pens deafened me. Miss MacDonald, middle-aged and puffy, stirred. Was she trying to catch my eye? Without seeing, I heard her heavy, round body trudge in my direction. As she approached, I bolted from my seat and across the front of the room. At the door, I heard

Vincent Phelps say, "Her little brother got killed by a train."

Somehow, I made it through my last year of high school. I should have failed chemistry. I couldn't remember the tables and weights, and I accidentally broke a glass beaker filled with chlorine. Mr. Stopher gave me the only "D" I ever got. Paying attention in class was impossible, and in study hall I sat, books unopened, staring at an empty stage.

Albert left school altogether. He claimed the vice principal, Mr. McKeever, struck him in the hall for cutting class. Albert struck back, knocked him to the floor, and was expelled.

Mama, distraught, demanded that he go back to school. "You don't even have to apologize. Just go back."

Despite Mama's tears and our chorus of pleas, Albert refused to return. Mama sat across from him at the kitchen table, pleading, "Son, you have only one leg. You, more than any of the others, need a college education. You have to finish high school."

Albert, uncharacteristically calm, waited until she finished. "I want to be a millionaire before I'm forty, and I can't learn how to do that from a teacher who only makes sixty dollars a month."

Albert never returned to high school. Instead, within a week he bought a truck with forty dollars he borrowed from his buddy Louis Martin and hired an old wino for a dollar a day.

The next Saturday he made rounds to a number of farmers who knew him from years of tagging along when Papa bought and sold fruit and vegetables from upstate farmers.

Albert bought a truckload of tomatoes, promising to pay the farmers within a week. At dusk, he carefully covered the tomatoes with a heavy canvas. Mama, avoiding eye contact and addressing the lentil soup, said, "Tomorrow is Sunday. There's no market. Put the truck in the barn. The air smells like frost."

Mama proved right. That night started a long cold snap. Temperatures fell below freezing, ruining the last of the season's tomato crop. On Monday, Albert's tomatoes were the only ones available. He had purchased them for one dollar a crate and sold them for six.

When he entered the kitchen, he yelled, "I feel like a millionaire." The next day he paid off his debt to Louis Martin and to every farmer who had trusted him. From then on, he worked day and night, parlaying his windfall into a growing business. In addition, he began to give Mama money to pay bills and for the rest of us to get twenty-five cents a day to buy lunch in the school cafeteria like most of our schoolmates.

Mama eventually accepted his decision. I thought she felt proud of her ruby. She said even in his sleep, Albert dreamed up schemes to make money. "He's getting ahead in this world."

CHAPTER THIRTY-EIGHT—CANCER

1937

T he reprieve from grief was not to last. For several months Mama had not been well, and now Francey worked with Albert after school, sorting through boxes of fruit, sizing and repackaging them for "more profit." Both helped to support the family and Francey urged me to get my driver's license. "You've turned sixteen. You can drive Mama for her doctor appointments." And that's what I did.

Dr. Banks, our family doctor, thought she might need surgery and recommended a young gynecologist who had opened an office in town.

She and I drove to town in silence. As we entered the specialist's office, Mama spoke, her tone solemn. She said I should stay in the waiting room. She wanted to see the doctor alone.

After what seemed too long—reminding me of Mama's story about Ellis Island and the sickly young boy who didn't come out of the examination room as soon as his brothers—Mama stepped from his office. Her face was ashen, her mouth taut, her eyes angry.

I waited until we were back in the car before I spoke. "What did he say was wrong?"

"He doesn't know anything. He's a shoemaker. He said I was having a miscarriage."

"A miscarriage?"

"I told him I hadn't been with a man for four years. I said he should take his sign down."

On the drive home, after a long silence, Mama asked me to stop at the neighbors. She wanted to talk to young Marion West-lake, who had become a nurse. "She can recommend the best doctor in the Hudson Valley. Nurses know."

A few days later Mama had her first examination with a specialist in Cornwall Hospital, about thirty miles away. After the exam he followed her out of the room to greet me, introduced himself, and asked my age.

"Sixteen."

Several questions flitted across his face, but he didn't ask. He turned and studied Mama, smiled, and patted her shoulder lightly before returning to his office.

Mama looked more frightened than before she had entered the examination room. I wished I had gone with her. We walked in silence to the car.

Once seated, she began to fold and unfold a handkerchief. "He said I have cancer. Cancer of the uterus. It needs to be removed. If I do it now, I have a chance. If I wait it could be too late. I'm bleeding too hard." Her chin quivered and she teared up. "I told him I have to live. My seven children aren't all grown."

Seeing her cry made my throat ache.

"He told me I was run down and that I needed to build up my health. He said I needed a blood transfusion."

This sounded ominous.

"I told him you were the oldest girl. You could do it."

I didn't know for sure what it was I was going to do, but I felt a surge of relief. I could help make Mama well.

"When do we do the transfusion?"

She acted like she hadn't heard me.

"I looked him in the eye," she said. "I asked what are my chances?"

I gulped to ease the pain in my throat. "What did he say?"

"He said he never knows, even the best doctors never know for sure." She paused. "He could schedule the transfusion and surgery for next week. He looked like he wanted an answer." Mama paused. "So, I told him, Truth is always in the room.

If I have surgery—the truth—what are my chances? The whole truth. Everything. Tell me the worst. He took a long time to answer and then he said said, 'The worst? One in a million.'"

I gasped.

"I told him. I'll be that one."

In the months that followed—before and after her surgery—Mama amazed us. The zeal she had shown in protecting us, in saving Bozo, in keeping the farm, in incubating dozens of chicks on our dining room table, in starting the fruit stand, in never giving up, she now applied to herself.

Once a day, sometimes twice, she would go to the chicken coop, pick up a few freshly laid eggs, put several in her apron pocket, and, before leaving the pen, crack one open, let the egg white slip to the ground, and in a single gulp, swallow the warm yolk.

Sometimes she swallowed two in a row. It was gut-wrenching to watch.

Her determination grew more convincing by the day. She napped three times each day, made herself beef tea, cooked chicken liver, whipped fresh cream into eggnogs, ate bowls of lemon custard, gnawed the knuckles and bit the bones of baked chicken thighs, sucked out the marrow, and sipped half a glass of red wine with her big meal of the day. We kids were mesmerized by her transformation, convinced she would regain her health.

Throughout this time, while recuperating from surgery, and during the weeks she underwent radiation, she kept gulping egg yolks.

Often, in the kitchen, when she cracked an egg in half, she would drop the white into Bozo's dish, then pour a trickle of red wine into the eggshell before gulping the yolk down.

She said it was the only perfect food. Had Mrs. Gould, the public health nurse, taught her this? No. She learned it as a child from the old woman in Chieti who milked her cow in a shed, the milk Mama carried in a pail to the other old woman who made cheese on her porch.

Mama said, "She lived past one hundred and four. And she ate at least half a dozen egg yolks a day. The perfect food."

Egg yolks may have been the perfect food, but watching Mama pick up a warm egg, crack it in half, toss back her head, and gulp it down in one swift swallow made something in my stomach heave.

Twice a week after school for six weeks, I drove Mama the thirty miles to Cornwall. At the hospital, Mama went into the radiation room while I waited near the nurses' station, made small talk, and took mental notes on how different nurses' caps were fashioned to signify rank. Mama seemed pleased to see me talking to them.

After a few sessions, on the drive home, Mama mentioned how impressive nurses were—she admired them for caring for her but also for their independence and self-respect. "You should think about becoming a nurse," she said. "That way, you never have to depend upon a man. You will always be independent."

I liked the idea of being independent, but nursing raised images of what I had seen when Albert and Francey were at St. Luke's: bedpans, sick people moaning, mangled limbs, old men coughing up phlegm. I was sure I'd be vomiting day and night. But I didn't say a word. I still had half a year before graduating from high school.

CHAPTER THIRTY-NINE—
PLANNING AHEAD

1937

As Mama regained her stamina over the next several months, she continued to remind me of the importance of a woman being financially independent. "Make your own money. Spend it how you like."

It was time for me to think about my future, and without money for college or Traphagan School of Fashion, she urged me to consider applying to St. Luke's Hospital.

"You could become a nurse like Marion or Mrs. Gould, the best teacher I ever had."

She knew I recalled Mrs. Gould with fondness, but the idea of carting foul-smelling bedpans for two years (or worse, for the rest of my life) sickened me.

But Mama had none of these thoughts. Almost daily, she dropped hints about how highly respected nurses were, maybe more important than doctors. The nurses really ran the hospitals. She prodded, "Fill out the application." I didn't openly protest, but Mama could read minds, and she continued with her efforts.

"You'll be close to your sisters."

"You'll learn things you can use all your life."

"This is a start. You don't have to do it forever."

She reminded me about the young nurse who rode her bicycle from St. Luke's to buy currants and peaches from our fruit stand.

"Remember, when Lucy graduated from St. Luke's, she gave

you her bicycle. She had a job waiting for her before she graduated. She went back to Connecticut to work in a doctor's office
close to her home."

Everything Mama said was true.

I hated the plan.

But I took the admission test at St. Luke's. Within a few weeks,
a letter came saying the hospital was pleased to announce I had
passed but could not enter until the following year. Hospital pol-
icy required applicants to be seventeen years of age before entering its training program.

Mama was crestfallen. I was ecstatic. I couldn't wait to tell
Miss MacDonald, who, other students hinted, treated me like
her favorite. Her subtle, ongoing support during the school year,
whether it was after-class meetings, individual assignments, or
outside readings, had gradually eased my silent grief.

When I confessed my relief at the postponement of nurses
training, she said she had news for me, too. "My friend Sid
Cohan, the editor of the *Newburgh Daily News*, mentioned he was
looking for a cub reporter. I recommended you."

Thrilled, I blurted, "Do I have to be seventeen?"

"No. You just have to do everything he says. His bark is fearful,
but he never bites. Tell your mother you'll have a career as a
journalist."

I hesitated. "Will I get paid?"

"Seventeen dollars a week."

A fortune in 1937.

The *Newburgh Daily News* occupied the second floor of a small
brick building in the heart of the city. The noisy, greasy-smell-
ing presses occupied the ground floor. During our workday they
printed ads for local businesses, and at night they printed the
next day's newspaper.

The rhythmic *tch-dom, tch-dom, tch-dom* reminded me of
Mama's Victrola when a record had a crack.

Mr. Cohan, a stocky, sandy-haired, middle-aged man who

wore his eyeglasses on the top of his balding scalp, sat in a wheeled armchair behind several stacks of paper, which sat on a huge, smudged wooden desk, his Royal typewriter a constant fixture on its pulled-out slab to his left.

Mrs. Carter, a round, middle-aged woman who almost never left her seat, was surrounded by trays of metal typeface near the back stairway to the press room. Amanda, who sat across from Mr. Cohan, did double duty as his secretary, but her official tag was "the Morgue." I assumed she wrote all the obituaries.

My job as a cub reporter lasted two years. Sid Cohan, growling from early dawn to midday, took me under his wing. He yelled at me for run-on sentences, for sprinkling commas like confetti, for embroidering. "This is a newspaper, not a handkerchief."

He had a way of snorting—my cue to look up. "Kid, did you ever hear of a topic sentence?"

Early on, he would beckon me to his desk and rewrite a paragraph. He corrected mixed tenses, challenged every opening and closing line. He forced me to use the typewriter. He never spoke a kind word to me.

I worshipped him.

After about six months, he told Ralph Aiello—his top reporter who doubled as story photographer—to give me my own camera, a Speed Graphic with a ground glass lens, so heavy I could barely lift it.

On my first photography assignment—a baby had been born with a full-size front tooth—Mr. Cohan raised his hand as I headed for the door. He asked me to demonstrate how I planned to prop the camera on my shoulder. He stood up, walked from behind his desk, and carefully leveled it.

"Get the picture in the sharpest focus possible. Then put yourself inside the camera and report only what you see in the lens. Imagine the camera has ears. Write only what the camera hears. Don't goo and gaa."

The following Sunday edition featured my photo of a three-day-old infant displaying a full-sized lower front tooth on the front page.

At home, Mama refused to take any money from my earnings, but now that both Albert and Francey helped with the bills, I insisted on giving her two dollars a week to provide cafeteria lunch money for Agnes and Gloria.

When she resisted, I reminded her of how she gave Aunt Angelina money when she got a raise for sewing double needle. She didn't budge. She reminded me of *las maestras,* who let her save her earnings in a jug under her bed so she could voyage to America.

Mama said she could manage the cafeteria lunches and that I needed to save the money to attend Traphagan School of Fashion on Broadway. "So you can become an American Schiaparelli."

I was less sure.

During the two years I worked for the *Newburgh Daily News,* I became more aware of life outside my family: Country clubs, elections, voting, sports, fraud, welfare, Democrats, Republicans, school boards, scandals, debutante balls, gerrymandering, fundraising.

The entire time I learned about the world outside, I saved until I had enough money to pay the one hundred and nine dollars for the first semester at Traphagan School of Design and twenty-five dollars a month rent at the Midtown YWCA.

On my last day at the newspaper, shortly before closing, Amanda invited everyone over to her desk to view a cake decorated with *New York, New York* in pink cursive writing.

Mr. Cohan said we should cut the cake so we could get home in time to hear Edward R. Murrow's report on Hitler's invasion of Poland. From his serious tone I guessed this seasoned newspaper editor knew hearing the world news was more important than my going-away party.

Mrs. Carter handed me a little package. It contained a shiny metal "E" selected from her special headline type sets. Ralph Aiello, the top reporter who covered all the important events, gave me a magnifying glass, reminding me to look for small details. The sports editor pinned a silvery miniature golf club clasp on my collar, "so rich guys might take a second look and believe I came from their class." Amanda's package held a hard copy edition of Strunk and White's *Elements of Style*.

Pressured by Sid's sense of urgency, the party ended early. Besides, this was a Saturday—payday.

As Mr. Cohan handed out the small manilla envelopes containing cash, he said to my empty desk that it was too bad I was leaving—he was about to send me out to fill in for Frank. I considered that my goodbye gift. But later, at home when I opened my pay envelope, it contained an extra ten dollars.

For my last day at home Mama rose early and made a fluffy sponge cake. I would leave for New York City to begin my studies at Traphagan. She said it would be a new tradition for her girls —a special cake for the day they left home and started their own lives, a sequel to the ritual chocolate cake she made when each daughter had her first period.

My brothers had said goodbye earlier in the day. Both were now buying fruit from local farmers and selling it in Wallabout Market. Mama had also been recruited to set up schedules for pick-ups.

When it came time for me to leave, my sisters busied themselves upstairs, putting together presents: a pair of fine scissors, a tube of lipstick, two fancy barrettes, a pair of leather gloves.

Mama and I were alone in the kitchen. Mama sat at one end of the table and cleared her throat. Her eyes welled with tears.

I told her I'd be home on weekends.

When she spoke, her voice was low. "I was too hard on you. I gave you too much responsibility as a child." Her voice faltered. "I should have been at the beach watching Charley. He was my child to watch. Not yours."

Our eyes met and we both began to weep.

Something unlocked inside me. The wordless link that had

tethered me from the day Louisa put Genevieve on my lap and said, "You the best lilla Mama," was released, and my feeling and thinking like Mama disappeared. I felt lighter. Taller. Free to be myself.

Too soon, my sisters jumped down the three steps from the landing into the kitchen. Almost in unison they asked why we were crying.

Mama answered, "They are tears of happiness."

And, as always, my sister teared up. Gloria, beginning to sob, said, "The Police Station Disease is incurable. We better learn to live with it."

It was almost two o'clock, time to leave and catch the Greyhound bus to New York City. Agnes asked how much money I had.

"Seventeen hundred-dollar bills."

"When you get to the YWCA, put sixteen hundred in the office safe. They do that. I asked Albert to find out," Mama said.

Genevieve said be sure to get a receipt.

Evelyn wanted to know when I would come home.

As I started for the door, I met my sisters' eyes. We knew what to do. Without saying a word, my sisters and I staged one last performance to make Mama laugh. Each of us did an imitation of Mama. We called it Kissing the Air. You leaned toward the other person's cheek and kissed the air, then swerved back and did the same thing on the other side. We did this several times, gyrating ever more theatrically as we exchanged partners, the air filled with kisses.

Nobody touching.

Finally, when the hilarity subsided, I headed out the back door into the driveway. Mama waved goodbye, her hand curling toward her heart, beckoning, her eyes glistening. "I know you'll do your best."

EPILOGUE

In 1950, Albert booked passage for Mama and Giulia on the *SS Atlantic*, a Mediterranean ocean liner headed for Italy. Aboard ship on the day of their departure, we seven siblings teased her with mock warnings that if she did not make peace with her seventy-six-year-old mother who still lived in Chieti, we too would never again set foot in her house.

Mama's face, flushed with excitement, looked wary, uncertain. She avoided eye contact and kept rearranging the bouquet of roses she held against her strong, solid body, pretending to ignore our merciless taunts.

"If you don't tell your mother you're sorry, we'll never come home for Easter . . ."

". . . never let you see our children . . ."

"Won't phone on weekends . . . not even on your birthday."

". . . we'll all change our phone numbers so you'll never be able to talk to us again."

We kept up the whooping and taunting until the loudspeaker called for all visitors to disembark.

As the ship slid past the Statue of Liberty, I wondered who might have stood on the dock when she left Naples that December morning almost half a century earlier. Was George there, waving goodbye to Mama, a naïve seventeen-year-old traveling under the watchful eye of Aunt Angelina while the *Prinzess Irene* drifted out to sea and headed for America?

As the ship continued to move farther away, my eyes were drawn to her strong hand waving goodbye in the mist, her palm facing inward, her slender fingers curling rhythmically toward

her heart, beckoning, Come back. Come back.
Veni. Veni . . .

* * *

Mama achieved her goal of total independence. At age sixty, she opened Mama's Italian Kitchen in a charming building of her own design to replace the small golf shed fruit stand. She ran the restaurant on her own terms, opened when she wished, and if she had few customers on a slow evening, she closed early.

Within a few months of opening, she became the darling of West Point cadets. She served wine yet refused to get a liquor license by convincing the authorities that the wine she served was given to her by her son who picked the Concords from her vineyard and made the wine in the basement of her house. She, in turn, gave it to her customers, a gift of Italian hospitality, she said. "I never charge."

Best of all, she paid her longtime debt. When the Township of Newburgh offered to buy or pay her for access to our lane so investors could develop housing on fifty landlocked acres, Mama said, "It's not for sale." She had a better plan, a counteroffer. She would *give* the lane outright on condition it would be named De-Vito Drive.

That evening she called all seven of us and said we had to come for Sunday dinner. It was important. The next Sunday, over homemade ravioli, she said we could make a toast. "Last week I paid off my debt to Mid-Hudson Electric for the electricity we stole during the Great Depression."

DeVito Drive is two miles north of Newburgh on the 9W Highway.

Under Mama's guidance the restaurant flourished. Gradually, she hired more and more help but continued to do most of the cooking. On crowded evenings she phoned our nieces and nephews, saying only, "I'm busy," before quickly hanging up. Without fail, within fifteen or twenty minutes, one or two teenage grandchildren arrived to pitch in.

Mama ran the restaurant until two months before she died in her sleep on her 97th birthday.

She never got a liquor license.

In 1942, Papa was found on a Florida back road, bludgeoned to death by an angry temporary employee whom he had humiliated and fired.

Since we had little or no contact with Papa for years, we didn't learn of his death until weeks afterward, when the Miami court notified Mama about the date of the trial.

The message seemed strange after our long separation from him, but Francey, Albert, and I took the bus to Miami and sat in on the trial. We were not called to testify. The assailant was convicted; due to extenuating provocation, the sentence was seven years.

I did not become a Supreme Court judge. Instead, I lived in Greenwich Village and studied and worked in various art fields for over a decade. I designed costumes for modern dancers and mounted fashion shows for Vogue and Simplicity pattern companies—and toured the country in *Life with Father* and Puppet Playhouse as a professional puppeteer. I married, moved to Seattle, and had two children. I earned dual master's degrees in anthropology and social welfare and was appointed associate professor in children's drama at the University of Washington. When my son developed schizophrenia, I left teaching and co-founded the Washington Advocates for the Mentally Ill (WAMI), which became a founding member of the National Alliance on Mental Illness (NAMI). I received numerous awards for my legislative advocacy.

As for the rest of the family, everyone married, and all the girls had babies nine months after their wedding date. Francey became an alcoholic but recovered before he died. Albert made millions, much through real estate. Agnes was featured in a *New York Times* article about her efforts to keep New York from demolishing a historic residence. Gloria became a whiz teacher of bridge. Genevieve became an X-ray technician. Evelyn saw a psychiatrist every week until she died in her eighties. We siblings stayed in touch every week of our lives. Now, only Agnes and I are here to phone each other every day.

I continue to live in my home in Seattle on Capitol Hill and hope this memoir reveals a period in history as remembered by a centenarian.

ACKNOWLEDGEMENT

The author wishes to thank the following people:

Elena Hartwell

Theo Nestor

The 10-year writing group: Ann Oxrieder, Steven Eck, Stephanie Erickson, Laura Hodges, Karen Klein, Mary Pringle, Heidi Schor, Robin White, and Maggie Corrigan.

The author also extends thanks to the following organizations for their workshops and conferences:

Hugo House

Pacific Northwest Writers Association

Allegory Editing

ABOUT THE AUTHOR

Eleanor Owen

Eleanor DeVito Owen is an American journalist, playwright, actress, and mental health professional. She founded the Washington Advocates for the Mentally Ill and co-founded the National Alliance for the Mentally Ill (NAMI). She studied acting and costume design at the American Academy of Dramatic Arts. She also studied journalism at Columbia University and holds a dual master's degree in anthropol- ogy and social welfare from the University of Washington. After a stint as a journalist, she worked in theater in New York and New Jersey. Moving cross country, she landed in Washington State, where she continued as a theater artist in Kennewick. Later relocating with her husband to Seattle, where they raised their two children, Eleanor taught at the Lakeside School and as associate professor at the University of Washington School of Drama. She taught creative drama to preschoolers at the Seattle Public Library. Known as "the Barracuda" for her advocacy efforts on behalf of mental health services, Eleanor has won multiple awards for her dedication to improve the lives of those struggling with mental health issues.